LOCATION X
A Quest for Place

Eva Rome

Blue Morpho Press New Mexico
SANTA FE, NEW MEXICO

Copyright © 2023 by Eva Rome

All rights reserved. No part of this publication may be reproduced, distributed or transmitted in any form or by any means, without prior written permission.

Eva Rome/Blue Morpho Press New Mexico
3201 Zafarano Dr., Suite C #218
Santa Fe, New Mexico 87507
www.bluemorphopress.net

Publisher's Note: *Location X* is primarily a work of nonfiction.

Book design © 2023 Laurie McDonald
Photographs © 2023 Laurie McDonald unless otherwise indicated

Cover design by Andy Bridge

Location X: A Quest for Place/ Rome, Eva. – 1st ed.
ISBN 978-0-9678995-7-2

Dedicated to
KENNETH DALE CONNER
June 27, 1946 – October 15, 2023
My high school art teacher, lifelong friend, and mentor.
"Live life on your own terms."

Your secret wish for your life to change completely is going to come true.
A fortune cookie prediction that's been in my wallet forever.

Also by Eva Rome

*Travel for STOICs: Empowering the Solo Traveler Who Is
Obsessive, Introverted, and Compulsive*

*What It Means: Myth, Symbol, and Archetype
in the Third Millennium, Vol. 1*

CONTENTS

Introduction 1
Diogenes 7
São Paulo 9
Customs 29
México City 33
Food To Make Your Mouth Water Burst 37
Santa Fe, New Mexico 43
El Paso, Texas 45
Airbnb Review: My Vacay in Your Travel Trailer ... 53
Guadalajara, México 57
Back in Santa Fe 85
Housesitting for the Holidays 91
Uncertain, Texas: A Housesit 95
Costa Rica 115
Arenal 141
IMAGES 145
Panamá 217
Portland, Oregon: A Housesit 239

Granada, Spain	243
Madrid	249
Rome	257
Grace	273
Walking the Camino: The Via Francigena	277
Florence	295
Porto	305
Lisbon	313
A Wild Goose Chase	321
Washington, D.C.	323
Can One Word Be Enough to Know Where?	331
San Miguel de Allende, México	337
Gratitude	357
The List: Relocation Criteria	359
Notes	361
About the Author	377

INTRODUCTION

LOCATION X

I am homeless. Or houseless, I should say. It's not that I can't buy a house, because I can; it's that I choose not to. In March of 2021, when the real estate market was in the midst of its manic rise, I sold my house—in twenty-eight hours—for far more money than it was worth and took to the road in search of a new life. I'd been wanting out of there practically since the day I moved in, ten years earlier, and over those years, a lot of inertia had built up. Although I love New Mexico, I knew Santa Fe wasn't the place for me, but I'm adaptable and, with varying amounts of effort, I can feel at home wherever I go. So where is home when it's everywhere and nowhere?

In July of 2022, I entered my eighth decade. Not all septuagenarians become devoted grandparents, contented gardeners, or avid pickleball players; some, like me, still crave risk and adventure. We're in that ticking-bomb stage of life, where we're wondering daily, When will our countdown reach zero? Our brains are shrinking to the size of walnuts, and we need to take advantage of what remaining intellect and muscle strength we have before it totally wastes away, sidelining us for the duration of the game. The prospect of turning seventy and embracing the stereotype is what finally got me out of the house and questing for Location X.

X is used to describe something vague or mysterious, like Mr. X, Brand X, X-ray. *X* is the place on a pirate's map that marks where treasure is buried. In an algebraic equation, *X* is an unknown quantity, and solving for *X* was the process to which I'd dedicated myself: locating that singular piece of real estate, in that singular city, in that singular country that said, This is where I envision living what remains of my life. *X* symbolizes a crossroads.

Location X is a chronicle of my eighteen-month quest and what I discovered along the way, a compilation of reflections and reactions to quotidian experiences, written in both diary form and in short fiction and presented in chronological order. Diary entries record travel challenges, the struggles and triumphs of adapting to new places, observations of unfamiliar cultures; my relocation criteria running in the background (see Appendix One). Told from the viewpoint of someone whose career working with museums and other arts organizations spanned several decades, *Location X* may appeal to the reader who loves the aesthetic experience. Sometimes a place or an event—in El Paso and in Rome, in a Fort Davis, Texas, travel trailer—inspired a piece of short fiction written in the third person using a proxy named Colleen. Colleen is derived from the Irish name Cailleach, meaning "old woman"; the Cailleach is a divine hag and wise woman who created the Celtic landscape. At an advanced age, don't we all want the freedom to create our own personal landscapes? These associations appeal to me.

Within the pages of this book, you will not find travel tips and advice, a rundown of the best places to retire, or best kept travel secrets a la *Condé Nast Traveler, Travel + Leisure*, or *International Living*. The descriptors that often appear in conventional travel literature—rustic, elegant, succulent, breathtaking, dramatic—and phrases such as "breakfast in your plush king bed; dreamy views from your spacious balcony with fruity frozen beverages in hand" are judiciously avoided. *Location X* is the meaning of "Truth in Travel," *Condé Nast Traveler*'s shrewd motto. I talk to people. I interpret my environment. It's the "doing" of everyday life and the accumulation of daily, discrete units of experience that creates the narrative thread and keeps *Location X* authentic and unpredictable. From the armchair globetrotter to the boomer looking for a soft landing in paradise, readers will recognize their unrealized relocation dreams in this compilation of travel exploits and perhaps be prompted to take on their own new adventures.

Relationships with friends and family are of course a priority, but game-changing Covid, Zoom, and good-enough internet have made those acts of relationship maintenance more flexible and not solely a function of proximity. Plus, over the years, clusters of friends have dug themselves in in various places worldwide, all reachable by internet and by air, so isolation is not the issue that it was a few decades ago. A bonus!

When rumination about life-changing decisions pushes you to the brink, input from elsewhere makes sense. You turn to friends and family for the wisdom of their experience and their views, but sometimes it feels prudent to look beyond the subjective to more impersonal (some might refer to as mystical) resources, like philosophy, astrology, the Tarot, a Brazilian *pai-de-santo* (priest), and augury. I availed myself of all five. After a friend retired from a physics professorship, he became an expert in Tarot and offered a reading. He explained, "Your thoughts (electrons) orbit the nucleus of the atom (the central problem), and you need a stray electron to knock an orbiting one to a lower level of energy to release a photon (insight). A reading is like that stray electron." For my friend, transitioning from physics to Tarot made perfect sense. The reading and its takeaways were spot-on: it is imperative to leave my current environment; be patient and disciplined, focused. Have conviction; there's no reason to resist. I will succeed. (The cards I selected and their meanings are included in the Notes section of *Location X*.)[1]

During the first few months of my quest, I spent an insane amount of time looking at online real estate in places I thought I might like to live, when I concluded that this was a lousy strategy. Naïvely, I thought I'd find the perfect house and everything else would fall into place. Photographic sleight of hand can deform an image of the most down-and-out shack and transform it into a great starter home, or make a two-storey colonial that's a few feet from the sidewalk look like it's sited on a sprawling lawn, so nothing compares to seeing it in person.[2] Sometimes an actual house doesn't even exist; some are architectural renderings with computer-generated trees, a pet dog, and a Stanley Tucci look-alike draining pasta in the kitchen sink. During one of those pointless, stochastic searches, images of the Santa Fe house I'd lived in for ten years popped up on my computer screen. I remember thinking, *Wow, I really like this one!* before realizing it was mine. As good as the internet is for nearly every kind of research, I realized I couldn't rely on any form of identifying Location X other than my own boots-on-the-ground investigation.

When you're traveling and you know you have a home to go back to, a fallback position, a different dynamic is in play than if you ditch your home and your stuff and just start wandering around. If you've planned a two-week vacation in, say, Provence, and after three days of being battered by the mistral winds you realize it was a mistake, you know you can run out the clock and be home in no time. But when you have no home, what do you do? Planning your life only a few weeks at a time quickly becomes impractical. For many reasons, committing to a place for a minimum of a month is advisable. And even if you relocate only once a month for a year, you must have twelve contingency plans because things happen. As it turned out, during those eighteen months, I relocated over forty times, sometimes returning to my previous home base, New Mexico. When I needed to conserve resources, I house-sat for vacationing pet owners.

After the ten-day mark, you can start assessing your priorities with more discernment, even though early on you may have wanted to turn and run. You have to give yourself time to become comfortable with the physicality of the place—is it easy to understand the layout and to get around, do you like the architecture, museums, infrastructure and other design elements, is the weather tolerable, is there a grocery store within walking distance, do its citizens seem happy and how likely is it that they'll be accepting of a newcomer, is your favorite brand of toothpaste available, etc., etc.? If a place can tick all the boxes, great; but it's not only about self-interest. It's also about finding a community where equality is more than rhetoric. It's about finding ways to contribute. If any of this is important to you, read on.

The peripatetic lifestyle can seem both chaotic and revelatory, depending on your outlook. What it does do, for sure, is force focus on priorities. During the process of discovering Location X, I kept these three simple questions at the fore: Can I envision living my life in this place? Can I connect to my adopted community in meaningful ways? Can I envision taking my final breath here without reservation?

In the following pages, I solve for *X*. DO NOT skip to the last page to find out where I ended up. When I wrote this introduction, I didn't know myself.

CHAPTER ONE

DIOGENES

In São Paulo, Brazil, the neighborhoods known as Alto Pinheiros and Alto Lapa are hilly, solidly middle-class enclaves of handmade, single-family homes and soaring high-rises. Pinheiros borders on a large park named for Brazilian composer/conductor/cellist Heitor Villa-Lobos, and close by are streets named for Berlioz, Beethoven, Bach, and Haydn. One of the longest, busiest streets that meanders through those neighborhoods, though, is named for the ancient Greek philosopher Diogenes.

Diogenes, a Cynic and proto-Stoic, was born c. 412 BCE. He rejected societal and cultural conventions and called out the hypocrisies and follies of the people and institutions of his day. Renouncing his material possessions, he lived in a large, overturned jar in the agora of Athens and carried a lantern around, shoving it in people's faces and declaring that he was "looking for a man," knowing it was a fool's errand when, in his estimation, none qualified. His philosophical antics didn't stop there. Supposedly he once encountered Alexander the Great in Corinth, a city west of Athens. Diogenes was reclining against a building enjoying the sunshine, and Alexander, thrilled to be meeting the famous philosopher, asked if there were any favors he could do for him. Diogenes replied, "Yes, stand out of my sunlight." Alexander then proclaimed, "If I were not Alexander, then I should wish to be Diogenes." Diogenes replied, "If I were not Diogenes, I would still wish to be Diogenes." If Oscar Wilde had been on the scene, he may have been inspired to author his clever dictum: *Be yourself; everyone else is already taken.*

Diogenes has renewed relevance in our era of extreme right-wing politics, the Covid pandemic, and the idiocy special to our times. He was partly the inspiration for the sale of my house and the drastic reduction of my possessions, but I haven't resorted to living in a large jar. Not yet. Today, Diogenes would be ensconced in a cement storm sewer drainage pipe somewhere in Los Angeles, and his lantern would be his cell phone. Instead of looking for a man, having given up on that idea, he'd be Googling the ideal place to live out his days in relative comfort and contentment, away from people and the possibility of being swept away in a deluge. Also a fool's errand?

Diogenes is credited with coming up with the word "cosmopolitan" (*cosmopolites* in Greek) because, in spite of his misanthropy, he claimed to be a citizen of the world. A radical statement for an ancient Greek, considering how important identity was to them. (Think the Peloponnesian War—the Spartans v. the Athenians—which concluded seven years before Diogenes was born.) I'm a citizen of the world, too, but what goes hand in hand with that is a sense of exile. Which I also feel. Cynicism encourages self-sufficiency and a focus on the things in life you can control, and in that spirit, I fled Santa Fe, New Mexico, in the United States, to find a place of reason, beauty, and tranquility, my own promised land. This was my quest, to hold my own lantern up to the world and my experiences and declare, "I'm looking for a place."

It's April, 2021, month one of my quest.

CHAPTER TWO

SÃO PAULO

Near the intersection of Rua Diógenes and Rua Pio XI (Pope Pius the 11th), at the Açai & Burger, a formidable hill leads up to a house designed in the style of Antoni Gaudí, the architect of the Sagrada Família Basilica in Barcelona. No other dwelling anywhere in the neighborhood resembles this house, a two-storey, pinkish-tan brick structure with curvaceous accents inside and out, fronted by a brick lattice wall and topped with a huge, decorative icosahedron on the roof. The windows downstairs are an oblong, amoebic shape with black burglar bars suggesting the roots of a strangler fig, and a large, flowering vine grows in a living room planter box, winding up the spiral staircase to the second floor. Life-size, leafless cement trees, painted gray, decorate the living room and an upstairs bedroom and served no functional purpose. The ceilings, made of red corrugated brick, are vaulted in undulating waves. This theme is repeated throughout the house, its designer accenting floors and bathrooms with patterns of broken white and blue ceramic tiles and interrupting the monotony of the brick walls with cement troweled in curves and painted white, suggesting the hilly horizon of São Paulo state's denuded countryside. In the space between the sidewalk and the street, an ancient avocado provides a refuge for São Paulo's city birds, mostly bright green parrots and great kiskadees, their calls—to Brazilian ears—inspiring their Portuguese name, *bem-te-vi*. Rua Jorge Felippe Sabra 26, a structure that looks like it belongs in a deep, dark stand of Atlantic Forest, is known locally as The Witch House.[1]

Saturday, April 3rd

After getting my suitcases inside, I went to the local Pão de Açúcar grocery (named for Sugarloaf Mountain in Rio de Janeiro) to stock the empty fridge. Store personnel were taking temperatures as people entered, but no one controlled the number of people in the store or whether anyone was wearing a mask. Special parking spaces with the word *idoso*, meaning "elderly," painted on the asphalt, and checkout lines for my demographic, make people over sixty-five feel seen. If you have even a hint of a slouch or are dabbing your dripping nose with a wad of tissue, Paulistanos let you cut in line. Clerks are friendly, maybe because they're allowed to sit while scanning your purchases. São Paulo gets points for that.

Sunday, April 4th

The next-door neighbors hosted a gathering that lasted all day and late into the night, a gab-and-energy-drink-fest, in the street in front of The Witch House. I hoped this was an Easter anomaly, not the weekend norm, and not an exorcism. To escape the noise, I walked to a neighborhood park where I discovered a large, wide terrace that provided a good overlook for the small corner of this vast city of twenty-two million people. As I got closer, I saw that the terrace was littered with dozens of used condoms and their packaging. Families were out enjoying the cool weather, and I wondered how parents were explaining the condoms to their kids. Maybe that a convention of clowns had been in the area, blowing up balloons and taking selfies at the overlook, then deflating the balloons and leaving them, and their packaging, behind. But kids who could read may be confused by the names of the balloons: Prudence Cores e Sabores (colors and flavors) Caipirinha (a yellow condom with a green tip—the colors of the Brazilian flag—that tastes like the popular cachaça and lime drink), the Sutra Aroma Morango. Kids might wonder, why would a balloon need to taste like a caipirinha or smell like strawberries?

Monday, April 5th

The buildings of Batman Alley (Beco do Batman)[2], in the Vila Madalena neighborhood, serve as canvases for some of São Paulo's best examples of its distinctive style of graffiti. The Beco is one of São Paulo's biggest tourist draws, but only a few of us were wandering the alley. A second wave of Covid is surging in Brazil, and this scarcity of people felt eerie. An excellent ancient cemetery is close by, and in this part of the world, people are often interred above ground in cement lockers, reminiscent of the Amazon package pickup stations in Whole Foods. The plaques that seal the lockers have expertly carved inscriptions and sometimes a photo of the person whose remains are inside. An old man whose job was to tend a small area of the cemetery was successfully removing a large hornets' nest from an empty locker and wearing nothing to protect himself in case they became angry and aggressive. When I realized what he was doing, I turned and ran, later Googling "can a human outrun a hornet?" The answer: no.

The neighbor across the street is an *idosa* woman who lives alone and spends much of the day staring at The Witch House from a front window. When I returned from Vila Madalena, she was outside picking up leaf litter that had fallen into her tiny, fenced cement yard. She asked how old I was, and when I told her, she said, "But you're still *forte!*" (strong) A funny thing to say, I thought, and I felt prompted to ask if she needed help with anything. *"Não, eu aindo forte também!" (No, I'm still strong, too!)* she insisted. Later in the day, when I passed by the living room windows on my way to the kitchen, I saw her struggling to put the garbage out for collection. Every step she took was slow and measured, working her way down the hill one fence rail at a time to the metal garbage basket on a pole, installed in the sidewalk and elevated to keep neighborhood dogs out of the trash. She tossed the bag but missed and, undaunted, slowly retrieved the bag and maneuvered it into the basket. She scanned Rua Jorge Felippe Sabra to see if she had an audience, saw me watching from the window, and waved triumphantly.

Friday, April 9th

Late in the afternoon, I walked to the neighborhood park, the one with the used condoms littering the terrace overlook, and on the way home switched my route to Rua Diógenes so I wouldn't be traveling poorly lit back streets. On Diógenes, bright orange temporary fencing was set up to direct pedestrian traffic away from areas under construction, and there was nowhere else to walk other than in between two strips of fencing. It was dark by then, and a truck carrying a large water tank was slowly making its way down the street. A guy sat on top of the tank, facing backward, sweeping one side of the street then the other with a firehose-strength stream of water, to control dust from the construction site, and I wasn't sure he could see me. I tried to pass the truck when he was spraying the other side of the street, which *he* was trying to time in between passing cars, and just as I was about to clear the truck, he saw me. I avoided getting drenched, but I couldn't help thinking that maybe he'd spray me for his own amusement. He didn't; more points for São Paulo.

Saturday, April 10th

It's like living next to a bar. The neighbors are having a testosterone-fueled motorcycle soirée tonight with dozens of their male friends. Straddling their bikes, they sing along with Brazilian pop tunes and Evangelical Christian songs, pausing now and then to rev their motorcycles' engines. Some of the men are good singers, and all enthusiastically belt out the music. I'm grateful no firearms are involved. The party shut down at 3:30

a.m., then at dawn, only an hour and a half later, a chorus of barking dogs and squawking parakeets started vocalizing. Maybe I'll get used to this eventually?

Thursday, April 15th

An 8 p.m. Covid curfew is in place in São Paulo, but it's not enforced. Tonight, I went out at 7:30 for food and didn't return home until 8:30, paranoid about getting caught. But now that I think about it, I haven't seen *any* police, not even in the daytime. For a weekly fee, a self-appointed security guard, who resembles a circus strongman, ostensibly patrols the neighborhood on his motorcycle, but the only time I've seen him is when he comes round to collect his fee. Surely I would have heard him cruising Rua JFS on a sleepless Saturday night?

Sunday, April 25th

The re-opening of the Museo da Casa Brasileira (Museum of the Brazilian House), after over a year of being closed due to Covid, was an opportunity to see some of the midcentury's most original, famously eccentric, and sensual modernist furniture. According to the museum's website, Brazilian furniture was banned for export during the military dictatorships of the 1960s to the 1980s, and the pieces on display represented some of the most important objects in the collection from those decades. As with many cultural history museums, visitors are led through an introductory exhibit.

On display were photographs of enormous Atlantic Forest trees being gleefully toppled by men with huge handsaws, and a sampling of these saws, weapons of arboreal torture and murder, were mounted on an opposite wall. A grainy black-and-white photo of a dozen smiling people linking hands at the base of a tree showed its immense girth. Another image included tiny, doll-like people standing in front of another giant. The size of the trees was so unreal I wondered if there was any photographic trickery involved. But no, these trees were over three thousand years old yet somehow expendable, their wood shipped to Portugal, the collection of hideously ornate, dark, and depressing Portuguese furniture on display in the museum likely hewn from their wood. The trees' venerable stories were written in the furniture: The headboard of a bed a tablet on which the history of a tree, and the health of a forest, could be read in rings and swirls, a history of rainfall and drought, insect attacks, lightning strikes, growth, famine. Armoires, chairs, and tables were unintended symbols of a ransacked Brazilian Eden. The sickened reaction I felt was like visiting a Holocaust museum for the first time. Finding the collection of Brazilian modernist furniture wasn't an option; I had to leave!

Tuesday, April 27th

Last night, a text arrived saying a book I'd ordered from Brazil's Amazon equivalent, Mercado Livre, had been delivered. (This is how it works here. A guy arrives on a motorcycle and stands outside the gate yelling your name, and if you don't appear within a few minutes and it isn't raining, the package gets tossed onto the porch. Or sometimes left with a neighbor.)

I went outside to retrieve it, searched everywhere and couldn't find it, and assumed it had been stolen. But this morning, I discovered the package neatly placed under a patio chair that sits to the right of the front door and is nowhere near the gate. When I went online to see how the package was delivered, a message said: "Left with a neighbor." Which means the unidentified neighbor has a key to the gate, at the least, and possibly one for the house, too. But which neighbor? I asked the woman across the street and she laughed. Given her physical condition, it could take her hours to cross the street, open the padlock, climb the three steps to the porch, place the package under the chair, and reverse those actions. I hope it's not the party boys next door.

Wednesday, April 28th

Today someone left a coin next to the mailbox, a five-centavo piece. Last week someone did this, too. Whenever I pocket them, they get replaced. I'm totally weirded out by the thought of someone having a key to the place and someone (else?) leaving these coins. Is the house being tagged? Are they good luck charms, offerings to appease the spirits of The Witch House? Not as far-fetched as it sounds. Brazil is home to a number of African syncretic religions: Macumba, Umbanda, Candomblé, Spiritists, and others, and offerings of money, flowers, fruit, and candles are common. Maybe The Witch House got its name for something other than its appearance.

Thursday, April 29th

Some musings about things domestic. Today I noticed that the carton of eggs I bought contains ten eggs instead of a dozen—because of the metric system? Milk here comes in unrefrigerated cardboard cartons, and just about everything contains an inordinate amount of sugar. The salt available in the stores has the consistency of an exfoliant or body scrub and doesn't really taste very salty. Crushed garlic and ginger are not available—you do the crushing yourself. Salad bags with a mix of lettuces are rare, but a shredded collard green called covey, kind of like kale but with a better texture, is available everywhere and is super delicious when cooked for a few minutes in a shallow pan with a little olive oil and garlic. Pre-made cakes in stores and *paderias* are long and thin, maybe twelve by three by three inches, not circular. The coffee here is surprisingly terrible. Scraps of food and otherwise stinky/dirty stuff generated when cooking are put in a plastic bag-lined, cylindrical-shaped countertop metal container and removed after the evening meal for the excellent *daily* trash pickup.

Clothes dryers here are an anomaly. Hanging up wet clothes, sheets, and towels is tedious and sloppy, and when the humidity is 100 percent, which is often, it can take three or more days for some items to dry, like towels and jeans. It's nothing like our grandmothers' backyard clotheslines with sun-dried sheets undulating in the breeze; here, peoples' clotheslines are installed in the ventilation shafts of buildings where no moving air ever penetrates, and rain frequently reverses the little bit of drying that's been accomplished. On a less humid day, if laundry is left out for more than eight hours or so, the dampness has absorbed the dust and air pollution, negating the cleansing the clothes just received.

Tuesday, May 4th

I cooked a chunk of salmon tonight. Sold with the tail still attached, it made me kind of queasy to cut it off, sawing away at it with a dull kitchen knife.

I located the source of an annoying sound that's been bothering me at night—a beetle that's worked its way into the ceiling fan lamp. It's been knocking around in there for a few days. It's not the first creature to get trapped; the lamp globe is an insect graveyard. Curious that insects are so compelled to be near a source of light that escape is not an issue and death is certain. A metaphor for something?

All my clothes smell bad now. Three days ago, I washed my single pair of blue jeans, and they're still slightly damp even after a string of sunny, low-humidity days. Inserting a leg expelled a musty-smelling poof, and when I turned the jeans inside out to investigate, they were streaked with mildew.

Tuesday, May 11th

Another five-centavo coin appeared near the mailbox, just inside the gate on a ledge, a place not reachable without a key to the padlock. There's a hardware store close by; I may go buy a new lock tomorrow.

Friday, May 14th

Tonight, I was downstairs lying on the couch snoozing when someone tapped the "shave and a haircut, two bits" rhythm on the window. My brain went into high alert. I couldn't decide what to do—should I investigate or pretend I was asleep? I lay there paralyzed. Eventually I got up. I couldn't find any evidence of someone being on the porch, and the padlock was closed and locked. The sound could have come from next door (our houses share a wall), but I know what I heard! The mysterious leaving of coins and now this convinced me that, definitely, something inexplicable was going on in and around the house. The guileless antics of my Evangelical neighbors, in their predictability and unambiguousness, seemed benign by comparison.

Sunday, May 16th

São Paulo is full of architecture that is neglected and decaying, covered in *pixação*,[3] a type of street writing inspired by heavy metal music and intended as an angry upbraiding of local government. But São Paulo's also a place of ultramodernity, distinctive buildings and neighborhoods, and fantastic graffiti.

I walked to the Parque Villa-Lobos, the location of a sad but beautiful ruin: an orquidarium[4] built in 2010, a giant dome greenhouse made of a metal framework grid and plastic sheeting. The yellowed plastic was in shreds and flapping in the wind like hundreds of small flags. On Paulista, one of São Paulo's most important and busiest avenues, the Museo de Arte de São Paulo, called the MASP, looks like it's been rotting in the rainforest for decades.[5] A glass and cement shoebox shape supported by heavy inverted beams, originally painted bright red and now streaked with mildew, the box looks like it's sagging in the middle. I'm curious why the engineers didn't compensate for this predictable effect, something the Greeks figured out two thousand years ago. They curved the bases of their temples by making each of the four corners droop, and the artifice created the illusion of a straight line. One of my favorite São Paulo buildings looks like it's been colonized by a giant strangler fig; another favorite building, Hotel Unique, suggests a grounded steamship.

Wednesday, May 19th

It happened again today—a book I'd ordered appeared on the porch under the chair. And I have no idea how it got there. I was around all day until 4 p.m., which is when I discovered it. Who has a key???

Sunday, May 23rd

Part of the fun of experiencing another culture is to visit big box retailers for a snapshot of the local interior design aesthetic. So I headed over to São Paulo's version of a Target/Home Depot hybrid, called Leroy Merlin. In any New Mexico Home Depot, imitation Navajo rugs woven in earthy, sandy desert colors dominate the flooring aisle; just looking at them made me sneeze. Here the rugs have cool '60s-inspired geometric patterns and bright colors. Mirrors and furniture styled in organic shapes and colorful throw pillows with vintage Portuguese tile designs were objects I could envision in a home. Bossa nova music played in my head accompanied by the clinking of ice cubes in a freshly made caipirinha. The door aisle was especially interesting—fun, modern designs, one that I liked with a basket weave pattern. Oversized doors. Doors that make a statement, suggesting what's concealed inside and the mood of the house, who the occupants are. I searched the appliance department to see if they sold clothes dryers. Nope. But Leroy Merlin peddles inflatable hot tubs, and a sample was set up, pool toys bobbing and swirling in the steamy water.

Thursday, May 27th

A young man (he shared that he was twenty-four) left a note in the mailbox, saying how much he liked The Witch House and that he'd seen me puttering around in the kitchen. He wanted to be friends. Back to Leroy Merlin for curtains. Has he been leaving the coins?

Sunday, May 30th

São Paulo's Covid risk assessment changes, arbitrarily, from Red to Orange to Yellow, and this week's yellow designation meant that the excellent Pinacoteca art museum was allowing 40 percent capacity. A special exhibit of the graffiti artist brothers Osgemeos (The Twins) included one of their signature characters recreated as a huge inflatable that filled the atrium of the three-floor building.[6] Their inflatables suggest string bean-thin disaffected youth that are the offspring of Mr. and Mrs. Potato Head, with a Yukon gold for a head instead of a russet. The twins are from São Paulo, and often you see their work around town where it's meant to be, on walls and buildings and in tunnels. The neighborhood around the Pinacoteca is sketchy, and a sign outside the museum warns people of a risk for cell phone theft, and of course I didn't see it until after I pulled out my phone to take a photo of a particularly good example of a Brazilian *calçada*[6] (the wavy sidewalks you see in SP, Rio, and Lisbon, where they originated). Men not affiliated with any kind of official security patrol the streets around the museum and when/if you find a parking space, they charge you twenty *reais* (a little less than four dollars) to watch your car. Was this the neighborhood security guy's day job?

Wednesday, June 2nd

The homeless man who sometimes hangs around the party house was on the street for a few hours. My elderly neighbor across the street said that he'd lived there in the past, and when she and I were talking, he gave us an evil-eye kind of stare and grabbed onto the party house gate, rattling it as if he were a caged chimpanzee. She said he robs people, but he is so thin, shoeless, and drug addled I questioned his ability to pull off a robbery. Later, I saw him rummage in a construction waste dumpster, find a Coke can, and try to extract some drops of liquid from it. I wanted to give him an orange, but the neighbor advised against it. If he's still hanging around later, perhaps I can figure out a way to leave something for him, anonymously, to eat. Maybe he'd benefit from a collection of mystery coins.

    Tonight at 8:30, as I walked up the hill from a restaurant on Diógenes, I passed a guy in the street timidly blowing a whistle, barely making a sound. A few moments later, a full-out protest erupted in the neighborhood, people banging on pans, on an instrument that sounded like a child's wooden xylophone, and blowing police-grade whistles, and you'd hear the occasional voice yell *Bolsonaro assassino!* The beauty of this kind of high-decibel dissent is that everyone protesting in earnest is in their apartments or their homes, protected, so there's a boldness you don't see on the streets. Such a perfect and powerful way to express your displeasure, anonymous and fortified in São Paulo's concrete canyons where sounds blend undifferentiated.

Thursday, June 3rd

This morning, a beautiful piece of embroidered cloth, bright colors, covered in big flowers, lay on the sidewalk across the street. On my way up the hill to the Pão de Açúcar, I crossed the street to get a close-up look at the cloth, and its shape suggested that a small dog could be lying underneath. I was tempted to poke it with the toe of my shoe but didn't and kept going. I bought a big, heavy bagful of provisions and walked home. Several hours later, no one had claimed the cloth.
    When I took out the trash tonight, it was gone.

Friday, June 11th

While cooking tonight, I remembered how my mother hated preparing the occasional shrimp boil for dinner. She felt compelled to peel those dozens of individuals for the five of us to eat and, by the end of the process, her fingers were lacerated, shriveled, and stinky. It never occurred to her that she should let US peel them as we ate them, and that was part of the fun of eating shrimp. This was one of many unnecessary labors she undertook that caused her a great deal of stress. She also used to break up uncooked spaghetti into bite-size pieces that she mixed in with the meat sauce; again, depriving us of the pleasure of twirling long lengths of pasta around a spoon or dividing it up ourselves. Given these behaviors, it would follow that she cut up tons of fresh vegetables, but if they didn't come already prepped or in a boil bag, they didn't get cooked. She did make salads, though, always iceberg lettuce and tasteless grocery store tomatoes. No wonder I was so delighted by my first bite of a homegrown tomato, straight from the vine, when we visited my dad's cousins in Bells, Tennessee.

Saturday, June 12th

Early this morning I was jolted awake by the sound of breaking glass, as if someone had thrown a rock through the window (it was intact). I'd been dreaming that a variety of dog breeds, even big dogs, were walking across the power lines outside, like squirrels and rats do. Enough was enough, so I decided to head over to the local Umbanda* temple for a consultation with the *pai-de-santo* (the spiritual leader of the group). His prowess with the *mesa radiônica*⁷ was legendary. The mesa consists of a board that resembles the TV test pattern of the 1950s (broadcast at times when regular programming wasn't available), and the process involves diagnosing and harmonizing energy fields, clearing and neutralizing negative vibrations, and attracting positive situations and outcomes. Evoking the names and special talents of both African and Catholic saints, the pai balances chakras and activates dimensional portals, borrowing from astrology and the mystical Jewish toolkit. It's a lot and it's complex. Mesa readings are an important part of Brazilian culture, and *brasileiros* rely on its insights for advice on the big four: money, love, work, and health. None of those things were my concern; most urgently I wanted to know about The Witch House, the mystery coins, book deliveries, and other strange goings-on and, secondarily, where I should be living.

The pai started by reading my energy. He said the force of the wind is my basis, and that one of my challenges is to tame that wind, be patient, and settle down. The color of my energy is blue. Archangel Michael[8] is my protector; he represents the capacity to change, and he confers the ability to transform, to turn a stone into a piece of gold (metaphorically). He is the angel of courage. I felt happy about this association with Michael; in Santa Fe I'd had an image of him on a wall in my bedroom, and looking at it had helped inspire the determination I needed to escape. In depictions of Michael, he stands in a classically inspired pose with Satan underfoot, his sword raised and ready to plunge into Satan's right shoulder. Michael is often depicted with flaxen hair and a feminized face, a picture of serenity mixed with determination. I wondered what his voice would sound like if we could converse.

Regarding The Witch House and the coins, the pai said that the bedroom wall I share with the neighbors' house is the source of the bad energy, that it's seeping through and permeating the house. He called the neighbors Satanists (gulp!) and suggested some rituals to perform and objects to place around the house to clear out the bad energy. He answered the where-I-should-be-living question like everyone else does—visit a lot of places and listen to your heart. Filter my experiences in order to focus on making the right choice. He added, "We are like white feathers floating here and there in our reality," a variation of the Taoist "I blow as aimless as the wind." It made me wonder, is my wind-ness blowing me around, neutralizing my control over my life? I felt vaguely disappointed in myself and in the reading.

After the consultation, I returned to my chair in the temple's outdoor waiting area, and a movement caught my eye. I looked up to see a downy white feather floating from above (but I was under a concrete overhang!), and it landed right at my feet. When I pointed this out to the woman sitting next to me, she said, "The pai works with white feather entities." I decided that going forward, my quest for Location X should be motivated less by expectations and lists and collecting certain kinds of data and more by the lesson of the white feather: by listening to my heart.

Monday, June 14th

Much of Brazil is in lockdown, but not São Paulo, and nothing has really changed significantly in the trajectory of the pandemic. It's as if the government decides arbitrarily when to shut down and when to open, to give the impression that it's closely monitoring the situation. I had errands to run on Paulista; my destination was the Martins Fontes bookstore for its architecture section, but none of the books I'd found online were there on the shelves. Both the street and the bookstore were packed with people; nothing signaled a pandemic except for the masks mandated to be worn indoors. Few Paulistanos wore them outside. To see the unmasked masses was to get a glimpse into São Paulo's long history of international migration and the blending of many cultures: Portuguese, Italian, West African, Lebanese, Indigenous groups, Arabs, Asians, Jews, people from almost everywhere. São Paulo has the largest Japanese expat community in the world. For an outsider, it's expectation-defyingly strange to hear Portuguese coming out of a mouth situated in a Japanese-looking face.

On the way back to The Witch House, the Uber driver and I listened to a government-produced news program that's broadcast on all Brazilian radio stations at the same time every day, preempting all other independently produced news. He said the first broadcast happened in 1935 and has been continuous to the present. It was pro-Bolsonaro, of course.

Tuesday, June 15th

Congonhas, São Paulo's inner-city airport, was spookily quiet at 8:30 in the morning when I arrived for a flight to Brasília, Brazil's capital a thousand kilometers to the north. GOL airline's boarding and disembarking procedures are far more enlightened than any airline in America. *Idosos*, pregnant women, and families board first, and when disembarking, nobody jumps up and grabs their bags so they can beat everyone else off the plane. A flight attendant announces by rows who can stand up, get their bags, and leave, and everyone is calm and follows the procedure. I thought only Americans suffered from triskaidekaphobia, but there was no row thirteen on the plane.

The Airbnb, an unexceptional flat in an ultramodern hotel, was not as described. I expected a kitchen and got a single-burner hot plate, two coffee cups, four coffee cup saucers, one set of silverware, and a bottle opener, the usual stuff you'd have if you were camping by yourself. And only half a roll of TP. But I'd come to Brasília for the brutalist architecture, and from the roof of the twenty-storey structure, the all-white Oscar Niemeyer National Congress building looked like a marble table set with two Crate & Barrel bowls—one right side up and the other upside down—separated by huge, monolithic salt and pepper shakers. The Niemeyer Cathedral and bell tower,[9] a crown of thorns and a giant pillory, respectively, and the dome-shaped art museum and reflecting pool, a 1950s B-movie spaceship look-alike, are icons of world architecture that, like the MASP in São Paulo, have seen better days. Brasília suggests an abandoned World's Fair grounds more than it looks like the capital city of a major world power.

Wednesday, June 16th

A sign at the hotel elevator says, "Before getting in, make sure that the lift is on the floor." So sometimes it's not, and people have plunged to their deaths? On the Airbnb listing, the owner of the space noted the interior dimensions of the elevator car, I guess in case you are a plus-size person or have an inordinate amount of luggage. To confirm, I measured the space with my feet, conveniently ten inches long, and arrived at four feet on a side.

I waited in the hotel lobby for a city excursion to see the Niemeyer buildings close-up and the residence of Bolsonaro himself. The house is located on extensive, heavily guarded grounds and isn't visible from the road, so you have to use your imagination. The tour ended at former president Juscelino Kubitschek's memorial. Kubitschek was responsible for greenlighting the whole Brasília deal, making it the federal capital of Brazil in 1960, and his memorial was a huge tomb-like structure filled with vitrines displaying the notable man's memorabilia. Medals and ribbons gifted him by royalty and politicians worldwide looked like artifacts from the Napoleonic era, and I wondered if this bestowing of medals still happens. Rarely do you see U.S. politicians' Brioni jackets festooned in medals and with garlands of ribbons, and I wondered why our forty-fifth president didn't think to revive this tradition. A collection of triangular felt banners, reminiscent of 1960s football banners students tacked on their college dorm walls, commemorated the creation of Brasília. I wished they'd reproduced them for sale in the gift shop—I would have bought them all.

Kubitschek's personal library was installed in a vast wing of the museum. Greeting you at the entrance were president and first lady look-alike mannequins wearing formal clothes and smiling, standing self-referentially next to life-size black-and-white photos of Kubitschek posing with famous people, including Castro, JFK, and Marlon Brando dressed as Mr. Christian from *Mutiny on the Bounty*.[10] Add a couple of vampire veneers on his canines, and Kubitschek would be a dead ringer for Bela Lugosi's Dracula.

Thursday, June 17th

On a day trip from Brasília to a colonial town called Pirenópolis, two smaller cities along the route were swarming with local and federal police and news reporters. Just past those places, the guide stopped at a sign that marks the original boundary that Portugal and Spain decided would delineate their respective territories—everything to the west of the boundary was Spain's and to the east, Portugal's. It didn't really work out that way but, at the time, no one knew the actual size and shape of South America. At a park bench in the Pirenópolis town square, tourists can snap a selfie with a friendly Minotaur, a seated human figure dressed in a bright orange sweater and green pants and topped with a cartoonish bull's head, the horns painted with colorful flowers.[11] The guide said that during Carnival, enslaved Black people disguised themselves as Pirenópolis's mascot so they could participate in the fun anonymously. Wouldn't that work only if everyone, Black or white, dressed as Minotaurs?

On the way back to Brasília, we saw an anteater crossing the road and stopped at a magnificent double waterfall where, while admiring the scene, the guide disclosed (he had known this all along) that a gunman was on the loose in the area, attacking and killing local farmers and terrorizing people in Brasília. All the cops and reporters suddenly made sense. Like spree killers in the U.S., the gunman had shot people at random, sometimes many at a time. Hearing this news put my amygdala on high alert—an indicator that I did not want to die in Brasília—and in that instant it fell off the list of possibilities for relocation. Actually, it never made it onto the list in the first place.

Thursday, June 24th

Today I walked to São Paulo's oldest bus stop, only 1.5 kilometers from The Witch House, to see a Renaissance-style work painted on its curved interior ceiling. But what I saw instead was a ceiling painted in glossy battleship gray that signaled the city's been at it again, obliterating its street art. I'd seen a photo online, taken of the ceiling only two weeks ago, with the painting still intact. Over five thousand *pixadores* and hundreds of graffiti artists prove over and over that the city's efforts to counter what it considers vandalism are futile and a waste of resources. Tags and murals are often repainted within days, re-establishing the ascendency of art over politics and restoring the true character of the city.

Friday, June 25th

June is the middle of winter in the Southern Hemisphere, but the weather was warm, and I was restless. So I went to the Shopping Cidade (city) São Paulo on Paulista to look for a pair of jeans to replace the mildewed ones, thinking that I may not have to wash them until I return to the U.S. in a few days. The best part of the trip was watching a member of the janitorial staff roaming the mall with a tennis ball installed at the end of an aluminum pole, cleaning up scuff marks deposited by shoppers' shoes. I snapped a photo of her from the back[12] as she erased a substantial and stubborn black scuff, vigorously and with determination. You could tell she loved her job.

Thursday, July 1st

Visited a favorite restaurant on Diógenes for lunch and ate a chocolate éclair that may have been topped with a dark brown adhesive. I managed to scrape most of it off without using a solvent, and much of it stuck to my fingers and ripped a few napkins to shreds. An hour later, I regretted eating it. I hope I don't have a heart attack in my sleep.

Saturday, July 3rd

The slog back to the U.S.—ten hours in the air—was today. I miss The Witch House already. The rituals the pai said to perform, and the objects placed around the house, had worked their magic, and The Witch House was cleared of all its negativity. I had a pocketful of five-centavo coins to remember it by. I missed São Paulo, too, a place I felt both attracted to and repelled by. But feelings can shift in an instant, and twenty minutes to touchdown a flight attendant appeared and asked, "Will you be needing a wheelchair?" Had I crossed the boundary into decrepitude, and it had escaped my notice? In a flash I cycled through six of the seven stages of grief: *shock and denial, anger and bargaining, depression and reflection*, and I rejected *acceptance* outright. I had been declared *forte* by my neighbor across the street only a few weeks earlier, and I was hanging onto that.

*Umbanda, one of many Afro-Brazilian syncretic religions, is a blend of Catholicism and traditional West African religions, practiced by close to half a million Brazilians.

CHAPTER THREE

CUSTOMS

Twenty minutes before touchdown, the flight attendant walked down the aisle handing out immigration forms. "Spanish or English? Spanish or English?" I'd filled these out plenty of times before and, even so, I'd forgotten that they make a big deal out of bringing food into the country. Two packs of my favorite cereal and a pound of Peet's coffee were in my checked bag. If I ticked the "yes" box, "Are you bringing in food," I would draw attention to myself. If I ticked "no," I risked getting caught. The consequences are severe: Mexican law imposes sanctions and penalties that are so terrifying that it's best left to the reader's imagination. I ticked "no."

As soon as I lifted pen from paper, I panicked. I questioned my decision and ran through several possible scenarios that could happen at customs. A tall, handlebar-mustachioed, bandolier-wearing *federale* would intuit that I'm a terrible liar, open the suitcase, find the cereal and coffee, and I'd land in a Mexican jail for the rest of my days with only bread and water to sustain me. Since I'm addicted to coffee, I'd soon be lying on the floor shivering with a migraine while my body adjusted to the lack of caffeine. I started imagining what I'd say to the customs official to avert this potentiality. "Coffee isn't proper food, is it? Food is something you chew." Or "Oh, gosh, I'm so forgetful; I packed my suitcase weeks ago and forgot it was in there!" Or "I couldn't read the fine print on your form and just ticked all the boxes 'no'." Or "I knew you weren't supposed to bring food into the country, but I'm on a special diet and I need this particular kind of cereal and brand of coffee, otherwise I could end up in the hospital with an anaphylactic response." Or I could own up to it and say, "I'm so sorry, sir, you're right; I've broken the law, now please handcuff me and take me away. Let this be a lesson to the other travelers who have witnessed my deception."

The plane landed. I pulled my carry-on from the overhead bin and marched down the aisle and down the steps to the tarmac, delivering myself into the jaws of fate. Once on terra firma, I had the urge to abandon my bag and run, but where would I go? Corralled between two parallel lines of ropes and stanchions, we travelers were given another form to fill out—a health declaration—printed in type so small I wished I'd brought a travel microscope. But when I saw that people much younger than me were also having trouble reading it, I thought that maybe we could collectively bargain for skipping this form.

After doubling up on reading glasses, I saw that another one of the questions could be a deal-breaker. "What other countries and cities have you been to in the past fourteen days? What was the date?" This was smack-dab in the middle of Covid, and I had been in one of the world's hot spots: São Paulo, Brazil. I was certain I'd be sent back to Houston for a two-week quarantine in an airport-area Super 8. The young woman ahead of me in line needed a pen, and I gladly loaned her mine, thinking that this good deed might count for a reciprocal good deed that I would experience in the immediate future. Like an immigration official discovering the food, winking, and looking the other way, for example. A man dressed in a white lab coat, suggesting that he was a health professional, was collecting the forms, and since I hadn't filled in the date (the question was ambiguous: did it mean the date you'd departed the country you were visiting in the past fourteen days? Were they wanting a date range?), I was prepared to ask for clarification but, again, I didn't want to draw attention to myself and raise suspicions. To my surprise, he took the form without even looking at it. Immigration obstacle number one: box ticked! We travelers were then fed into a line in a narrow hallway that led somewhere else that we couldn't immediately see. At the end of the hallway, a huge poster on the wall reminded us that FOOD IS NOT ALLOWED TO BE BROUGHT INTO MÉXICO. As examples, there were pictures of fruits and vegetables and uncooked meats of all kinds floating on a background of blue sky with fluffy, cheerful clouds and, to my relief, there were no images of bags of cereal or coffee. A new strategy came to mind: if questioned, I could say, "I thought the items referenced in the 'no food' rule were only agricultural products in their raw form, as depicted on your poster, plus things like seeds or worms that might drop to the ground from these products and replicate and become invasive. Or the meat might not be actual harvested meat, and the animal might still be alive, reproduce, and overrun México like rabbits and cane toads did in Australia. Really sorry, sir!"

After we rounded the corner at the end of the hallway, two immigration officers stationed at their kiosks came into view. They were rubber-stamping everyone in, and I relaxed a little. The irrefutable proof that I'd been in Brazil only a few days earlier was right there in my passport, but I, too, was rubber-stamped, and I thought I was home free. Immigration obstacle number two: another box ticked. At the next checkpoint, I saw my bag. A baggage handler had removed it from the carousel and positioned it in a neat row with three or four other bags. Was it flagged for inspection? It might as well have had a flashing red arrow hovering over it that said Eat at Joe's. I smiled at the man guarding the bags, hoping to communicate friendly calm via sparkly eyes and confident body language because, of course, everyone was masked, and he pointed to the big X-ray machine, the final obstacle. It's the last opportunity the federales have to discover the boxes of Pop-Tarts you're smuggling into the country or the twenty computers you intend to sell at the Saturday market. Do cereal and coffee show up on an X-ray? I had no idea. As I placed my checked bag, carry-on, and purse onto the conveyor belt, managing my nervousness had become nearly impossible. But something unexpected happened. An elderly Mexican couple behind me was struggling with their huge bags, and I saw this as an opportunity to cluster all of our bags together so that maybe they would look like one big undifferentiated blob as they passed through X-ray, and my food would go undetected. So, while hoisting their bags onto the conveyor and arranging them around my smaller bags looked like I was performing another good deed, it was totally selfish and calculating. As the bags came out the other end, I was a little too quick to grab mine and head for the *salida*, and another customs official stopped me. Entry into México was within my grasp, only a few yards away, and I'd been caught. She said something to me that I didn't quite catch, and then said it again in English. "Push the red button." It didn't make sense in my native tongue either. But a kiosk stood to my left with what looked like a big red panic button, and pushing it meant the sliding glass doors would open to freedom. But it wasn't working. People were clustered at the exit anxious to escape, and finally the customs official sauntered over to the kiosk and pushed the red button herself. I guess you had to have the right touch. Miraculously the doors opened, revealing a sea of smiling brown eyes and black masks anticipating the arrival of their loved ones. Welcome to México!

CHAPTER FOUR

MÉXICO CITY

Friday, July 23rd

Before boarding a tourist hop-on-hop-off bus, I wondered if we'd spend lots of time stuck in traffic, and from 3 to 5 p.m. that's exactly what happened. We were immobilized in a tunnel for over twenty minutes[1], thirty people on the upper deck breathing fumes and somehow managing not to pass out. I was sitting next to a guy probably not that much younger than me who took selfies almost constantly, and sometimes making a gang symbol with the hand not holding the phone. Once I caught him looking at the thumbnails of his pictures, and he was scrolling through hundreds of them. I wonder if the Diagnostic and Statistical Manual of Mental Disorders has an entry for this behavior, specifically related to cell phones and the compulsion to take one's own photo incessantly.

The bus often stopped at places I had no interest in, like huge, modern shopping malls. The hop-on-hop-off day did have three highlights, though: lovely Alameda Park, established in 1592, its pathways paved in marble; the spectacular art nouveau/art deco Palacio de Bellas Artes[2], an early twentieth-century architectural wonder known as México's Cathedral of Art; and the Basilica of Our Lady of Guadalupe. I was also the recipient of two kindnesses. A park employee took the time to lead me to the departure point for the bus, and a young girl working in a drugstore in a micro mall across from Alameda who, when I asked where the bathroom was, gave me a spare receipt to get into the one downstairs. Not just anyone off the street can use the bathroom—you need to have shopped in the mall—and a dour woman at the entrance checks everyone's receipts for interlopers.

I walked the entire perimeter of the Alameda looking for the Diego Rivera Museum, asking random people where it was, and no one could tell me; it didn't even register on Google Maps. When I finally found it, an official guarding the entrance pointed to a sign: *CERRADO*. I was clearly disappointed and later wondered why he didn't tell me that Rivera's most famous mural, *Man at the Crossroads* or *Man, Controller of the Universe*, was installed in the Bellas Artes at the other end of the park.[3] I discovered it totally by accident. Not only does the palacio house several extremely famous and valuable mural works, but the building itself is an architectural sensation, inside and out.

The Basilica of Our Lady of Guadalupe is a place of pilgrimage, an opportunity for México's nearly ninety-three million Catholics to see the miraculous image of Lupe on a cloak. In fact, each year ten million people from around the world visit the shrine, making it the world's most visited Marian destination and second only to the Vatican in popularity. In December of 1531, her image imprinted itself on the tilma (an outer garment) of a man named Juan Diego and, to this day, nobody can explain how it got there and why, in over 450 years, it still hasn't crumbled into little bits. Even the Aztec locals wrote, pre-1531 in the Nahuatl language, about seeing a similar apparition, and

> There is plenty of historical evidence that after 1531, the number of Aztecs seeking Baptism jumps through the roof:
>
> "This miracle precipitated the greatest flood of conversions in the whole history of Christianity. In the seven years fol-

lowing this miracle, approximately eight million Aztecs converted to Christianity [...]"[4]

Prior to this event, the Aztecs were offering thousands of human sacrifices per year in central México, including child sacrifice. The conversion of the Aztecs to Christianity ended the brutal practice of human sacrifice..."[5]

And no doubt reduced the numbers of Aztecs brutally massacred by the Christians.

Lucky *chilangos** can make a pilgrimage without needing to travel to one of Europe's many caminos and walk hundreds of kilometers in all kinds of weather. Plus, to see the famous image, you board a moving walkway that conveys you past Our Lady and keeps the line from stagnating, so viewing the miracle image places practically no physical demands on pilgrims at all. Maybe a sore neck, from needing to look up, is all anyone suffers.[6]

Later in the day, I wandered around México City's main square, the Zócalo. A guy rode past on his bicycle recording himself on a cell phone he was holding at arm's length. Laughing, he said, "Six thousand people here are lovin' on me!" "Aztec" reenactors were performing *limpias*** and dancing, and I indulged my tourist side and had my photo taken with two of them dressed as skeletons (photo not included, too embarrassing). Their dress and makeup were so compelling, I couldn't help myself.

A driver I hired to take me to a popular restaurant asked, unprompted, if I was afraid to travel alone in México, and I said no, that in the United States being anywhere in a public place was a special kind of scary because anyone can own a gun, even people who are still legally children. He was stunned by my answer.

---

* Residents of México City

** A limpia is a cleansing ceremony performed traditionally by Mexican healers using eggs, the smoke from herbs and special plants, oils, and sound to clear negative energy, obstacles, and confusion and to instill a feeling of well-being.

CHAPTER FIVE

FOOD TO MAKE YOUR MOUTH WATER BURST

The ReadMyGrub app translates a high-end México City restaurant menu from Spanish to English (sort of), and I provide descriptions of these dishes.

From coolapps.com: "Listening to someone speak another language can be daunting enough but interpreting menus in other languages is often a downright herculean task. ReadMyGrub allows you to point your phone's camera at the inscrutable menu in front of you, and instantly translates it to the language of your choosing."

THE CHILI OF SEPTEMBER OF CHOLULA

Chiles en nogada with the recipe of the nuns of the convent of Santa Clara. "Tribute to Mexican food, thanks to them."

Chiles boiled in the sacred wash water of Cholula's nuns' wimples, veils, and undergarments, stuffed with the crusts of day-old bread and discarded shoe leather, a tribute to the oldest city in México and the women who walked its streets, genuflecting with each step.

DUCK OF RED ROSE MOHOSO

Juicy lacquered Canadian duck, bathed in crunchy rose petal syrup. "The miracle is fulfilled, sings the fragrant wine of fragrant matter."

Duck slathered with the highest-quality lacquer that money can buy, procured at the local Sherwin-Williams. We collect the crunchy rose petals left at the gravesites of our forebears, only red ones that are completely desiccated and slightly moldy, that will crumble to our touch. Marinated for fourteen days in Ombre Rose perfume. Cuidado: hot!

CHILE PALMA DE MALLORCA

Ancho chili stuffed with pasta, shrimp, and pumpkin flower sauce with crispy onion. "Sowing in an afternoon in the lost garden, spell and fertile of luminous creatures."

The recipe for this peyote-inspired dish was conveyed to Chef de Cuisine José Maria José by the god Quetzalcoatl himself. We found JMJ in the late afternoon light, lying in the jardín público, staring up at the dappled light filtering through a strangler fig, blabbering about fairies and elves orbiting his head and reciting this recipe.

CHICKEN THE DELIRIO

Filled with huitlacoche and nopal bathed in its pineapple and sesame sauce. "Share your appetite for delirium and the smile trickles between your lips."

While it's still running around with no head, a chicken flash-cooked in a vat of boiling oil, then stuffed with sauteed magic mushrooms. For those of you who love being in a disturbed state of mind, this dish is for you. If you're lucky, you'll be transported to an ecstasy never before imagined and, after the scary first rush, your partner will wonder what the huge grin on your face is all about.

THE ADOBADA OF DON LEONARDO

Grilled marinated pork tenderloin jerky. "History repeats itself."

Don Leonardo is the mummified relic lying in a vitrine in the Church of the Bautizado en la Tierra (Baptized in the Earth). But don't worry; this jerky is not made from Don Leonardo's flesh, it is only named for him. And rest assured, Don Leonardo won't reincarnate as a pig, Catholics don't believe in that.

CHICKEN WITH MOLE DE PUEBLA

Exquisite poblano mole with the authentic version of the grannies accompanied by red onion, topped with sesame. "Recreation of kitchen angels."

Our grannies are long dead and cremated, but we saved a cupful of their ashes for this special ingredient, one of twenty-eight, of our subtle but flavorful mole. We often feel the presence of these two beautiful angels in the kitchen, slapping us upside the head for drinking too much mezcal while cooking.

THE VILLA ELENA FILLET

Prepared with butter on a bed of hibiscus and roasted potatoes. "The flavor exists, you are missing."

Yes, the missing ingredient is you and your tongue (but don't worry—it will remain attached to the floor of your mouth!) Your taste buds will thank you; the dish is meaningless without them.

THE SAN MATEO FILLET

Grilled in a sauce of twelve dried chilies with a bed of nopal. "History of the brave bull, seed of livestock."

Cuts of meat for the San Mateo are harvested solely from bulls killed by a matador maestro. Garnished with a reduction of bull semen, collected the day before the contest between man and beast. Bull penis medallions by special request.

STEAL OF HAVANA

Bathed in a delicious sauce of pumpkin seeds and nopal trotters. "Grain of sand collected between the sky and the sea."

We are doing our part in climate change mitigation by collecting particulate matter from the air, filtering out everything but the finest-grain sand, and sprinkling it over your nopalitos. (Not responsible for cracked teeth.)

BEEF EMPTY

With a cilantro and pistachio pesto dressing, topped with a coriander sauce. "The rest of the gods and silence."

Indulge, but conservatively, in this delicious dish, and you will feel emancipation of the mind, a state of not-self. Eat too much, and you may experience emancipation of the bowels. But don't worry: the gods are not watching and laughing, they're resting.

THE CROWN OF QUEEN ISABEL

Giant shrimp in lobster sauce and fried spinach. "The miracle is accomplished, sings the fragrant lobster of fragrant gray matter."

Served in a life-size Día de Muertos sugar skull, with the top of the skull lopped off; shrimp line the perimeter, and a gelatinous, pink lobster sauce fills the cranium. Rice balls are fitted into the eye sockets, with a slice of green olive, black pits for pupils. Presented on a bed of crispy spinach.

FRESH SALMON JEWELRY STYLE

Salmon steak bathed in a sea of saffron and white wine. "A sigh to meditation."

A generous slab of salmon floating in white wine and saffron, presented in a giant lotus flower and surrounded by a string of cultured pearls (yours to keep!). The pearls, 108 of them, can be used as a mala for your personal meditation practice.

LANGUAGE IN MOLE DE CUALE

Rich chunks of beef tongue in sweet mole. "Your name ends in Puerto Vallarta."

Regardless of what tongue you speak, don't venture out after dark in PV or you may lose it!

CHAPTER SIX

SANTA FE, NEW MEXICO

At 3 a.m., Colleen woke up needing to pee. She liked to sleep with the door closed, and earlier in the evening when she climbed into bed after shutting the door, something had felt off about the mechanism. The doorknobs in her friends' house had never worked that well, and now the one in her hand spun aimlessly. Her friends were out of town, she was alone, and panic slackened her bladder. Peeing in the trash can, a loose-weave Navajo basket, wasn't an option, and neither was the small, felt souvenir teepee whose shape reminded her of the travel pee funnel she kept in her car. Fortunately, the house was only one storey, and the windows in the bedroom that faced the street didn't have screens. But the garden path was six feet down from the windowsill and, in the past, she'd broken her foot under much more innocuous circumstances, from merely stepping off a curb.

She slipped into a pair of blue jeans and a T-shirt, grabbed her phone and glasses, and found a spare key to the house in a dresser drawer. She stuffed it into a back pocket and stood at the window looking deeply into the early morning blackness, weighing the possible outcomes. By then her need to pee was more than desperate. The (empty) recycle bin was positioned slightly to the left of the window, and she decided to ease herself onto the top of the bin and jump down from there.

A long crack traversed the bin's flimsy plastic cover. The application of her weight presented a risk of collapse, and once inside the bin, butt down, legs and arms up in a jackknife position, she'd be stuck until someone discovered her. Or the bin could shoot out from under her, and she'd end up on the cement, broken and bleeding. She hoped no gun-toting insomniac was walking down the street as she exited the window, thinking they were seeing a burglary in progress. None of these scenarios were good, but she took the gamble.

Moving slowly and deliberately, she was clear of the house and sitting on top of the bin, the crack holding enough to prevent her from slipping through. But the greater challenge was getting down; she could still end up lodged inside or sprawled on the sidewalk. She realized that the afternoon's monsoon rain had filled the bin with a substantial amount of water, and she thought of herself as the bikinied woman sitting on a dunk tank's collapsible bench at a county fair.

Grabbing the opposite edges of the top of the bin, she leaned forward, counted to three, and launched herself into the air. Time warped into slow motion, as it does during life-threatening situations, and somehow, she landed on her feet. A few minutes later she was back inside the house, jeans still unsoiled. After visiting the bathroom, leaving the door ajar, she disabled both the bedroom and bathroom doorknobs, crawled back in bed, and fell into a deep, dreamless sleep.

CHAPTER SEVEN

EL PASO, TEXAS

Driving into El Paso on I-10 traveling east, Colleen was reminded of a graveyard. Italian cypress trees, a scrawny, compact tree she had always disliked, populated parched, crumbling neighborhoods and reached to the sky with their pointed tips. She associated them with cemeteries, dark green sentinels guarding the dead, and homes surrounded by chunky rock walls suggested family burial plots. Pollution wafting over El Paso from Ciudad Juárez and from a large, local oil and gas refinery created a thick whiteness that hung in the sky, draining the landscape of color, even muting Juárez's famous landmark, a 200-foot-tall bright red X^1 just south of the international Bridge of the Americas.

Colleen was in town to explore El Paso as a possible place to live. Six months earlier, she sold her Santa Fe house and had been wandering ever since, searching for her special place on the planet. Someone told her about friends who loved El Paso, and that was enough for Colleen to dedicate a compulsory ten days to research the area and its offerings. Staying in Airbnbs for six months had nearly depleted the funds she set aside for her quest, and each new place created both heightened expectations and bigger disappointments. Ten minutes into her arrival in El Paso, things were already looking inauspicious.

Coffee may help, she thought, so she pulled off the highway and into a crowded Walmart parking lot, wondering if this was the one at which a mass shooting had taken place three years earlier. A white supremacist had driven over six hundred miles from Dallas to El Paso specifically to shoot Mexicans. Instead of searching for "coffee near me" on her phone, overcome by curiosity she Googled "El Paso Walmart massacre." Waiting for the results to load, she noticed a Starbucks across the street, its familiar logo comforting. The thought of dark roast coffee coupled with a bagel helped mediate her anxiety. She canceled the search, placed her phone on the passenger seat, and navigated across a busy street crisscrossed by gargantuan trucks and modified sports cars emitting predator-inspired screams from their mufflers.

Even though she was the only customer inside the Starbucks, her order took over fifteen minutes to fulfill by five staff members. Bagel and coffee in hand, she went outdoors to escape the intrusive sound system playing the refrain of "Just the Way You Are" but was quickly overwhelmed by a swarm of aggressive flies. Back indoors, something that had escaped her notice earlier now drew her attention. At the drink pickup counter, the employees had constructed a memorial to the troops who'd recently lost their lives in Afghanistan during the shutdown of the American occupation. There, on the protective acrylic shield that separated staff from customers (this was during the height of Covid's Delta wave), someone had written "For the U.S. Troops killed in Kabul, Afghanistan, 8/26/2021." Flanking the shield were two small American flags, and underneath were thirteen tall-size Starbucks cups arranged in an arc and filled with coffee beans, each cup labeled with a soldier's name written above the Starbucks logo.[2] With Fort Bliss right around the corner, it seemed likely that soldiers and support staff were patrons of that particular Starbucks and, using what was at hand, likely that the employees sought to attract more customers (and boost sales) with their unintentionally whimsical memorial. People's lives represented by a cup of coffee beans? Colleen found it disrespectful and trivializing and, given the huge Mexican American population of El Paso and the fact that Fort Bliss is the home of a notorious migrant children camp, bizarre in the extreme. But was she missing the point? Maybe the disrespect was intentional; the Mexican American employees of Starbucks choosing to represent the deceased Fort Bliss soldiers as inconsequential cups of dark roast beans a comment on the inhumane treatment of México's innocents. She found herself imagining the memorial on a large scale, the Starbucks CFO running with the idea and green-lighting funding for an installation in downtown El Paso. The cups six feet tall, rendered in Carrera marble and topped with a dome of polished obsidian coffee beans. And to clarify the metaphor, with one of the cups knocked over as if in a moment of carelessness, the spilled beans symbolizing the instant loss of life. She thought of a related idea expressed by an hourglass, the grains of sand inexorably running through its wasp waist, their depletion symbolizing a life lived predictably and ending as expected. An hourglass memorial the size of the Washington Monument, filled with coffee beans representing the grains of sand.

 Revived by the caffeine and bagel, Colleen walked to her car that, by then, had heated up to 115 degrees. She slipped into the driver's seat and entered the address of the Airbnb, her destination, into Google Maps, while the air conditioner strained to mediate the heat, forcing ever-colder air into her face, drying out her eyes and lips. She removed the sunshades from the windshield, the intrusion of white light temporarily blinding her.

 Google Maps routed her through El Paso's historic district past mansions that hinted at more prosperous times. A few homes still maintained their former glory, but most had been appropriated and neglected by the impecunious. Hippies had moved in, installing tie-dye curtains in elegant windows and strewing debris in front yards. Staircases, window frames, and Ionic columns were rotted, and roofs were covered with bright blue plastic tarps. A Greek revival two-storey came into view, catching Colleen's attention, the words "International Art Museum" written in the entablature that four Corinthian columns supported. She wondered, what does International Art Museum mean exactly? She turned the corner and pulled into the parking lot.

    Colleen was no stranger to the art world and the world of museums. For more years than she cared to ponder, she had worked for a vanity museum in a big city creating a video archive of artist interviews. Over the years, these interviews gained in importance as their iconic subjects died one by one. After selling her home in Santa Fe, she felt like she was severing ties with her career, too, although it was never stated formally. She merely had informed her contact at the museum that she was taking a break from home ownership and would likely be resettled somewhere within a few months. In her heart, she knew this wouldn't come to pass, and she hoped he would forget about her and find someone new to assume her role. Because of Covid, she hadn't been in any museum for over a year, so investigating the International Art Museum felt like a minor adventure. An experience with a touch of familiarity but full of possibility. She liked the acronym it created: I AM.

    As she approached the entrance to the museum, the door opened and an elderly gentleman wearing a Toulouse-Lautrec tie emerged. They began talking to each other as if they were old friends. He was an expert at extracting information from Colleen, and within a few moments knew her history with the vanity museum in a big city. Even though the I AM was closing for the day, he insisted on giving her a tour. They started with an installation of a local painter, a transplant from Russia, who was having an opening the following night. His work was a mishmash of styles: Monet, Van Gogh, cliché Southwest, cliché cowboy, and fellow Russian Marc Chagall, as if he couldn't get a fix on a specific painterly identity. Then he showed her the Mexican Revolution room in the basement, with a statue of Pancho Villa that looked like a Madame Tussaud's Palace of Wax reject, passing by a case of antique Buddhas, Bodhisattvas, and Boehm porcelain birds on the way. The museum owned a collection of astronaut Alan Bean's paintings, and Colleen couldn't help but think how worthless they would be without his name attached. A small sitting room displayed objects collected by the original owners of the mansion, and a few antique rocking horses were scattered here and there, all with a fine coating of El Paso dust that dimmed their former beauty. After twenty minutes had passed, the man asked Colleen if she wanted to be the museum's new director.

The next night Colleen attended the opening, and the man acted as her escort. He introduced her to the Russian artist, telling him (falsely) that she had driven the six hours down from Santa Fe expressly to see his show. He introduced her to the current director and to members of the museum's board of directors and to a wealthy patron who bragged, in the presence of the Russian artist, that she had bought several of his paintings as party favors to give to her friends. The director herself pleaded with Colleen to assume her role. She said, We probably don't have the money to hire someone else to do it.

That night, at the Airbnb, Colleen spent way too much time crafting a letter to the man, in which she declined the offer, suppressing her anger at the insensitivity of both the wealthy art patron and the director. In case it needed revision, she intended to send the letter the next morning.

Dear —,
Thank you so much for being my personal escort at the opening last night and for introducing me to your colleagues. I enjoyed every moment and especially enjoyed your company. I gave your proposal a lot of thought last night, and while I'm honored to be offered a position with the organization, I believe you would be better served by someone who has a degree in museum administration and/or development or experience in those specific fields. What I heard last night from multiple people is that fund-

ing is the number one issue, and although I have grant-writing and fund-raising experience gained at three different nonprofits, my professional interests lie elsewhere.

I also understand that additional staff is sorely needed. I'm sure it's crossed your mind, but what about offering internships to students from the University of Texas at El Paso or the New Mexico State Museum Studies programs and to area artists or other interested locals to give them firsthand experience in museum operation? Or advertising internship opportunities to a wider pool of candidates? It seems to me that there could be a lot of response, both locally and nationally, and not just among those interested in art museum practices; you might attract history buffs and archivists, too. The IAM is a hybrid of both an art and a history museum: the Mexican Revolution collection, the Alan Bean painting collection, eclectic personal El Paso collections donated to the museum coupled with exhibits of individual artists' works suggest this. Internships could serve these two important purposes: to relieve the pressure on you and the few others who shoulder all the responsibility, and to allow you to groom someone for the positions you need to fill. You could even advertise for positions not currently in place at the museum but needed; for example, a staff historian/researcher, an art installer, a conservator, or a social media and web content developer, offering candidates the opportunity to develop these important roles with an autonomy not available to someone working at a larger institution.

Here's another thought: what about offering personalized docent tours staffed by volunteer high school or college students who could earn credit by their participation? These internship and docent initiatives, while infusing the organization with "new blood" and fresh vision, could result in the invigoration of the museum and the emergence of an ideal candidate for the position of director, albeit not contributing any cash to the coffers. I'm assuming you will appoint an interim director to relieve the desperate rush to fill the director position? This, of course, could buy time until you find exactly the right person.

Thank you again, I really appreciate the fantastic introduction to the IAM and to its stakeholders, and I wish you every success in identifying a new director.

Warm regards,
Colleen

Colleen was softhearted and never wanted to disappoint anyone. And even though she was drifting aimlessly on a vast ocean, looking for her next port of call, she wasn't about to take the helm of a sinking ship, especially given that she was trying to identify the perfect place to drop anchor. (Desiccated El Paso–inspired water metaphors.) After drafting the letter, she was exhausted and hungry. She headed for the kitchen to warm up a bowl of soup, and her Airbnb hostess Yolanda was emptying the dishwasher. As Colleen ate her soup, Yolanda told her a story from her El Paso childhood.

As the youngest of a very large family, Yolanda had many household responsibilities, and the morning collection of eggs was one of them. One day, she discovered that several of the hens had laid their eggs in the *horno*, the beehive-shaped outdoor oven where Yolanda's grandmother baked bread. Yolanda took her egg-collecting bucket and crawled into the horno to gather the eggs. After the bucket was full, she discovered that she couldn't get out without tilting the bucket and spilling the eggs. She twisted and turned, positioning herself and the bucket in every configuration she could think of, but she was stuck. She cried out for help, but her grandmother and siblings had gone into town to sell their produce at the farmers market, and they would be gone all day. Yolanda began to panic when no one responded to her cries. But she was determined not to lose a single egg and decided to wait. After twenty minutes or so, her legs started to cramp, and her back was sore. She was hungry and thirsty. Just then, she heard the neighbor's dogs playing and fighting close by. *¡Ven acá, ven acá!* They stopped, perking up their ears. One of them ran to the horno. With some difficulty, Yolanda removed a shoe and thrust it toward the dog. He grabbed it in his mouth and shook his head as hard as he could, but Yolanda wouldn't let go. The other dog's relentless barking drew the neighbor's attention, and when she came over to whip him and take him home, Yolanda began to yell and pound on the sides of the horno. Then the neighbor understood.

"I'll get a basket; hand me the eggs one at a time, then we can tilt the bucket and get it out," instructed the neighbor. Yolanda did as she was told, the eggs were sitting in the basket in the yard, and the neighbor pulled her out feet first. Not a single egg was broken or even cracked, and after the neighbor fed Yolanda a lunch of tortillas and honey, Yolanda resumed her chores.

Coffee cups full of beans honoring fallen soldiers, a soon-to-be-orphaned museum, stuck in a horno with a basket of eggs, what was the universe telling me? wondered Colleen. She excused herself, went to her room, opened her computer, ended her stay at the Airbnb effective immediately, and left El Paso.

CHAPTER EIGHT

AIRBNB REVIEW:
My Vacay in Your Travel Trailer

Thank you so much, everything was great! 😊 I'm thinking of buying one of these, so I thought I'd try yours out first. All I can say is, wow! I arrived during the heat of the day, and when I opened the door to your adorable trailer, I was greeted by a blast of lukewarm air that said *moldy refrigeration coils!* After bringing in all my stuff, I checked out the rural Texas flea market décor: cute, oversized plastic flowers in a Mason jar painted black, plastic stick-on butterflies, and all those old 45 records with psychedelic flowers painted on them glued to the walls, how fun! And the records, "Frontier Christmas" by Hudson & Landry, "Fat Man's Prayer" by Victor Buono, and "Moonlight in Vermont" by Sam Butero, some of my favorites! Speaking of vinyl, the tablecloth was a great touch, with its Target store-logo motif and numerous coffee cup rings that complemented those exact shapes. And the slits in the cloth that said, someone got in a hurry and cut their BLT in half right here. The two-tone curtains featuring the midcentury's most popular colors—avocado green and harvest gold—looked original, given the years' worth of spaghetti sauce splatters and Cab Sauv stains, or is that grape Kool-Aid? 😜

The toaster oven and stove looked like they'd been left out in the rain, wind, and sun for a few years before being brought inside, but the rust gave them a great patina that said "country camping." So did all the flies whose numbers I could never seem to reduce, no matter how many I smacked with the flyswatter. I got a really good feel for the other guests who preceded me when I saw all the greasy fingerprints on the fridge and microwave—thank you for providing this little bit of history! But I was wondering, doesn't anybody cook anymore? The pots and pans were covered with cobwebs, and the holes in the colander were plugged up with what looked like red mud. Maybe somebody's kid was out panning for gold, haha! Oh, and the toilet, rustic to be sure; indoor plumbing with an outdoor look (and smell)! The bedroom was a delight—pillows that were well-broken in—I always like to take a peek inside a pillowcase to see those infusions of other people's head sweat and drool—it's comforting! An afternoon nap was out of the question, tho, since the west-facing bedroom was uninhabitable for five hours or so in the afternoon. But that's okay—I just drove around in my air-conditioned car waiting for the sun to go down. You know that massive gash in the balsa wood wall behind the head of the bed, and those huge gaps in the walls and floors where pipes enter and exit? They made me think I might be visited in the night by a raccoon or a possum, exciting! I love how raccoons look when they're sitting on their haunches eating your food, their nimble little hands and short legs remind me of my Aunt Dolly. ✓

You know you're REALLY out in the country when you get up in the middle of the night to pee, take the four steps across the bedroom carpet to the toilet, and end up with lots of those West Texas sand burrs in your feet, ouch! But no problem, I had pliers in the car that I removed them with. Did I mention the shower? No hot water or water pressure, but no worries. All I wanted to wash were my bleeding feet, anyway.

When I woke up the next morning, I squealed when I noticed I HAD had visitors during the night but missed the patter of their little feet. Mouse droppings were all over the towels, in the sink and—this is so doggone cute—they had eaten through my plastic bag of chocolate chip cookies and taken a bite out of each one! I'd forgotten that out here, you have to put <u>everything</u> in the fridge or they'll get to it, even all the paper products. They LOVE Charmin Ultra Strong (maybe it's more of a challenge than the cheap brands of TP 😊); it's their favorite nesting material. 'Course you have to plastic bag-up all the paper before putting it in the fridge or you end up with a big, soggy, useless mess.

When I got cold during the night and pulled an extra blanket down from one of the cabinets, a pack rat nest came down with it. You wouldn't believe the stuff that was in there! A lipstick tube, a five-centavo coin (did the critter go all the way to México to get it? 😊), the usual matted hair and masticated steel wool, and somebody's keys. You know how pack rats can reconstruct their nests overnight? I do have one suggestion: you might want to check that, in between guests. I left the lost keys sitting on your book *We Want It All: An Anthology of Radical Transpoetics* because it has that bright pink and black cover, and I thought it would catch your eye. BTW, the cozy quilt on the fold-out couch, was that your grandmother's? And did she bear all her children on it? There's a substantial accumulation of history on that quilt!

Well, thanks again for the perfect vacay, and for sure I'll be back this way again. Don't you dare change a thing! 10/10
✨✨✨✨✨

CHAPTER NINE

GUADALAJARA, MÉXICO
with side trips to Guanajuato, Tlaquepaque, Querétaro, and Lake Chapala

Sunday, October 10th

Last night, the drive from the airport to the center of Guadalajara was not what I expected. Many of the buildings on that route are decaying, abandoned, and tagged with people's names and gang symbols, and since you never really know what your Airbnb neighborhood is like until you arrive, I hoped the buildings in mine had roofs, glass in the windows, and locking front doors. The place was a surprise: a palace, comparatively, with multifoil Moorish-style windows and arches and a central courtyard that opened to the sky, the courtyard planted with trees and a fountain its central feature,[1] reminding me of the riads I'd seen in Morocco. The soaring living room ceiling was painted in French art nouveau designs, and the bedroom was cool and cave-like. Built c. 1890 at Calle San Felipe 39, it's right on the edge of a transitioning neighborhood, not quite solidly middle class but not a slum, either, and within walking distance of Guadalajara's cathedral and main square.

Before leaving the house in the morning, I tried to find the local provisioning places on Google Maps and what came up were three balloon stores. At 8 a.m. I struck out on my own to look for a corner tienda—in México, they're usually on every other street—to buy milk for the cereal I'd brought with me. Nothing was open, and strangely, the streets were deserted except for a few homeless men. I ended up at an OXXO a mile away, crossing a wide avenue that I later learned was the boundary between safe and not-safe and next to one of Guadalajara's most dangerous public parks. When I returned to the riad, I spent an inordinate amount of time searching on the internet for grocery stores and found Soriana, not within a comfortable walking distance. Requested an Uber, got the reusable bags from the kitchen (with "Soriana" printed across them in huge letters, doh!), and struck out again.

Monday, October 11th

This morning's city tour was cancelled; I was the only person who had signed up. While searching the internet for things I could do on my own via walking or Uber, I came across a local Spanish language-only tour website. I clicked on "translate this page?". *¡Estamos a tus órdenes!* = "We are on your disposition!" In a section about Lake Chapala, *Bellezas naturales como la laguna de Chapala* translated as "Enjoy the nature of its lagoon all over the river." I could have wasted at least a few hours searching this website just for fun.

I walked to the Palacio de Gobierno, a stunning baroque-era building, and even though the website said it was open, it wasn't. Tomorrow *a las once*.

After a delicious lunch of a fish that may have been tilapia, half an avocado, and some broccoli, I walked to the Mercado San Juan de Dios, claiming to be the largest indoor market in Latin America, using vague directions from Google Maps. It routed me down a short street called Aguafria; no balloon stores there, only neighborhood prostitutes. All the young women wore outfits that unambiguously signified their profession: platform shoes that are the antithesis of "sensible"; a short, ruffly skirt; a tube top; garish makeup. When I walked back from the mercado, most of them were gone. Inside seedy buildings with their clients?

To get to the mercado using this route requires climbing two flights of urine-soaked stairs blackened by the exhaust of constant traffic and the fallout from airborne tire bits and city dirt. Once you ascend, you're on the Plaza Tapatia and the Instituto Cultural Cabañas is at the far end, one of tomorrow's destinations. The mercado is truly a wonder of the capitalist world, a dense and labyrinthine outdoor mall, with products representing the spectrum of Mexican offerings. A guy followed me around demonstrating, on a head of cabbage, an impressive and lightning-fast vegetable peeler, and if there's anything I hate most it's a vegetable peeler dull from years of use. My side-eye glances at his skillful wielding of this superior product encouraged him to pursue me relentlessly, and he almost made a sale before I reminded myself of my limited luggage space. Did I really want one of my souvenirs of México to be a vegetable peeler?

Tuesday, October 12th

This morning I walked to the Instituto Cultural Cabañas, and at 11:10 when the entrance area was still suspiciously inactive, a nice university student told me, in English, that he and his companions had looked it up on their cell phones, and it was definitively closed. The Palacio de Gobierno was also closed, contrary to what yesterday's guard asserted. The student suggested I walk to the MUSA, the Museum at the University of Guadalajara, because certainly it was open, but when I looked on my phone, it said *cerrado*. Damn Covid! Since you can seldom rely on anybody's website info these days, I decided to walk to the museum anyway. I stopped at one of the many churches along the route, and a toddler not more than two or three years old was not going to let me in if I didn't give her some money. I didn't have any coins in my pocket, and I wouldn't have given them to her anyway. Encouraging a two-year-old to beg is just wrong.

To my delight, the museum was open. Inside is a wood-paneled auditorium featuring two murals by José Clemente Orozco[2], one of the triumvirate of important Mexican muralists that includes Diego Rivera and David Siqueiros. As a young man, Orozco suffered a horrific accident. Gunpowder he was using to make fireworks exploded, and his left hand became gangrenous and had to be amputated. When you know this about him, in any photograph of the artist, first and foremost your eye goes to the left sleeve of his shirt or jacket to confirm there's no hand emerging from it. Often he was so adept at posing in ways that obscured his left side altogether that there's no way you'd notice an absence of a left hand. Did having this bit of biographical information affect my appreciation of his work? Or make me like it even more because I felt empathy for him? Not one bit, I think. Neither does knowing that Van Gogh was missing his left ear, or that Frida Kahlo was impaled by a streetcar handrail, "the way a sword pierces a bull," as she put it. In all three cases, the work stands on its own merit.

At the busy intersection outside the museum, a mother held her infant in one arm and juggled three balls with her free hand, in traffic, soliciting donations. Two other small children played with toy walkie-talkies and made a game of dodging cars. I wondered if the juggling metaphor was intentional. Across the street, a trombone and sax player performed jazz numbers and a young violinist played Bach. My pockets were drained.

Thursday, October 14th

New occupants have moved into the riad—a noisy boy and his permissive parents—and for over twenty minutes this afternoon they were going in and out of the front door, slamming it every time. The kid is in the courtyard wailing and shrieking, refining new ways in which he can irritate the adults around him. Like in its Moroccan counterpart, reflective surfaces are not dampened by rugs or draperies or acoustic foam, so sounds merge and amplify. I wonder if people can hear ME when I'm cursing at the unreliable internet connection. Combined with the muffler-less buses that pass by every few minutes, creating a green blur in the frosted glass windowpanes, and the ambulances dispatched, noisily, several times a day, the riad has become sonically challenging. As I write this, a monotonous low-pitched tone, the kind that vibrates your chest uncomfortably, is coming from somewhere, a machine or truck or manufacturing process. How I long for a few moments of silence in an anechoic chamber.

    I tried going to a restaurant called La Fonda de San Miguel Arcángel, near Centro, and when I arrived, it was closed for a special event. I've come to expect that it will take two or three tries before I can enjoy an experience I set out to have. For now, I'm content to spend a few moments lying on the living room couch thinking about my twenty-year-old self and how these experiences I'm having as an almost seventy-year-old have been nothing like I'd expected. If I'd known this was in my future, maybe I would have been happy instead of stuck in an endless existential quagmire. But what rational human being thinks, *I will be happy in the future; therefore, it should inform my happiness now, because at that future time of happiness I will consider my younger self and wish she were happier?*

Friday, October 15th

I woke up today stressing about where to get food. Soriana was only as good as an upscale 7-Eleven. Since I've been here, it's been on my mind way too much, and strangely, it was before I arrived. Somehow, I knew it was going to be challenging to find, and get to, grocery stores and to identify something I wanted to eat. I've got to figure this out soon. Today's only meal was a tiny bowl of cereal, and I think the milk may have gone bad. I definitely don't want to live in a place where food security is on my mind more than necessary.

In Guadalajara, garbage collection is street theater. I plugged my ears as a massive cowbell dragged along the cobblestones and ran to the window expecting to see an ancient mega bovine lumbering down the street. But the cowbell was tied to the back of a giant, stinky garbage truck and a team of energetic guys in bright orange jumpsuits ran back and forth across the street tossing our refuse into its maw. In México (and Brazil) various services are signaled sonically, luring you into the street to buy kitchen towels or have your knives sharpened or get your ears pierced or whatever by a man playing a pan pipe or singing in a lovely operatic tenor or by cowbell-dragging trucks. After enough repetitions, you can ID the service by the sound. You also hear earworm-creating jingles sung in major thirds such as "Next stop, next stop, Zeta Gas!"

During the past hour I've been indulging in a fantasy of rescue, a kind of intervention enacted by my sister Suzie. (It's guaranteed not to happen because Suzie seldom leaves her comfortable zip code and devoted mahjong-playing friends.) But concurrent with that, I feel a fear of committing to a specific place again. Whenever I think of how many years I spent in Santa Fe—fifteen total—and how I knew it wasn't the place for me, yet I stayed, I feel like there's a teeny angry man in my head running around kicking my gray matter, either trying to tenderize it or striving to reconfigure a tangle of synapses into something more operationally efficient. (Back to my rescue fantasy.) Suzie, who has been incommunicado for a while, decides to check in and discovers that I'm on the brink of losing touch with reality, living in some tiny fishing village-turned-tourist haven in México, and despite her reluctance to travel (and fears around it), she gets on a plane with an old Berlitz pocket Spanish book from junior high school and, after traveling by air, then in a beater taxi, finds me languishing under a mango tree, lying on a makeshift bed made of bright red plastic Coca-Cola crates with an old horsehair mattress tossed on top. I've long ago run out of my favorite lip balm, so my mouth is crusty and shrunken, and my once-luxurious silver gray hair is caked with grime and beer and beset by flies. I've passed out from hunger and thirst, but she revives me with a sip of Aquafina and helps me to one of the canopied beds that the luxury hotel, at which she is a guest, has installed on the beach. I open my eyes and look into hers—soulful, pitying, the green of Picholine olives—and she insists on overseeing my convalescence. But we don't return to Fort Worth, Texas, our native land, she's set us up in a beautiful house in . . .

And there's where the fantasy stops, abruptly. I can't see the house, I can't see the city, and I can't see the country, although I know it's somewhere on planet Earth. It's as though I'm swimming through water clouded with sediment or flying through fog so thick I can't tell which way is up.

I keep returning to an image that popped into my head at some indeterminate time in the past, of a second-floor apartment seen from a cobblestone street, bathed in the golden light of sunset, a hilly, friendly, flowery old-world village. Maybe Guanajuato is this place?

I visited the Basilica of Our Lady of Zapopan, a thirty-minute Uber ride from the riad, with the added intention of going to the Huichol Museum and walking the neighborhood. I'd read good things about all three activities. The basilica, magnificent from the outside like all Guadalajara churches I'd seen so far, was a little aesthetically ambiguous on the inside. Its soaring ceiling, vaulted arches, and pendulous chandeliers were textbook baroque, but the place was festooned with garish bright red and gold pennant flags that looked like they belonged at a NASCAR racetrack finish line. I sat down in a pew behind a tiny old woman, solo like me, who, from behind, looked like a hybrid creature, a pigeon crossed with a human. Or a skeleton of an extinct bird, its bones with skin and clothes draped over them. Her little shoulders were hunched and through the thin cloth of her gray dress you could make out their outline. She had a long neck and a slim head that was slightly cocked. She sat absolutely still, a kind of profound sadness exuding from her form. In her youth, she would have worn a lace head cover or a humble Kleenex.

Another woman and her daughter, both in bright pink polo shirts, came slowly down the aisle toward the altar. At first, I thought they were two children, but then I saw that the mother was shuffling along the veined, dark gray marble floor on her knees. She was wearing blue jeans and tennis shoes. I wondered at what point she'd assumed that posture. At the entrance to the basilica? When disembarking the bus? All the way back at her flat?

In a side room, a figure lay face down on a folding table in a kind of modified grasshopper yoga pose, his feet pointed and legs slightly curving up, supported by a fluffy red pillow encased in clear plastic. The figure was draped from the waist up; three surgeons were at work on various parts of his body under bright lights that illuminated his form. The soles of his feet were black, as if gangrene had taken root and was starting to creep up his legs. But there was no visible blood. The surgeons poked at him with long Q-tips, and a young man wearing red Converse sifted through powder he'd scraped from the figure's side. This ad hoc conservation team was working on one of the basilica's Jesus figures, pre-crucifixion.[4]

Saturday, October 16th

I've been wondering what "gua" means in Spanish, since many places other than Guadalajara start with the "gua" spelling: Guadalupe, Guamúchil, Guanajuato, Guasave, Guayabas, and Guaymas to name a few. The internet seemed to agree on the interjectional meaning of "gua." *¡Gua! ¿Qué fue ese ruido?* Wow! What was that noise? *¡Guácala!* Ewww! Like when you step on something you wished you hadn't. (After learning that meaning, I couldn't eat guacamole for a long time without wanting to hurl.) So what about the rest of the name, the "dalajara" part?

Later. . . I did a little more digging and found this: the name comes from the Arabic وادي الحجارة (wādī al-ḥajārah), which means "Valley of the Stone," a phrase Spanish speakers revised into something they could pronounce: Guadalajara. I hear a marching band playing in the distance. Time to abandon this insignificant research project and go investigate.

For a late lunch, I settled on a tourist favorite annexed to the sublime neoclassical Teatro Degollado near the cathedral in Centro. I had tried patronizing the (closed) La Fonda de San Miguel Arcángel restaurant for the third time and gave up for good. Then something that could only be described as miraculous happened. I was contentedly sitting in the tourist restaurant enjoying a delicious bowl of tortilla soup, grooving on the crunchiness of the tortilla pieces and the saltiness of the cheese, when the Archangel himself slid into the chair opposite me.

The radiance of his face and golden hair was blinding. I grabbed my sunglasses. Michael said, "Look, I know you haven't noticed and, admittedly, you're seeing me for the first time, but I've been following you around for the past seven months to every single blessèd location. Enough is enough; you're exhausting! What's all this indecision about, anyway? You've NEVER been an indecisive person during your entire life! Except about this. Why can't you just declare a place, move your stuff there, and call it your forever home?"

His voice! What a surprise. It was countertenor, quiet, and modulated with a windy, whispery kind of tone. Endearingly, he had a slight lisp. It wasn't at all what one would expect from a powerful warrior angel.

"Remember that woman you met on the bus from San Francisco to Providence in 1974? She threw a dart at a map of the U.S. and was in the process of moving to the place where the dart landed? Yes, I was there, too. I admit that Pittsburgh wasn't the best choice, but throwing a dart at a map at least identifies a location. 'X marks the spot,' you know? As I see it, you've visited too many places in the world and that's a problem. There's too much choice. Two hundred years ago, you wouldn't have traveled even twenty miles from your home! That place is a part of you, and no amount of traveling will ever change that."

I realized I'd stopped breathing. I couldn't speak. When I didn't respond, he dialed back the brilliance. "Has all this traveling around moved you any closer to your goal? Well, has it?"

"Not significantly."

"Okay, then, what will?"

"A pilgrimage to the place where I grew up? Would it give me any insight?"

He rolled his pale blue eyes. "Try to dig deeper. Somewhere that connects you to what gives meaning to your life *now*. Think about it; I gotta run."

And with that piece of arcane, unsolicited advice, he vanished. I paid the check and was on my way.

Sunday, October 17th

A four-hour bus ride was the perfect way to process yesterday's meetup with Michael. The idea of revisiting my childhood environs—no, too painful—was the easy part. But the person-place bond and how that attachment forms warranted more thought. How was it even definable? I hoped Michael's appearance wasn't a one-off so we could discuss this. I had the feeling, though, that it was something I was supposed to discover on my own.

At the outskirts of Guanajuato, strange highway signs began appearing. One featured a silhouette of a steaming cup of coffee with the text Black Coffee Ahead. These were official highway department signs, not the Mexican version of Stuckey's advertising Pecan Log Rolls; Two Eggs, Toast & Jelly for 99¢. The closer the bus got to Guanajuato, the more frequently this sign appeared, as if it were a not-to-be-missed tourist attraction. Another bizarre highway sign had a silhouette of an elephant superimposed on a blue background. No text. Did we need to watch for them crossing the road?

Wednesday, October 20th

Guanajuato is a university town known for its silver mining history; extensive underground roadway system hewn from solid rock; colonial architecture; hilly, narrow, winding streets; and a museum populated with mummies, bodies of locals whose families could no longer afford to keep them interred in the local cemetery. For visitors disturbed by the prospect of recognizing a desiccated grandparent, seeing a mummified toddler, or the obvious parallel to images of the Holocaust, best to pass on the experience.

People here are friendly and kind. Walking down Juarez Street on a crowded sidewalk (a typical sidewalk is no more than thirty inches wide), a chubby man wearing Day-Glo orange tennies and a big smile chivalrously turned sideways and said, in a beautiful bass voice, *Pase*. I would totally write a story about Mexican passing-on-the-sidewalk etiquette if Dostoevsky hadn't penned the definitive examination of this already ("Apropos of the Wet Snow"), where he considers the politics, class hierarchies, and signifiers involved in who turns sideways to let the other pass, and who doesn't. But it's not that complicated here. Mexican sidewalk real estate is at a premium, the inconveniences and dangers of the street—uncollected pet droppings, cobblestones, cars, trucks, and motorcycles—are sometimes a single misstep away. So sidewalks are where good breeding and graciousness are practiced in one of their highest forms. Mothers with children and/or strollers, really old people, the very poor, and the blind have dibs on the sidewalks at all times. Others must drop to the street or stand in a doorway and wait for them to pass. The rest of us turn sideways, torso facing torso, while one says *con permiso* (excuse me) and the respondent says either *gracias* or *por nada* (no problem). Walking a Mexican sidewalk, with everyone practicing these rules, restores one's faith in humanity.

Like New York City, Guanajuato never sleeps. A few nights ago, the wandering horn sections of competing mariachis passed directly under my window, their overlapping music creating utter cacophony and making me nauseated. Last night, at 3 a.m., a group of students congregated, protesting in earnest, but who was the audience, I wondered? Maybe they were rehearsing for a future demonstration somewhere more relevant, or maybe it was spontaneous theater. Whatever it was, it kept me awake. Plus, I was obsessing about the idea that our Airbnb host was locking us in at night with a giant baby blue padlock I'd noticed hanging on the outside of the heavy, ancient wooden double doors at the entrance to The Conquistador, the coffee shop that occupies the first floor. (Six Airbnb rental units are located on the second floor.) I was waiting for an Uber when I noticed the lock, and it followed that whoever left the coffee shop at closing would be responsible for securing the place. But what about us, the people upstairs? What if we needed to evacuate because of fire or an earthquake? We'd be trapped in the building, unable to save ourselves. A leap from the second-floor balcony was out of the question unless a delivery truck happened to be parked below and we could land on its ample roof.

To confirm my suspicion, I planned to go downstairs to check the lock after The Conquistador closed at 10 p.m. Lying in bed looking at the ceiling, listening to the hiss of the espresso machines being cleaned and the trash taken out, it was well past 11:30 p.m. when they finally closed. By then I'd been in and out of consciousness multiple times and decided to postpone the inspection until 6 a.m. Or if the protesting students were back at three, I'd give it a shot then. When six arrived, I got dressed, activated the flashlight on my phone, and headed downstairs.

The two heavy doors were closed and locked. My heart pounded. Like in many old wooden doors in México, you could see the evidence of multiple former locks. A sizeable hole in the wood likely opened with a bulky skeleton key that my Airbnb hosts hadn't provided. But then I saw the kind of lock I'd encountered elsewhere in México: a state-of-the-art, super well-designed, seamlessly operating lock, and I inserted the smallest key on my keychain into its lubricated slot. I turned the key, and the door swung open, effortlessly. I felt like an idiot, closed the doors, and slinked off to bed, hoping there wasn't a guy in a back room somewhere watching me via a slew of security cameras. I revised the Airbnb review I had already written in my head from BEWARE! Kidnappers Masquerading as Airbnb Hosts to I highly recommend this wonderful apartment, but bring earplugs.

Thursday, October 21st

The street below continues to be a popular venue for personal expression. Early this morning, again at 3 a.m., a group of guys and a single woman were assembled under the balcony talking and laughing, occasionally shouting at each other as if a fight were imminent, and finally at 4:30 a.m. they disbanded. Things were quiet up to the time I left for the bus station, two hours later. When do G-tiños (I made up this name) sleep? From 7 to 10 a.m., and is this the norm? Can't people have these emotive outbursts in the privacy of their own homes?

On the return trip to Guadalajara, when the bus entered the outskirts of León, every hundred feet or so a man stood near the side of the road slapping the air with what looked like a small white bath towel. The last man we passed waved a bright red towel. I wish I knew how to ask someone what that was about.

When we were close to Guadalajara, a group of federales stopped the bus, and a handsome young man wearing an impeccable uniform boarded to inspect everyone's ID. My passport and immigration form were in my cargo pants pocket, just by chance. A few people were removed from the bus. Later I Googled "Can Mexican law enforcement stop someone at any time and ask to see their passport?" The answer: yes. "Can I be detained if I don't have it?" The answer again: yes. The experience taught me that I should always carry my passport, because sometimes I don't.

Something else I didn't know about: only taxis operate from the Guadalajara bus station, Uber is forbidden, and I was short on pesos. The bus station had two ATMs, and the agent who replenishes the money had both machines open and stacks of cash sitting on the floor. He was guarded by two AK-47-toting accomplices, and if this were happening in the U.S., the sight of these guys would have cleared the place out. The agent couldn't get the key that opened the money trays to work, and if I'd been that guy, that would have been me, too. I decided to reassess. I scoured my purse for coins and came up with an additional twenty pesos, just enough for the cab ride and a tiny tip for the driver.

In the process of researching the passport question, I also found this:

> When stand-alone ATMs are being re-filled, you might see armed guards surrounding it. We recommend you find another ATM instead of waiting around for it to be filled: it can take up to an hour for a machine to be re-filled and tested before it becomes operational again.

Useful!

A guy with an extremely loud, low, and gravelly voice paced the street in front of the riad tonight, saying "Whore! Whore!" and "F*ck your mother!" I sneaked a peek at him through the window, and the veins in his neck and temples were the size of my little fingers. Did he, too, have a high-caliber firearm? Would he glance in my direction and see me, smash the glass windowpanes to get to me, the closest woman on whom he could visit his rage?

Friday, October 22nd

Today I saw a display in a store window with two dozen flesh-colored shoes on their own little pedestals, and the shoes were all the same. A strappy sandal with sparkly things glued to the straps. No other styles of shoes were available for sale. I wondered if other stores sold only one kind of thing: a Panama hat, one brand of 32" TV, one shade of lipstick, one book.

Saturday, October 23rd

Today marks the end of two weeks in Guadalajara, and I woke up with that "I'm running out the clock" dread. I stayed indoors most of the day. It was nice to just sit in a chair and feel clean, but I had to go out for water and a walk in the late afternoon and that was the end of that. But while walking around Centro, I noticed a sense of connection, a swell of contentment. It may have to do with familiarity and predictability: the more you know a place, its people, and its rhythms, the more comfortable you become. That sounds obvious, but it can also have the opposite effect, in a *Groundhog Day* kind of way, as if you're living in a space-time quantum weirdness where *everything* is predictable, down to the banana peel you narrowly missed slipping on when rounding the corner of San Felipe and Liceo. You know you'll see the tattered old mexicano, catching the rays of the setting sun, who leans up against the third column from the left of the Teatro Degollado, raising his punched tin lantern at passersby and shouting something you'll never quite understand.

Tuesday, October 26th

On one of the balloon streets, customers mobbed three popular Día de Muertos stores, clogging the sidewalk. Near one of those stores, a woman in a wheelchair, an amputee, made her way down the street. As we passed, I thought about giving her money when she blew an eardrum-bursting whistle and picked up speed. I did a double take; she was a policewoman in pursuit of a lawbreaker.

Thursday, October 28th

Guadalajara's historic limestone buildings in Centro are sparkling clean. Men on scaffolds dislodge accretions of pollutants and bits of tire by tapping gently on the limestone with small hammers, and when the light is right, you can see the particles floating through the air and down to the ground.

Guadalajara is the hometown of superstar architect Luis Barragán, designer of the Parque de Revolución—a large urban park—and three simple houses. One of those houses hinted at the Bauhaus-Mexican-Arab fusion that he would become known for, but the other two looked like any other 1920s era middle-class Mexican home and were shockingly in disrepair. One had been transformed into a taqueria, its white stucco façade covered in red, blue, and black gang tags, a vulnerable part of the building fitted with a chain-link fence topped with razor wire.[3] Barragán may have approved of the use of red, but probably not the razor wire, a symbol of the exclusion of the disadvantaged classes by the elite. The other house is a small hotel called Petit María José.[3] (María José is a convenient name to have if you didn't identify with the gender you were assigned at conception. If you are born female and your parents included the names María José with the half dozen family names that constitute your full name [see Diego Rivera], and you want to transition to male, you may simply reverse the order and call yourself José María.)

None of the houses were remarkable, but what about the Parque?

Saturday, October 30th

To prep for a visit to the Parque de Revolución, I read that the property was a former orchard that belonged to a Carmelite order and that the land manager donated it, in 1845, to the city to build a penitentiary. But by 1935, the complex was demolished, and the space was designated a green area. Barragán was invited to design the park and supervise its construction.

The park is split by mega street Calle Juárez, and two statues on tall, black pedestals, one on each side of the street, are backgrounded with white walls. Or at least that was the original intent. Any time you erect a white wall somewhere, someone is going to take that as an invitation to express themselves. "The police doesn't (*sic*) take care of me, my friends take care of me" was painted on one wall. Well, yeah? Would you really *want* the police to take care of you? The guys who drive around in their ATVs intimidating citizens with their machine guns, their loudspeakers, their suffocatingly tight black uniforms, and smug looks? Would you trust these guys to babysit your three-year-old or help your aged mother across the street? I'll take my friends any day. The wall on the opposite side of the street was whitewashed, but someone had since stenciled "You Deserve Healthy Love" in red letters. (Thank you for that sentiment!) Red is also the dominant color of the Parque. Red walkways, red benches, red playground equipment, red walls. Red symbolized the blood shed during the revolution.

The Parque's design was also unremarkable. After it was completed, Barragán left Guadalajara for México City. Was he run out of town?

Guadalajara is a city of statues. Minerva, the virgin goddess of war, wisdom, justice, law, music, medicine, kind of an all-purpose goddess, stands in the center of one of the city's main roundabouts. I'd seen it from a tourist van a few days earlier, this Statue of Liberty of Guadalajara, and I wanted to have a closer look. I hopped into an Uber, and when I arrived at the roundabout, I saw that Minerva was a lot smaller than I'd remembered, not even eight meters (twenty-six feet) tall. The face wasn't what I'd remembered, either. In my mind, it was classically Greek, but it looks more like a tired Mexican housewife with bags under her eyes and ill-fitting clothes. As if the artist dressed the family housekeeper in this fetishistic costume and made her pose for the statue. Handed her a staff and placed one of those iconic Roman helmets on her head, borrowing the bristles from one of her brooms. She doesn't look all too happy about it, either. A stirring sentiment is engraved on her pedestal, though: "May justice, wisdom, and strength guard this loyal city."

The Mayans represented their monuments of gods in more abstract ways. At Chichén Itzá, in the Yucatán Peninsula, they constructed homages to the planet Venus (which they referred to as a star, and male): platforms twenty-five meters square on each side, with steps leading up to the platform on all four sides. Glyphs associated with Venus appear at each of the corners[5] and, in another section, he emerges from the mouth of a jaguar. The Mayans studied the rotation of Venus closely, his movements used as signposts for rituals and agrarian cycles, and I wondered if any crack Mayan astronomer had ever mapped Venus's rotation in relation to the Earth, one of our solar system's greatest works of art, a lovely, loopy pentagram. It looks like it was made with a Hasbro Spirograph, a favorite childhood toy.

Most cities have questionable public art, but the Mayans got it right.

Of course, many statues of Greek and Roman gods and goddesses populate U.S. museums, but classically inspired art has never been much of a thing outdoors. The Atlas sculpture at Rockefeller Center, a kitsch Jupiter at Virginia Beach, plus a few minor Minervas, and that's about it. Since public works are signifiers of a city's identity, this says a lot about U.S. cities' disinterest in the Classic past and acceptance of a muddled, sometimes violent present. (In Houston, twin statues sit outside a downtown performance hall, one a short, squat pile of what looks like human feces, the other a taller complement, which I call

Laurel and Hardy Blow Mud.) Until recently, the United States had plenty of monuments glorifying racism and tyrants and grand wizards of the Ku Klux Klan, and my former state of residence New Mexico honored Don Juan de Oñate, its first Spanish governor, with two statues, one in Albuquerque and another in the small town of Alcalde north of Santa Fe. In the late 1500s, Oñate wanted to colonize the Acoma pueblo near Albuquerque, and when their leader learned of Oñate's plans they engaged in a battle that killed a dozen Spaniards. Oñate responded by massacring eight hundred Acoma natives and chopping off the right feet of twenty-four young men, keeping them alive and enslaved.

The equestrian statue of Oñate in Alcalde also lost a right foot when someone sneaked into the heavily fortified compound and sawed it off. The foot was replaced, and the original was never returned. Vandalism has a four-year statute of limitations in New Mexico, so if you're reading this and you're the person who did it, please let the world know because we want to create a statue in *your* honor.

Many places have interesting stories and things to recommend them. It's not only the light and the architecture and the design of a city that are important to me for a place to live, but it's the stories, too. I want to live in a place whose stories I like. Albuquerque didn't make the cut.

Sunday, October 31st

Delightfully, on Sundays Guadalajara closes two and a half miles of Avenida Adolfo López Mateo Sur to traffic, starting at the Minerva statue, for bicyclists and skateboarders and walkers to use. The sky was overcast and the temperature ideal, so I walked from the Minerva statue to Guadalajara's central historic district and back to the riad. The juggling mother was on the route, and when I asked if I could film her amazing one-handed-juggling-while-managing-three-kids routine she said, "No." I gave her a twenty-peso bill, and she allowed me to take her photo. I felt bad afterward; I could have parted with a hundred or two. Or just left her alone.

The Parque de Revolución was also on the route, and Sunday was Hula-Hoop day. Vendors rented out large, plain, black ones, and people of all ages and abilities were gyrating to loud, distorted music. Hula-Hooping is somehow associated with Día de Muertos, but I haven't been able to find out how, so I'm going to take a wild guess. Maybe the Hula-Hoop is a symbol of the circle of life, wholeness, completion, with no beginning and end, the black color symbolizing the place from which we arose and to which we will return. But I needed help, so I Googled "semiotics of the hula hoop" and an abstract of a relevant paper popped up:

> This paper will seek to operationalize in a salient to consumer culture manner the Heideggerian notion of Being-towards-Death as a primordial mode-of-Being and the Lacanian phenomenological opening up of the Freudian death drive in the light of the consumption performance ritual of Hula Hoop dancing. The consumption ritual of Hula Hoop, a cultural practice with a rich historical background and multiple practice occasions (from gymnastics to circus performances), marked by the celebration of an official annual Hula Hoop day, will be deconstructed according to a product syntactic approach (Holbrook & Hirschman, Kehret-Ward) and mapped out alongside two axes/continuums, viz. individual/collective consumption and proximity to physical death (i.e., minimal danger vs. high danger).[6]

This academician was definitely onto something, and I think Heidegger, Lacan, and Freud would agree. Watching people Hula-Hooping was like seeing time speeded up, a person "consuming" a lifetime with each rotation of the hoop—a Freudian death drive. And they were laughing about it! But was it possible that families were just enjoying a fun day in the park?

We all have something to learn from México, a place that really knows how to party and that celebrates death.

When I arrived at the Zócalo, mariachis were playing in the bandstand, and a local dance group, 99 percent prepubescent girls, performed on the rough concrete, jumping, spinning, doing the splits and managing not to reduce themselves to a bloody mess. Caught in a crush of people, I was trying to be careful not to step on the head of the sleeping man directly in front of me on the grass. You see this a lot here—men contentedly sleeping in the most public of places and everyone else just going on about their business. They don't look indigent, just wiped-out tired, I guess.

Monday, November 1st

The Museo Panteon de Belén is an ancient, historic cemetery that is an immensely popular destination on the first day of Día de Muertos. All over México, families visit the graves of ancestors and loved ones and decorate them with flowers, candles, and objects meaningful to the deceased. Picnics are shared with the spirits who visit Earth for that single night when the veil between worlds lifts. Anticipating a huge line, I arrived at the cemetery at 9 a.m. sharp to buy my eighty-one-peso ticket. I wondered why eighty-one; who usually has one peso in their pocket? The ticket seller was stressed—nobody had change. I wondered if she was required to contribute her own money to make up for the dozens of one-peso shortfalls every day.

I hope our tour guide didn't notice that I stared at her mouth when she spoke. She hardly ever closed it, so I could see how her tongue moved as she pronounced her words, tobogganing around the inside of her mouth, sliding from side to side and up and down, vibrating when she rolled her *r*s. I wondered which vibrated faster, her tongue or a hummingbird's wings?

We stood at the tiny concrete casket of a two-year-old who had died, surrounded by offerings like small toy trucks, laminated prayer cards with the portraits of protective saints, coins, baby shoes, tiny plastic dinosaurs. He'd been afraid of the dark, so they placed the casket on an above-ground vault, positioned so his resting place would be in sunlight and, at night, in moonlight when available. The tour guide led us to the place where an alleged vampire was buried. A mysterious European man, no relation to the neighborhood halal butcher, was seen leaving dead animals drained of their blood in the cemetery, and townspeople started showing up in the same condition. He was captured, slain via a stake through the heart, and buried. A sapling sprouted from the stake and grew into a huge strangler fig that overwhelmed a nearby mango tree. So the story goes.

A well-fed resident black cat followed us around, eyeing us suspiciously and slinking away when we reciprocated.

Tuesday, November 2nd

The highlight of Día de Muertos is the catrina parade, where women wearing skull makeup and elaborate dresses and headgear proceed down the main street in Tlaquepaque (about ten kilometers southeast of Guadalajara) but, thanks to Covid, the parade was cancelled. Disappointed and wandering around aimlessly, I found a store called Dicake, bathed in the loveliest pink light and exuding an intoxicating bakery smell and saw the freezer full of ice cream. I entered the store and asked for vanilla in a cup, and the young man pointed to a poster on a wall. I was to choose from various shapes and sizes of penises and vulvas to which ice cream was added. The genitalia were made with waffle batter poured into molds, and chocolate or vanilla icing drizzled over the tops of the penises as if they had just orgasmed. Same for the vulvas. Penis on a stick was also available in Day of the Dead designs: a mummy with vanilla icing bandages, a Frankenstein with bloodshot eyes and sprinkles for hair, and a catrina with a skull penis head. I had walked into an X-rated ice cream store. How had I missed seeing people walking the streets with these erotic treats? I wondered if they delivered so I could try one semi-anonymously. I tried my best not to react and lingered as if

I were thinking about my order. After a few minutes of being indecisive, a young couple stepped up to the counter, hand in hand, and I bolted.

Thursday, November 4th

If you're spending any amount of time in México, there's no excuse not to explore places within a four- to five-hour "executive" bus ride from your home base. To travel by executive bus is to luxuriate in one of the few air-conditioned spaces in México, in a seat reminiscent of a La-Z-Boy recliner, while watching TV, snacking, snoozing, and texting your friends. So I took the bus to Querétaro to experience the architectural highlights.

While exploring the historic colonial area, someone threw a partially full plastic water bottle at me from their car as I passed the Neptune Fountain, which drew my attention to it. Instead of being a larger-than-life, Jason Momoa Aquaman figure, with an outrageous upper carriage and sinewy arms, wearing an I'm-the-king-of-the-sea crown and wielding his trident, the figure looked like someone's down-and-out hippie brother who hadn't shaved or cut his hair in years and was kind of stooped from harboring an inferiority complex. Both the Neptune and Minerva statues look like regular folks, a quality I found appealing and that said to the viewer, Look, you could be up on this pedestal, too.

Friday, November 5th

I left the Airbnb by 8:30 this morning and walked to the closest end of Querétaro's aqueduct, Los Arcos, an extraordinary 4,200-feet-long construction roughly the height of a nine-storey building.[7] Started in 1726 and finished twelve years later, it carried water along its seventy-four arches into Querétaro from six miles away to supply fresh water to an order of Capuchin nuns, its construction team scoring major points in heaven. Snaking through the empty countryside, casting late-afternoon arched shadows onto the desert floor, the aqueduct must have looked surreal to the local *campesinos*. Almost three hundred years later, it dwarfs the city that engulfed all six miles of its length and is still in excellent condition.

In the opposite direction, the Capilla de Maximiliano, a tiny chapel dedicated to Emperor Maximillian, is tucked in at the bottom of a hill below the sprawling Benito Juárez plaza. Maximillian, an Austrian archduke installed in México in 1864 by Napoleon III, was executed at age thirty-four on that plaza, on Juárez's orders. Basically, France had invaded México because México owed them money, and the execution of Maximillian symbolized a thumbing of the nose to the French. Maximillian gave each member of the firing squad a twenty-peso gold coin, a lot of money at the time, to shoot him anywhere but his head so that his mother back in Austria could see his face one last time. He didn't die instantly and had to be shot again in the heart. A huge statue of a scowling Juárez stands stiffly on a massive pedestal, looking in the direction of the execution, leaning forward slightly as if he'll step off the pedestal at any moment and crush underfoot anyone occupying his plaza.

Saturday, November 6th

The journey back to Guadalajara, not on an air-conditioned executive bus, was exhausting, my seatmate leaning into me with her left thigh and torso, heating up my entire right side, and a guy behind me blowing his nose and coughing for most of the five-and-a-half-hour journey. The bus made a loud squeaking noise, like a couple having vigorous sex on an ancient brass bed. Once we descended from the higher, cooler elevation of Querétaro, the bus became even more claustrophobic and hot. A familiar face peered over the seat directly in front of me. It was Archangel Michael.

"After you get some food and water in you, things will start looking brighter."

Tuesday, November 9th

Lake Chapala, about an hour's drive south of Guadalajara, is México's largest lake, and the tiny village of Ajijic that sits on its north shore is known as a Shangri-La for American and Canadian expats. Not a place I would normally visit, but I wanted to see what all the fuss was about. I booked a room in what looked like a Mexican Taj Mahal, complete with reflecting pool, and to get there, the taxi navigated streets clogged with huge American cars, driving past sprawling walled compounds, no doubt the residences of wealthy expats.

    At 4 p.m., I strolled the deserted lakeside promenade while the smart people were indoors avoiding the intense sun and enjoying siesta. Seated on a bench, I watched a man wearing a broad-brimmed hat wading in the lake about ten feet from shore. The water was full of algae and mixed with an oily sludge from nearby boats. Shirtless, his brown skin glistening, he was fishing with a small net, maybe eight feet in diameter, and I thought, How can he catch anything here in these shallow, disgusting waters? His wife sat on the retaining wall, also watching. His first cast resulted in a yield of hyacinth roots and other tenacious lake debris, which he patiently removed from the net. On the second cast, he caught a good-size fish, held the net up to show his wife, removed the fish, and handed it to her. She placed it in a large red woven bag, and he went back to work. I felt like I was witnessing the last vestige of Ajijic's fishing village past, life before the gringo invasion. I also felt sure that he thought I was watching as some form of entertainment, and maybe I was. No doubt the couple's sons and daughters were the restaurant workers, gardeners, taxi drivers, and housekeepers that service the Canadians and Americans who have overrun the area. Not my kind of place!

    At night, from my room at the Airbnb, I hear the clomping of horses' hooves on the cobblestones outside, their riders returning home after a long day's work. Or maybe it's a group of Mexican Foley artists paid to sonically entertain us gringos.

Wednesday, November 10th

Even though I'd seen enough already, I'd committed to staying for a few days, so I taxied to the close-by town of Chapala to investigate. I was glad to be walking conventional streets and not breaking my feet into little bits on cobblestones, and glad to see that Chapala wasn't another retirement enclave. A group of *voladores* were performing, five guys who climb a thirty-meter pole, attach an ankle to a rope wound around a contraption that's like a garden hose reel, and spin in ever-widening circles around the pole to the ground. I wondered how they transport the pole to a venue—it's about twice the height of a conventional streetlight and made of wood—and how they install it, sometimes in parking lots. How would they negotiate a sharp curve in a road? How could they get the pole to stand upright? How would the weight of five guys affect its stability? What if it's excessively windy?

When I returned to Ajijic and tried to open the metal door, with its well-functioning lock, to the grounds of the Mexican Taj, it would open only a few inches then get stuck. From the time I'd left, maybe three hours earlier, to when I returned, a rock in the driveway inside the compound had dislodged, and I couldn't reach inside to remove it. Lucky for me the host was home, and as I explained the situation via an intercom, a huge, sound-masking cement truck pulled up a few feet away. She'd gotten the message, though, and appeared a few minutes later to remove the rock. The universe had sent me a tweet. *An insignificant rock kept you from your bed and bathroom, food in the fridge, and the giant TV where you've been binging "Luis Miguel." Consider what could be next.* #SMDH*

The universe was right. My future was tenuous, the comforts of home obstructed (by me) and just out of reach, and I'd lost focus. I needed a reset.

*Shaking my damn head.

Friday, November 12th

Only three more days in México. Running out the clock, again, in Ajijic. Took a long long long shower, trying to see if I could deplete the hot water, and gave up after twenty minutes. Irresponsible, I know.

When you're running out the clock, little things can become big sources of irritation. I know I hate touching wet coffee grounds, but I really noticed it today with a new intensity. They have a way of lodging under your fingernails and sticking to your skin in clumps, like a slime mold composite creature that forms a collective out of its individuals. Even with soap and vigorous scrubbing, they don't wash off easily, I guess it's the oil in the coffee; nothing a little naphtha or kerosene can't take care of.

I sat on the bed and reread recent phone messages. "Hey, this is Sean calling you back." I get at least one of these a day. From Hawthorne, California; Gallup, New Mexico; Tampa, Florida. Sean has homes in all these places? It's always the same voice, and it's always about a $50,000 loan I qualify for because of my exceptional Dun & Bradstreet rating. I wondered how marketers settled on the name Sean for their robocall voice and did some Google research.

From the Urban Dictionary:[8]

> Sean is a wonderful, caring guy who will never hesitate to tell you the truth. He's rough around the edges but if he trusts you, you're someone special and you'll see the person he is underneath. He's the kind of person who will laugh with you and cry with you. If he sees you in any kind of emotional distress, it will make him sad if he cares for you. He will make you smile on days you think you will never smile again. He's a fighter and will fight for what he believes in. He'll be the best friend you ever had and will make your heart soar. Oh yep, and his d*ck is so long it drags on the ground.

And this from myfirstname.rocks:[9]

> Sean is a name that indicates a gift of gab—the ability to persuade others effortlessly. You are expressive, optimistic, outgoing, and inspiring. Charming and cheerful, you are the life of the party for any social event. You fascinate others with your creativity, especially in speaking. You have the innate ability to explain complex concepts in a way that is easy to understand.

If this is how Seans are perceived by others, then good call on the part of the telemarketers. A truth-teller with the gift of gab, the ability to persuade, easy to understand. But a large, ground-dragging d*ck; do we really care?

A few moments after I left the Airbnb for the morning, the phone rang. It was Sean calling from Miami, offering me a pre-approved $500,000 line of credit at 04.8% interest. Adding that the offer expires soon. But knowing Sean, he'll call back again tomorrow.

Monday, November 15th

The plane was delayed taking off from Guadalajara. The captain came on the intercom and said that a plane ahead of us had blown a tire on takeoff and was circling the airport near the tower so they could see if any fire was involved. Cleaning crews were removing tire bits from the runway, and as soon as they were finished, we were next. They didn't make the disabled plane come back. What about their destination, how will they land safely with one less tire? I wanted to know the missing pieces of the story.

Coming back to the U.S. through Texas means you're greeted by the grumpiest immigration employees on the planet. Terminal E at Houston's Intercontinental is beautiful, though; it's shaped like the bow of a huge ocean liner that opens up to the sky. Good restaurants near the gates, too.

CHAPTER TEN

Back in
SANTA FE

Thursday, November 18th

In Santa Fe for a reset. Plus, all my worldly belongings are in storage here, and I need to change out my clothes periodically depending on the climate of my next destination.

Got a haircut today; I asked for Helen Mirren and got Nancy Pelosi.

Friday, November 19th

Maybe while I'm here, I can find someone to do a shamanic journey with—the two other times I've done it, it was helpful. You may not get the answers you're seeking, but frequently you get some kind of clarity.

Friends have loaned me their house for three weeks while they're in San Francisco. A crow is walking the length of the leaf-filled gutter by their apricot tree, scraping out the autumn leaves looking for fruit, grubs, or other insects, I guess? Hey, here's a business idea: corvids are smart; you could train a dozen crows to do this for hire; no ladders required, no dangerous roofs for humans to fall off of, all you'd need is a rake and bags to collect the debris on the ground. Animal-centric businesses are already a thing in New Mexico: rent-a-goat herds to eat unwanted vegetation, cat cafés, service dogs, llama farms, this might just fly.

Friday, November 26th

A message from Archangel Michael came in today, and he said, Don't bother doing the shamanic journey, just keep looking. So okay, I'll keep looking.

Monday, November 29th

This morning I dreamed about a suitcase I'd returned to storage yesterday filled up with miscellaneous items not needed on the next leg of my journey. In the dream, it's garbage collection day, and I see it sitting on the sidewalk of a large city next to a mound of black trash bags. I realize I need to get something out of the suitcase, so I venture outside in my bare feet to get it. What is this object? A pine-scented air freshener tree that hangs from a car's rearview mirror. This kind of scenario constitutes the non-profound content of my dreams. Why can't I dream about where I'm supposed to be living? Paul McCartney famously dreamed some of his best songs, like "Let It Be" (every Beatles-loving septuagenarian in the Western world knows the story: Mother Mary came to him in a dream to offer comfort), and "Yesterday," the melody arising from the delta waves of REM sleep. I'm not asking for creative inspiration from dream-space, all I want to know is where I'm supposed to live. Is that asking too much? Archangel Michael's quiet, lisping voice echoed in my head: *There will be an answer.*

Wednesday, December 1st

Today was one of those perfect early fall days, except that it's December first. One of the best ways to spend these days is to take a long walk in the middle of the afternoon when the day is at its warmest—upper 50s, low 60s—and enjoy the supersaturated blue skies and the cute faux-adobe houses festooned in Tibetan prayer flags and decorated for the holidays with chile ristras. Santa Fe can be deceptively genial and welcoming; it's not uncommon to pass a walled compound with a "My security system is a colt-45" sign nailed to a weathered wooden door.

Today's destination was Santa Fe's most beautiful park, the Cornell Rose Garden. I walked the perimeter of the garden, looped back up Galisteo Street, and wove in and out of traffic for sport. Everyone in the neighborhood drives as if it were a school zone for paraplegic kids, so this behavior didn't pose any danger.

Halfway to my destination, a woman in a beater car pulled up next to me. She rolled down the window and pleaded, Could I talk to you for a sec? I said, Sure, but I kept my distance. She asked if I knew of any casitas for rent, six hundred square feet or so, under a thousand a month. I thought, Yeah, right! Don't let the modest look of this neighborhood deceive you; you're driving through the Beverly Hills of New Mexico. I explained that I was no longer a resident of Santa Fe but had friends who might have friends who might know of a vacant casita. She said she'd lived in the neighborhood for ten years, renting, and was kicking herself for not having bought before the market went crazy. To legitimize herself in my eyes, she reached around to the back seat and produced several laminated poster boards of her garden design work, which was truly outstanding. I mentioned that I'd faced a similar dilemma ten years back, when I sold my money-pit house in the summer and was looking at living under a bridge because nothing was available to rent. I ended up buying a cookie-cutter tract house, thinking I'd be there the minimum amount of time required by tax laws to live in a place without penalty. Since then, the Southside of Santa Fe had become a place of hideous urban sprawl. I reminisced about the time when Santa Feans were opposed to these kinds of neighborhoods, rightly arguing water issues and aesthetics. But capitalism won out, and Californians and Texans fleeing their polluted, violent, conflagrant hometowns were arriving in droves.

She mentioned she was living on the fringe of the Southside and hated it. I wanted to commiserate, but I didn't want to encourage a discussion that would make me feel angry all over again about the years I wasted there, hating the neighborhood and my tract house. I suggested Albuquerque. She said, *I can't stand that ugly place*. I resisted the urge to argue the point that ABQ has some beautiful neighborhoods but, all things considered, she was right. I took her business card and told her I'd ponder her dilemma, thinking to myself, Who are you kidding? You can't even figure out your own situation, the seeds of which were planted at least ten years ago. We parted ways, and I silently thanked my Santa Fe friends who unquestioningly take me in, or let me borrow their homes, when I want to spend some time here to remind myself why I left.

I can't stand that ugly place triggered an annoying Albuquerque memory. In September I'd stayed at an Airbnb owned by an elderly woman from England, and from the moment we met, I knew she was fastidious and distrustful. I was on my guard. The next morning, while she was still asleep, I was in the kitchen using a small Le Creuset saucepan to boil water for coffee. The water began to boil, I turned off the gas stove, and to my horror I noticed that the wooden handle on the saucepan was burnt to a crisp. I thought, Did I do this?? Was I so inattentive that I let the handle sit in the flame, and now it's a piece of charcoal? I rushed back to my room and ordered a new handle from Etsy, and shipping (from England) was twice the cost of the handle itself. Le Creuset replacement handles were not available anywhere locally or even nationally, so if I wanted to do right by her, I had no choice. By then, she was in the kitchen unloading the dishwasher, and I expected to hear a sigh of exasperation when she noticed the burnt handle. I clicked "buy now" and cheerily joined her, announcing that a new handle for the saucepan, sent from Dear Old England, would arrive in a week. I was about to apologize for the damage I'd caused when she said, "Yes, it's been that way for a while now—that pan is really old but it's one of my favorites, and I've been wondering how I could get it fixed."

Of course! The handle had been cooked to a crisp over many years. A new one set me back forty bucks.

Thursday, December 2nd

Six hours of cleaning restored my friends' house to near-pristine condition. But last night while talking on the phone and pacing the living room, I noticed lots of little scratches in the floor that were in high relief because of the overhead lighting. I started noticing other flaws: a coffee stain in the TV room rug, impressions in the leather couch left by the hip bones and heels of reclining nappers, nicks in the walls where they join in 90-degree angles, a few gouges in the dining room table. I had a nagging feeling; did I create any of this damage? Did I carelessly walk across the wooden floor in golf cleats, pound studs into a leather jacket on the dining room table without protection underneath, forget about a lasagna cooking in the oven? I wondered if my hosts, on their return from San Francisco, would notice these flaws when they first entered the house after their long absence, during those first few moments when you can see your home with objective eyes. I wondered if I had altered the home's own distinctive smell with my *eau de âgée*. I said goodbye to the crows, still busy with their own cleaning tasks, smoothed out my footprints in the gravel walkway from the front door to the car, and left New Mexico for Uncertain.

CHAPTER ELEVEN

HOUSESITTING FOR THE HOLIDAYS

Hi Colleen! Thanks so much for agreeing to be our house sitter for the holidays! Your profile made us go, oh my gosh, she is the perfect fit! We sooo look forward to your arrival and, in the meantime, here are just a few extra things we'd like you to know about.

As you saw in our profile, we have two dogs and a cat. I'd like to introduce them to you now. Roger is our rescue pug, eight years old, and as you probably know, pugs can make these hilarious breathing snorts and grunts that just keep us in stitches all day long. Speaking of stitches, when you arrive, Roger will be recovering from abdominal surgery, and are you okay with taking his stitches out? Since it's Christmas vacation, and our house is out in the middle of nowhere, access to a vet will be pretty limited so it'd just be easier if you could do it (if you don't mind!). We ordered some scissors designed especially for this purpose, and we'll send you a link to a video so you can see how it's done. BTW, he's a "leaner," if you stand still long enough, he'll waddle up to you and lean on your leg (he's not a humper, though). He's easy to trip over and loves to snooze on the stairs, so be careful.

Squeaky is our Chihuahua-dachshund mix, and she is a pill! Like a typical Chihuahua, she loves to dig holes in the backyard, and we've never been able to break her of the habit. It sure doesn't make for a very attractive expanse of St. Augustine! So what we do is we keep a supply of poultry manure (more about this in a sec) and grass plugs under the back stairs and fill in those holes as soon as we notice them. I hope you don't mind that we've added this little task to the list! Eventually the backyard will start smelling like the chicken coop, and we keep hoping that this will deter Squeaky, because she HATES the chickens. (We mentioned them in our profile, right?) Like dachshunds will do, she barks at them all day if you let her. But I (Stacey) got this great idea for an invention that I'm in the process of patenting: it's called the Bark-B-Gone Dogapult, like CATapult, you know? It's basically a pole with a rotating wheel on a timer that you load up with hot dogs. Every ten minutes, it tosses a hot dog into the yard away from the chicken coop and distracts Squeaky long enough that we (and the neighbors) get a respite from her relentless barking. You'll find the packages of hot dogs in the freezer in the garage.

Conveniently, the coop is also around back, so hauling their manure isn't a big deal. We've left you a whole bag of nose clips next to the back door, because, honestly, the smell can be pretty intense. Even better, if you've got some personal protective equipment on hand, like a respirator or full-face mask, some cut-resistant gloves, oh, and some really heavy-duty rubber boots, you might want to bring those things with you. It may be hard to resist, but be sure not to cuddle or kiss the chickens because they can carry salmonella or, heaven forbid, avian flu. One thing that's good to know is that the chickens will rush you when you open the gate to the coop, and some of them can be downright aggressive. They respond to "GET BACK!" so, if you remember to scream this first, you should be okay.

Our precious little calico is named Darlene and she will follow you around and jump in your lap the second you sit down.

She loves to walk around on your computer if you give her half a chance. Once she tried sharpening her claws on the keyboard and pulled off the T, Q, and V tiles before I noticed, but I jus (oops! see, I pressed the "t" and nothing happened!) couldn't get mad at her because she's so adorable. She sleeps on Tom's face; I hope you're okay with this, too, but if you're not, just put her out in the hall and close the door. She may scratch at the door and meow for a few hours, but eventually she'll wear herself out and give up. Be careful, tho, when you open the door the next morning, because she usually leaves a little "present" right in your path.

None of our canine or feline pets are trained to respond to any commands other than "NO," but this should suffice for most situations, like when the dogs gang up on Darlene or when Squeaky manages to catch a chicken by the neck and starts shaking it. For goodness' sake, those chickens are bigger than she is!

We have no trash collection, no cell phone service, no internet, and the closest grocery store is 45 minutes away, but there's a pizza place about 20 miles from here that makes the most delicious broccoli and medallions of bull penis pizza. What we do have is beautiful sunrises and sunsets, and the occasional convict from the local prison looking in the windows. Let us know if you see the Sasquatch roaming around ;).

Make yourself at home!
Stacey and Tom

CHAPTER TWELVE

UNCERTAIN, TEXAS: A Housesit

Saturday, December 18th

Once you leave Interstate 20, near Marshall in far East Texas, the rolling grassland prairies give way to dense bald cypress and white oak forests draped in Spanish moss, looking like an army of stick figure zombies with long, gray hair and beards. I was heading toward Uncertain, Texas, near Caddo Lake, meandering along asphalt roads that looked like they were laid back when Texas was a republic and not updated since. Litter-filled ditches flank these roads. Rusted-out cars and farm equipment, splintered wooden pallets, discarded doors, 55-gallon drums that held who-knows-what, strings of tangled Christmas lights, rotted boats sitting on trailers with flat tires populated the landscape. Was Harrison County completely lacking in trash disposal services? Tattered Dixie flags tacked to the mildewed walls of mobile homes signaled their occupants' nineteenth-century politics and mindset. Feral hogs were as plentiful as West Texas cattle. What was I getting myself into? Did the people who selected me to house-sit fake their identity and their home, and I will be greeted at the door of a dilapidated trailer by a pair of meth heads and their pack of snarling pit bulls? Either I took a detour through time and space to the *Deliverance* movie set, or I'm the doomed heroine of a Stephen King novel.

I crossed a bridge into the neighborhood of the housesit, the bridge being the only terrestrial escape route should I need to make a quick getaway. Wooden-frame houses constructed on stilts began to appear, with massive diesel trucks parked in the driveways proudly displaying their support of our forty-fifth president. Just as I was seriously considering turning back, a majestic, white, three-level, early American-style house, also on stilts, came into view. The number on the mailbox matched the number I'd entered in my phone. A kind of Father of the Bride house in the middle of the Amityville Horror.

Sunday, December 19th

I had agreed to take care of three dogs, two cats, half a dozen chickens, and a modest tank full of fish. One of the cats lived next door and was owned by the brother of the woman for whom I was sitting. All the animals, including the betta in the fish tank, have separation anxiety, and my amygdala has been in a constant state of high alert. I think they're going to figure it out (that their owners are gone long-term), and the dogs are going to take it out on me. The owners will return to find my decomposed, partially eaten body lying in their bed, my pajamas ripped to shreds and my liver missing. My right ear will become Sven the miniature dachshund's favorite chew toy, and Spencer the Doberman will have dibs on both femurs.

The homeowners mentioned a Christmas float parade passing by the house at 2:30 p.m. that was not to be missed. Chugging down the bayou, the transvestites of Caddo Lake come out of hiding once a year, and it's agreed by all that they will not be used for target practice. A Miss Uncertain, Uncertain being the name of the closest town, has a float all her own. I watched the parade from the windows flanking the front door because I was afraid that if I left the house, the dogs would forget that I was the person who had fed them only a few hours earlier and tear me to pieces when I returned.

    The owners strongly suggested that they wanted the little dogs to sleep with me, but tonight Weevil the rat terrier-Chihuahua mix tried chasing me away so he could have the bed to himself. Sorry—I'm the alpha being for the next three weeks.

Monday, December 20th

I made it through the night without having my face torn off by Weevil, the terrihuahua. The dogs are more chill today, but they seem to be switching personalities by the hour. Weevil is calmer—he even lay belly-up for me to pat him—and Sven, who's been the model dog, has been barking at me aggressively. I guess I'll figure out their patterns eventually; that is, if I survive the next few days. The house doesn't have a dog door, and the little dogs must be watched like a hawk when they're outside because, well, of the hawks and owls that would love to make a meal of them. So far, that's meant I've spent half of my waking hours on dog guard duty. And some early morning hours, too, when I'd rather not be awake.

    The chickens have a great setup: a big coop that they can run around in and be safe in and a ramp that leads up to two houses where they lay their eggs. The eggs are accessed from the outside by three sturdy doors that open directly to the nests, and the eggs are eye-level to someone about five foot eight. I'm five five, so I have to stand on tiptoe to see them. Also, to see if any egg-stealing snakes are present. Today, I shut door number three too hard, and the door inverted on its hinge. I nearly wore my knuckles raw trying to force the door back into its normal position so I could latch it. No such luck. I wondered, Could a chicken-killing raccoon open the door itself, with their tiny, dexterous, humanoid fingers? Are they stronger than a nearly seventy-year-old woman?

    When I was a kid, my parents took us to the State Fair of Texas where a favorite exhibit was a chicken that played tic-tac-toe. Chickens can also learn card tricks, like how to identify a specific card in a spread of many cards, the Queen of Hearts, for example. But these chickens aren't going to card identification school any time soon.

The cat stays out of everybody's way, and I've noticed that I forget she's here. I hope I don't forget to feed her.

Tuesday, December 21st

On the Northern Hemisphere's shortest day, I woke to a dense fog. I considered walking the neighborhood to snap some moody photos of dripping moss, but I heard gunshots close by. Hunters, no doubt. I didn't want to be mistaken for a feral hog, so I went back inside and walked a few miles on the treadmill instead.

By afternoon the sky had cleared and it was a beautiful day. Spencer the Doberman and I had been in and out of the backyard several times, and I needed more stimulation than running up and down the stairs yelling "Spencer!" had to offer. I was rapidly depleting the homeowners' bottled water supply, and drinking the well water wasn't an option. I knew the closest Kroger was a thirty-minute drive away, and argued with myself about making the trip just to buy water, but by 3 p.m. I gave in, crated up the dogs, and got in the car. It was the first time I'd ventured out of Uncertain since arriving at 5 p.m. on Saturday, nearly seventy-two hours earlier. I was hoping to find a 7-Eleven or some version of a convenience store close by, but none of the dilapidated structures I passed seemed to be places of commerce. Or at least not ones I would patronize. But then a brand-spanking-new Family Dollar appeared at an intersection, and I was spared the thirty-minute drive to Kroger that I was already ten minutes into. It's fun to peruse small rural stores to learn what the neighborhood folks consider essentials, and Family Dollars are among the best places to do this kind of research.

This is what I discovered. In far East Texas, lots of sugary and salty snacks—Moon Pies, Dum-Dums, Pringles, and the like—occupy the most shelf space, along with several brands of chewing tobacco, Velveeta single-serve shells and cheese, Chef Boyardee, frozen pizza, and an entire wall of refrigerated soda and beer. Water was mysteriously absent. I walked up and down the aisles, feeling like one of those characters in a Western who's just crossed the Mojave, walks into a saloon, and collapses from thirst. I'd almost given up when I saw a partially opened box of gallon containers of Crystal Geyser, "alpine" spring water bottled at the source in Norman, Arkansas, elevation 692 feet. I couldn't believe my good fortune and grabbed two jugs. I had a hankerin' for ice cream, too, and, astonishingly, they had exactly two pints of Ben & Jerry's Half Baked. My favorite.

The exact person I had imagined would meet me at the door of the housesit stood at the counter paying for his cigarettes, handing the aged, toothless cashier a ten from fingers covered in death-themed rings. Thick chains cascaded from his neck and belt loops, and his filthy white T-shirt, both sleeves chewed off—probably by the pit bulls waiting for him outside in his Dodge Mega Cab—revealed spider tattoos on both elbows. He was polite to the unruffled cashier, grumbling a "thank you" when given his change. She was probably his grandmother.

No matter how much I wash them, my hands smell like Spencer.

Thursday, December 23rd

The first time I took a shower here, I noted that the floor seemed coated either with Teflon or a high-tech lubricant. Even though I was taking such care, this morning I slipped and fell. This was a full-on fall, feet sliding out from under me, and thank goodness my butt landed first and I didn't break anything. Synchronistically, several hours later Spencer slipped on the back porch and got stuck in a sitting position, and I had to try to help him up by lifting him at the waist, if that's what you call the part of a dog's anatomy immediately forward of its hind legs. "Did we forget to tell you that Spencer has hip dysplasia and is on pain meds?" the pet owners had asked. For a moment, I panicked because he wouldn't budge, but then he put in some effort and the two of us got him back on all fours. Loading up a disabled, ninety-pound Doberman into a truck I've never driven before, in the pouring rain, and racing to the emergency vet an hour away was not an option. Also not in my housesitting agreement.

The rain cleared in the afternoon, and I took a boat ride on Caddo Lake with a man named Patrick. When he gave me directions to his place over the phone, he said, Look for the yard with all the Trump flags. I thought he might be pulling my leg, but he wasn't. As I drove down Doubtful Drive East to Patrick's place, there they were, unfurled and undulating in the humid Republican breeze. Hundreds of ducks hung heads down from the tin ceilings of several shacks on the riverfront property and, at first, I thought duck hunting was his priority business. That would explain the presence of the extended Chinese family I kept running into wherever I went; they had to be restaurateurs on a business trip to check out their major supplier. But Patrick said the ducks were decoys. I asked him why a person would need so many. He explained that to attract the real thing, you create a synthetic flock. I wondered how you could tell the real ducks from the plastic ones when out on the lake, but maybe it doesn't really matter if you're just into randomly shooting whatever.

Friday, December 24th

When I went next door to feed the brother's cat, I was greeted with a flood of feline upchuck, and it was fresh. It looked like the three-quarters of a cup of cat food that I had fed her earlier had expanded to twice the size of the cat, so no wonder it had nowhere else to go. As I was cleaning it up, I imagined the scenario that produced this abundance of ejecta, her little body heaving and contracting, her sweet little voice possessed by a demon making guttural, choking sounds. Disgorging her dinner, then happily hopping up on the couch to clean herself. I texted her owner to ask if this was normal, and he replied, Oh sure, she's quite the old girl. I looked it up: eighty in human years.

So that we house sitters can be prepared for any eventuality, I think house sitter-solicitors should be *required* to divulge the conditions, habits, and proclivities of their pets in detail: most important, including whether they can reliably control their digestive systems and bowels. Additionally, in the case of Spencer, his back legs. An army of fact-checkers should be deployed to their homes for verification.

I'd also want to know if someone's pets masturbate. While I sat on a barstool at the kitchen counter and worked at the computer, Weevil retreated to the crate to my left. The crate began to rattle, and I glanced down. He was sitting up on his back legs and leaning against the rear bars, holding his penis in between his front paws and rubbing it up and down as fast as he could. We made eye contact, and he stopped instantly. I could tell he felt shame, so I looked away. But I wanted him to keep going. Could he make himself come?

Late morning, Spencer tried climbing the outside steps and fell, tumbling down four of them and landing on the concrete deck with a thud. Thank god he's okay; and thank god for pain meds. We're going to use the outside elevator exclusively from now on. I don't recall elevator operator included in the house-sitting description?

Even though his owners said that Spencer *may* have an "accident" in the house, but rarely, he's been defecating indoors predictably, every day. At least he's regular. His poo is almost perfectly spheroid and not gooey; golf ball-sized, unlike the little dogs'. But he lets loose all over the living room, and I suspect his excrement has touched all carpeted and upholstered surfaces over the years. Thus, I always sit at the kitchen counter to work and to eat and enter the open-concept living room/dining room, the dogs' domain, only to address accidents or to tidy up.

Are things spinning out of control?? I had to get away for a few hours or else go crazy, so I drove to Jefferson, a cute Texas town that must have been prosperous during the steamboat days when cotton was shipped via the Red River, through Caddo

Lake, to New Orleans. I was on a quest for treats for the dogs and a bath mat to prevent future slips in the shower. My first stop was a Brookshire grocery store. No bath mat and limited treat selection: only Oinkies—some kind of "highly digestible" stick wrapped in a chicken-like substance. The kind cashier recommended the Family Dollar just down the road and across the bridge, and it was the place to be seen on Christmas Eve. The Dollar was jam-packed with Jeffersonians and just about everything you'd find in a Walmart Supercenter, except in a space one one-hundredth the size. Beefeaters sweet potato sticks wrapped in chicken (a smiling dog in a chef's hat graphic is what made the sale); Dream Kabobz—again, a stick wrapped in chicken, pork, and duck; and DreamSticks, chicken and vegetables solidified into a dog chew, were the offerings. They all claimed to be "The Healthy Alternative to Rawhide," which made me suspicious. These dog treats come from Vietnam, China, and Thailand, and who knows what's really in them? I didn't see any vegetables I recognized, unless you consider rubber a vegetable.

On the way back to the house, I stopped at the (recommended) Big Pines Lodge to check it out and maybe eat lunch there, but it was closed. The Chinese family was there, too. A chubby eight- or nine-year-old boy was chasing his two younger siblings around, trying to keep them corralled and entertained. When he saw me he said in a kind of exasperated way, "I'm taking care of the toddlers." I said, "You're a good sport."

The property was on a bayou with a wooden dock that led to a half-sunken paddleboat. I'd heard about the legendary paddleboat from several people; it's like what the Statue of Liberty is to New York, the one thing you must see when you visit the Uncertain area.

Saturday, December 25th

Had spaghetti and meatballs for Christmas dinner and Half Baked for dessert. Eighty degrees here. A very low-key Christmas in the East Texas Heart of Darkness.

Sunday, December 26th

The dogs woke up at 5:30 a.m. this morning wanting to eat and go outside. After all this activity, I dragged myself back upstairs and by some miracle went back to sleep. Sven, and eventually Weevil, joined me. I dreamed that I needed to take the dogs with me to New Orleans on a bus. The bus driver said I had to hold Spencer the Doberman on my lap, and we were trying to make this work when I woke up.

Monday, December 27th

Today is day ten. I've lowered the minimum number of days I tell myself must elapse before I make a definitive judgment about the livability of a place. I knew Caddo Lake and Uncertain didn't make the cut within ten minutes.

I am utterly exhausted. The dogs woke me up at 3:30 a.m. and wanted to go outside. We were back inside by 4, and between then and 6:15, I got twenty minutes of sleep. I'm not used to lying in one position and not moving; whenever I lie on my side, Sven uses my stomach as a pillow and Weevil cuddles up to my back. He likes to lick my legs and last night he was licking my (clothed) butt.

On one of our many excursions down the two flights of stairs to the backyard, I filled the dogs' outside water bowl and when I bent over to pick it up, the remote for the elevator fell out of my shirt pocket and into the water. I retrieved it in a split second, dried it off, and my racing heart calmed when it still worked. The elevator is Spencer's lifeline to the outside world, the world of the backyard dog toilet and the occasional squirrel he tries to chase. I'd wondered what I'd do if the battery gave out; the owners didn't mention a backup remote. I can't even find a screwdriver in this place. They have what they called a tool kit but all that's in it is a tiny hammer, a level, and a roll of braided wire: a picture-hanging kit.

I'm desperate for a nap. Every time I think I may be able to sneak one in, something happens.

The weather for Wednesday is predicted to be rainy, and I'd arranged for a boat ride with a different captain to take sunset photos. I called him to see if we could change our ride to tomorrow, Tuesday, which is supposed to be mostly cloudy but not rainy. I told him my goal was to get some photos with nice light, but I wasn't too worried if there were a few clouds hanging around. He said, I can fix that. Was he pulling my leg?? I almost suggested he see someone about his God complex, but after last week's Trumpster boater and his bunting of flags, I think the new guy was serious. So okay, let's see how Mr. Zeus controls the weather. I've asked for his address twice now, and both times he's given me vague directions. What about a street name and a number, please? I know how to use Google Maps.

Tuesday, December 28th

Mother and daughter housekeepers are coming today; I may go to the Walmart Superspreader, uh, Supercenter, in Marshall to buy pansies while they're here. The homeowners had bought some for the front porch pots but hadn't actually planted them. Set in the pots, plastic container and all, with a little dirt thrown on top, they had all dried out and died. I might wait until next week, though, because the temperature's predicted to dip into the upper twenties for a few days over the weekend. I know pansies can survive that, but it may be prudent to wait and see.

The daily disaster happened first thing. I'd let the dogs out at 5:30 a.m. and, as usual, Sven and Weevil wanted to go back inside before Spencer. While Spencer and I were outside, the cat jumped up on the kitchen counter and knocked over several bags of dog treats, and when we made it back upstairs, Sven and Weevil were having a free-for-all eating what had spilled onto the floor. When Spencer saw the bonanza, he shoved the other two aside, mopping the floor with his massive tongue. Even after gorging themselves on treats, they were still able to gobble their breakfast. For a miniature dachshund, that was impressive.

When the housekeepers came to the door, I wasn't sure the mother was wearing any pants. I hope she didn't see me staring, but I was trying to figure out if her legs were covered in a tattoo pattern of some kind, top to bottom. Then I realized she was wearing flesh-colored tights with an animal print. She had augmented lips and breasts; not something I expected to see in rural East Texas. When I returned from Walmart, the house smelled like lemon Pine-Sol and was satisfyingly clean. That won't last.

This welcome tidiness triggered a memory, or maybe it was the Pine-Sol? Virgo is my rising sign, and believe in astrology or not, I am a textbook Virgo. We are perfectionists, dependable, predictable, fastidious, self-effacing, practical, and are frequently stressed, tense, and overthinking things. These Virgo qualities started to emerge some time before my fourth birthday, and by kindergarten, I already knew this was my MO. At that age I was a budding artist with some visible talent. But I couldn't stand to get dirty, to color outside the lines, to represent something in the abstract. I'd had my first one-preschooler show of individual bird portraits, each sitting on a generic tree limb, and I remember a drawing of a magpie that I was particularly fond of. But something very non-Virgoan got into me one day. Each student was given a book of newsprint drawings that we were supposed to color, and on one page I lost control and attacked the page with frantic scribbling, effectively obliterating the original drawing. Later in the week, Principal Tunstil planned to visit our class to see our work, and it was possible that I'd be the focus of his attention because I'd heard my teacher telling him that I was a good artist. When he arrived, my classmates and I were standing in a large circle and our teacher commanded us to show him each drawing in our book, one by one. He entered the circle and stood in its center. All my other drawings were controlled and well executed, which he noticed and commented on, and I'd decided ahead of time what I would do when we came to the page in my book that was just a bunch of scribbles. I flipped the page in the book and stepped slightly to the left so that I could hide the drawing behind the girl next to me. And the ruse succeeded. No one noticed, but the anxiety was so intense that I never colored outside the lines again. Ever.

A few days earlier I'd been playing in our family's rather feral backyard when I lifted a rock and discovered a scorpion underneath, pincers raised, threatened. During the principal's visit to our class, I was this threatened scorpion, hiding the evidence of my rebellion against the Virgo oppressor behind my classmate.

Here at Caddo Lake, every day has challenged my perfectionism. I've broken a cherished Christmas ornament, failed at winding the grandfather clock in the living room, dropped the irreplaceable remote control for the outdoor elevator in the dog's water bowl, killed the pansies, and more! To neutralize the cortisol invading my stressed-out body, I imagined indulging in passive-aggressive behaviors that wouldn't be discovered until I'm long gone. Like collecting the Doberman's perfectly spheroid stools, letting them desiccate for a week to reduce the smell, and placing them in a Waterford cut-glass bowl along with a few handfuls of potpourri. Allow the cat that so desperately wants to discover the outside world to escape. Fry up one of the chickens. Replace the pansies with their plastic counterparts from Michael's. Of course, I would never do these things, but imagining them was such diabolical fun.

"Did you just mention me and reference my nemesis in the same breath? A familiar, lispy voice whispered in my ear.

"I said I'd never actually DO those things."

"Well, be careful what you put out into the universe. You don't want to conjure you-know-who. You really don't want to go there."

At 4:30 this afternoon, the dogs and I were outside when the two teenage boys next door appeared with their .22s to shoot squirrels. We were right in the line of fire. I tried hustling the dogs inside, but have I mentioned that they don't behave? Spencer could easily be mistaken for a deer, and Sven a feral piglet.

During a late-night foray outside, I decided to start a music experiment. I'd been humming "Jupiter" from Holst's *The Planets* for much of the afternoon, and I wondered if the dogs would like to hear the orchestral version on my phone. And they did! All three of them stopped, froze, and perked their ears. They stayed with the music for the entire seven minutes. Next, I wondered if they'd like "Les Voix Humaines" by Marin Marais, and none of them were at all interested. Maybe they're just not fans of the viola da gamba.

Wednesday, December 29th

Can attachment to pets induce a mild form of Stockholm syndrome? As of last night, I noticed I've developed irrational, and somewhat powerful, feelings for the dogs, Sven in particular, and it occurred to me that I could be trauma bonding. When I examined the conditions under which a person develops this, it made perfect sense. First, you have to be held prisoner, meaning you're in a situation from which there is no escape; and you have to see yourself as a captive. For the first week at Caddo Lake, that's exactly how I felt: I was being held hostage. Plus, fear of the dogs—they can be unpredictable, right?—was a factor. Eventually I began to develop positive feelings toward my captors; they were funny and entertaining sometimes, but like in a prisoner/abductor situation, these behaviors could turn on a dime, especially with Weevil the terrihuahua. He could be enjoying a tummy rub one minute and the next, act like he was going to tear your face off. But over time, with lots of affection (and treats), he dialed back the aggression and our positive bond strengthened.

In classic Stockholm syndrome, if the abuser is kind in any way, the captive clings to this as a coping mechanism for his or her very survival. But how are the dogs "kind," exactly? After a very long day of tolerating their barking, their demands to go outside several times an hour, and their insatiable appetite for treats, when we pile into bed at night, they clearly are grateful and want to demonstrate this by humping your leg and licking your mouth. Then they slam their little bodies up against yours and pass out, trusting that you won't sneak off into the night, roll over and crush them, or toss them out the third-storey window. If you're not careful, feelings of sympathy for the dogs will lead to empathy, a desire to protect them and, eventually, love. It's all very confusing.

This morning I was imagining life without Sven and how bereft I will be. I've been here for twelve days, eleven with the dogs by myself. About half my stay. Will I be ready to be released by my captors in another eleven?

Later in the day, the dogs dug up a large crawfish, aka a mudbug; I think that was what all the vigorous hole digging had been about over the past few days. I saw the three of them surrounding something in the grass, and when I went to investigate, the poor crustacean had reared up on its back legs with pincers extended and open. No match for the gnashing jaws of the two little dogs. I chased them away and tried to figure out how I could rescue the crawfish. The only available tools nearby were the dog's water bowl and a broom, and I figured if I could distract the dogs long enough to grab those two things, I could get the crawfish to safety. In the meantime, I took a closer look. His eyes were transparent globes, and his body was coated in slimy red clay from which he had emerged. His antennae were almost as long as his body, and his serrated, paddle-like tail suggested a good swimmer. He was determined not to let anything touch him. At an opportune moment, I ran for it, emptied the water bowl and grabbed the broom. I'm not sure how, but I got the crawfish into the bowl, fending off the dogs, and took it outside the fence. I put it in a flower bed, away from any predators and in friable soil, so maybe it could dig its way in to safety. Putting that much effort into rescuing a crawfish had something to say about my state of mind. I was enacting my own need to escape.

Thursday, December 30th

One of the weirdest things about sleeping with two little dogs is that, at times, it's like sleeping with a very horny, very sloppy little man. If I'm lying on my side, Weevil licks the bottoms of my feet and would love to chew on my toes if I'd let him. I've tried sleeping in my heaviest winter socks, but I can't stand wearing socks to bed so that never lasts long. Sven snores just like a human, and right in my ear. And Spencer is still shitting in the house like clockwork, an hour after he's eaten. When he barks to be let out, I open the door, but he won't budge. I can't exactly carry a ninety-pound Doberman down the steps into the yard, and I foolishly think, Well, maybe he's not going to foul the carpet this time. Maybe it's a false alarm. I start looking at emails or reading the *New Yorker* or whatever, then the smell hits. Today I watched the time more closely, swiveled on my barstool a few minutes before an hour had elapsed, and caught him in the act. I shamed him into going outside, but he refused to get in the elevator to be conveyed into the yard. I've managed to crush my middle finger in the latch, twice now in the last twelve hours, in the same spot.

The dogs were up at four; I've already cried once today, and it's not even 7 a.m. I reminded myself to embrace the more positive tenets of Cynicism and decided to see how (or if) delving deeper into its philosophy could help my current state of mind. Wikipedia offered some surprising info.

> There are four reasons why the Cynics (cynic means "dog-like") are so named. First because of the indifference of their way of life, for they make a cult of indifference and, like dogs, eat and make love in public, go barefoot, and sleep in tubs and at crossroads. The second reason is that the dog is a shameless animal, and they make a cult of shamelessness, not as being beneath modesty, but as superior to it. The third reason is that the dog is a good guard, and they guard the tenets of their philosophy. The fourth

reason is that the dog is a discriminating animal which can distinguish between its friends and enemies. So do they recognize as friends those who are suited to philosophy, and receive them kindly, while those unfitted, they drive away, like dogs, by barking at them . . . Diogenes, in particular, was referred to as the "Dog", a distinction he seems to have reveled in, stating that "other dogs bite their enemies, I bite my friends to save them."[1]

I'm supposed to be learning these lessons from the dogs, now I understand! My canine friends have been preparing me for reentry into the human world with a more thorough immersion in Cynic philosophy. More indifference to what happens, less shame, guard what I believe in, be discriminating. In moments of utter boredom and inattention, pacing the yard and waiting for the trio to relieve themselves and finish chasing squirrels, I've found myself trying to imitate the high-pitched, ear-piercing cry of Weevil, the deep moan of Spencer, and the sharp, staccato bark of Sven, with some degree of success.

Friday, December 31st

I ate lunch at the Catfish Village of Waskom, the local catfish restaurant go-to, and yeah, it was great. The smallest order of catfish came with four fillets, mashed potatoes, red beans, coleslaw, hushpuppies, and I also ordered a side of fried okra. Enough food for at least four people. The building and décor are intended to resemble a fishing camp, and the restaurant was full of a type of man distinctive to the area; I'm not sure exactly what inspires this look but my guess is either the MAGA, QAnon, or White Supremacy movements. Tight T-shirts, lots of tattoos, closely shaven heads and voluminous but neatly trimmed beards. Huge guts. Loud voices. A swagger that says either chapped butt or I've got a handgun in each pocket and I need to walk cautiously so as not to discharge either of them by accident.

Uncertain's New Year's Eve fireworks started after dark, and the little dogs went berserk. At 11 p.m. we piled into bed, and I started reading them a children's book. It calmed them down, but periodically they'd hear a loud boom, triggering their out-of-control barking. But they liked being read to, and we wrapped it up at 1 a.m. I suspect the same thing will happen tomorrow night because it's the night of the local Caddo Lake fireworks. I'm ambivalent about leaving them alone; the owners are insisting that I see the fireworks, but what about the terror that the dogs feel? Plus, I can't convince Spencer to get in his crate, and just last night his owners confessed, via text, that he usually crates upstairs in the office. They moved his crate downstairs because they thought it would be more convenient for me, but what they didn't do was accustom him to its new location before they left. He's confused, no doubt. I suggested a two-inch-thick cut of top sirloin to lure him in, haha, but honestly I'm kind of annoyed. Counter to my nice Southern girl need-to-please upbringing, someday I hope to acquire the skills needed to call people on their sh*t. You'd think I'd have earned a PhD in this field after nine years in Yankee (Rhode Island) re-education, but all it did was modify my accent to one more neutral and comprehensible, altering the way I communicated (sonically) and making me a better listener.

Saturday, January 1st

Welcome, 2022! Beautiful pink light this morning and a red-tailed hawk screaming outside. I'm determined to get Spencer out the door before he blows mud... succeeded!

Sunday, January 2nd

A cold front arrived last night, and this morning it's twenty-eight degrees and windy. The well insulated chickens survived and even produced four eggs overnight. Ice on the stairs, the grass crunches when you walk across it. Gray sky, gray trees, gray Spanish moss. It looks like a hurricane barreled through New Orleans, Baton Rouge, through Shreveport and up to Uncertain, bringing with it these cities' dust bunnies and depositing them in the trees.

Spencer was such a bad dog today. I had to crate him (a time-out) to get him to stop standing right beside me and barking in my ear. Five more days.

Monday, January 3rd

Today Weevil pulled a small bat out from under the gap between the door and the floor of the upstairs screened-in patio the owners call "The Café." I don't think he was bitten, but the bat was injured, and I didn't want to get near it. In the meantime, Spencer was eating prodigious amounts of grass and throwing up. The happy ending is that the bat crawled back into his home and Spencer seems to be okay.

The owners shared that earlier in the year, Spencer had survived a cottonmouth snake bite in the face.

Tuesday, January 4th

Two red-tailed hawks were circling above today, one very close to the house. It dive-bombed something in the front yard. Sven was barking his little head off out in the yard and refused to behave when I called him to come inside. I had to carry him up the stairs and into the house. I didn't drive anywhere today, and didn't get much done either because of dogs, watering plants, trying to keep the place somewhat clean. At least I did a good deed—I boxed up two dozen eggs and left them in the next-door neighbor's mailbox and in the mailbox of the family with three kids across the street. I figured that in both instances, those eggs would disappear fast.

Wednesday, January 5th

Spencer deposited a huge crap, a brown dotted line along the walk space between the couch and the kitchen bar. Right in front of me. Couldn't he have signaled that he wanted to go outside?

Thursday, January 6th

It was another sleepless night, the dogs squirming a lot and walking on my chest periodically. When Weevil does this, it's like he's wearing doggy stiletto heels, sliding around on my ribs. We're in a king-size bed, and my guess is that we use about an eighth of bed real estate, teetering on the left edge. I worry that Sven will fall off because he positions himself on the left side of me. Sometimes in the middle of the night I'm able to sneak away to the right side of the bed to enjoy a few minutes away from them, but that never lasts long. Last night I was worrying about whether I was lying on Sven's very large and flimsy ears—the kind that invert with the slightest gust of wind. Then I thought, how strange to be worrying about lying on someone's ears.

 I woke up thinking about friends who coach me on situations I already know how to manage, point out details in photos that, of course, I've also observed, give advice about things that are self-evident to a reasoning person with his or her wits still intact. Alzheimer's sufferers are allowed to inhabit their own universe without their loved ones correcting, contradicting, or supervising their reality; why shouldn't the rest of us be treated with that courtesy? I'm planning a trip to Costa Rica, and a friend advised, "Be sure to bring sunscreen." Another friend said, "Make a list of what you want and don't want in a place to live and see how it matches up." Why would I have not thought of those things on my own? Have I behaved in ways in the past that suggest I can't grasp the obvious? I'm sure their advice was offered in a spirit of helpfulness, but it's annoying. In the name of friendship, I should inhabit their universes, too, and let it go.

 I feel guilty about the things I've ordered lately from Amazon. It's all necessities, like the kind of floss I like. A waterproof map of Costa Rica. A new suitcase to replace my beloved carry-on whose handle broke during the last trip, making it nonretractable. Waterproof shoes for walking in rivers and in the ocean and reef-friendly sunscreen. Covid tests. Nothing frivolous, that is, if one considers a trip to Costa Rica essential.

But I'm adding to the suffering of people who work the supply chain, from sailors on container ships who ferry the stuff here, unload it at docks, load the ships back up, and sail off to somewhere else without a break, to Amazon workers and their well-documented repetitive motion injuries and twelve-hour-on-your-feet shifts. UPS, FedEx, and Amazon truck drivers. I need to learn to survive with less. We all do.

Friday, January 7th

I never thought this (penultimate) day would arrive. I've been cleaning like mad, packing as much as I can so I'll have a minimum number of tasks to do tomorrow. This morning I noticed a particularly foul smell coming from Spencer's crate and when I investigated, I saw that his comforter was stained and when I removed it from the crate, several balls of grass-impregnated poo fell out. Not that fresh, fortunately. I removed all his bedding, held my breath, and carried it upstairs to the washing machine. At some point during the next hour, the weight of the water-soaked bedding caused the washing process to pause. Why was there no cheerful washing machine tune to signal the problem? I went upstairs thinking his bedding was ready to be put in the dryer, and that's when I discovered I hadn't found all the golf ball-sized poo hidden therein. Poo and grass were evenly distributed throughout the wash, so I ran it again and could have run it a third time, but I decided to throw the whole mess in the dryer to see if the drying process, and the lint collector, would remove the rest of the grass. And it did.

Saturday, January 8th

I cuddled Sven most of the night, gosh I'm going to miss him!

I locked up and left Uncertain in the pouring rain. At last, I was released from captivity, and I cried all the way back to my sister's house in Fort Worth. Next time I have a housesit that includes pets, I hope they're living in an Uncle Milton Giant Ant Farm.

CHAPTER THIRTEEN

COSTA RICA

Tuesday, January 11th

The airport shuttle arrived at 3:25 a.m. on the dot. The driver offered me the front seat and, when I hoisted myself up, I saw that I shared the van with only two other people. By the time the driver finished his rounds, the van was packed, half masked and half not, and my carry-on containing an expensive camera and computer, with data that had never been backed up, was at the bottom of a pile of ten other people's luggage. On the way to the airport, I stole glances at the driver, and I was never sure if his eyes were open. We arrived at the departure area with only an hour to go before the flight. Everyone's bags were removed from the back of the van, revealing my carry-on and its collapsed corner, and I imagined all the broken electronic bits it now held.

The check-in line was long, and (break my) Spirit Airlines was understaffed. To avoid getting a migraine, I wore sunglasses to moderate the airline's Day-Glo-yellow-and-black color scheme. Finally at the counter, with passport in hand, the ticket agent asked to see my PCR test results. Just yesterday, I'd checked to see if I needed a test, and when I yelled NOT REQUIRED through my mask and their plexiglass barrier, she gave me a look and grabbed her cheat sheet. Then she asked for my QR code. She was referencing a mandatory health form that generates a unique QR code for entry into Costa Rica, a requirement I hadn't seen mention of anywhere. I asked for a paper version of the form, and she handed me a well-used laminated sheet of QR codes that connect travelers to the health forms of the airline's eighteen international destinations. It was the only option for filling out the form. So if you don't have a device with a QR code reader, you don't get to go? Then I understood. If printed out, the form would use half a ream of paper and, if rolled up, would create a scroll six inches in diameter.

I had no idea how to answer some of the questions, like, "What is your seat assignment?" I hadn't thought to note that on my detailed travel schedule, but now I know to do so in the future. For the question asking, "What is the address of your stay in Costa Rica?" it wouldn't accept the address of the Airbnb, so I picked a random hotel from a drop-down list. The form crashed four times, always when I'd reached the final page: the page asking for proof of health insurance, another requirement I hadn't seen when researching entry to Costa Rica. Thanks to a Christmas miracle, I'd updated my travel health insurance policy on December 25th, and the coverage letter was in my email. I took a screenshot and uploaded it to the form, but it crashed again. Precious minutes were ticking away, my flight left in thirty minutes, and I still had to clear security. I couldn't afford another crash. I was starting to accept that I wasn't going to Costa Rica when a nice Tico (what Costa Ricans call themselves) stepped up to the counter and offered to help. I relinquished all control to him and, on the sixth try, was awarded my code.

On the connecting flight from Ft. Lauderdale to San José, I got half an hour of the kind of deep, quality sleep that fortifies you for what's next. Which was the customs line at the airport. I was one of at least four hundred tourists, and sometimes it wasn't clear that the line was moving. I'd been talking with a middle-aged surfer dude when out of the crowd, an airport official materialized and said, "There's a problem with your papers." I thought, How does she know who I am and that I lied about where I'm staying? She instructed me to get on a bus that would take me to Gate 17. Gate 17 was not really a gate but a huge, carpeted room, empty except for three card tables. At each table, a uniformed official sat behind plexiglass. The one with a take-no-prisoners face signaled for me to approach. I was about to admit to my lie when he asked to see my vaccination card, which I produced. He looked at it and said, "Okay, you can go back to the customs line." But there was no return bus. Fine. I needed the exercise. And maybe the surfer dude would kindly let me back in line. Two and a half hours later, I was at the Avis counter waiting for delivery of the car. My computer and camera survived the trip.

Thursday, January 13th

My home base Sarchí is accessed via a road I would have loved as a ten-year-old go-kart driver: winding, sharp turns, up and down inclines, the heady aroma of diesel. I've rented a small, prefab minimalist bongolow, as the Airbnb owner calls it,[1] that came with a giant spider wedged in between the screen door and the sliding glass front door. Which meant I couldn't open the glass door to let in fresh air without also inviting the spider inside. I hope those deadly Brazilian wandering spiders haven't wandered this far north.

    A remnant of indigenous forest surrounds the bongolow but, clearly, a lot of things were planted to fill in, often the same tropical exotics imprisoned in containers and decorating over-air-conditioned U.S. office buildings. Beyond the boundary of the property, the neighbor is scraping his land down to the red dirt, and the front-loader's constant, low-frequency rumble rattles the bongolow's glass façade. Every now and then I catch a glimpse of bright orange moving behind the greenery and suffer loud beeping, that universal signal that a dangerous piece of equipment is backing up. When I close my eyes, I imagine a downtown Los Angeles construction project.

There's something really hypnotizing about certain leafy tropical plants that grow here, particularly the ones whose slender leaves shaped in long scoops radiate from a center point. When the wind is blowing slightly, these scoops catch the breeze and bob up and down in a regular rhythm, as if you were watching a time-lapse video of multiple automatic gate arms, like at a parking lot toll booth. When you see several plants doing this mechanical bobbing thing, your head starts to bob along with it. You can't help it. Banana leaves don't do this—they waver more side to side, like an elephant dislodging flies from its ears.

Four hours later, the giant spider is still on the screen. Maybe she thinks she's found a fancy spider condo that she can just hang out on and catch insects, without having to exert herself to make a conventional web. I could brush some honey on the screen to help attract her dinner. She's become my new pet, and her name is Ursula.

My neighbor next door, a Jehovah's Witness, and I drove into town to eat lunch. She doesn't have a car, so I offered to drive her wherever she needed to go to provision herself. She filled me in on all the good restaurants, groceries, and fruit and vegetable stands, and bought me a pipa, a tiny coconut that is punctured and intubated with a plastic straw. Since I was a captive audience, I was expecting a lecture on the imminence of Armageddon, but it never came. I did get to hear her life story, which was harrowing, and was grateful she didn't ask about mine.

Sarchí is known for its expert woodworkers, Ticos who make beautiful rocking chairs and continue the tradition of making wooden carts for hauling coffee, even though there are no more small-farmer coffee plantations in the area. They're all operated by monster multinationals that appropriated the land, deforested it, planted huge monolithic plantations, and pay the locals a pittance to harvest the coffee that they were already in the business of doing before the capitalists came along. The coffee carts and their large wheels are painted with elaborate geometric designs, brightly colored florals, and curlicues that look like they were created by Thangka painters flown in from Nepal.[2]

The late afternoon light here is transcendent. In the U.S., between 3 p.m. and just before sundown, it can be harsh and depressing. Here it's soft and calming, filtered by clouds and foliage.

Saturday, January 15th

Today's destination was the Rescate animal rescue/zoo, specifically to see Central American animals I may not see otherwise. I'd read that the Rescate had a resplendent quetzal on-site. A quetzal looks like a cuddly plush toy bird, with a greenish-turquoise face and a shiny black button for an eye, a crown of fuzzy, wispy feathers, and two absurdly long tail feathers, possibly twice the length of its body.[3] The Rescate's quetzal sat on a perch for a long time and didn't seem to mind that a human was four feet away staring at him with a big glass eye. I managed to get a few decent photos, but shooting through a metal mesh fence has its limitations. You'd think Costa Rica would make this fantastic creature its national bird; that honor goes to one of the most boring species imaginable, the clay-colored thrush, a bird with such great camouflage that you rarely see them.

The traffic was bad on the Autopista, the main highway between San José and Sarchí, and as I rounded a curve near the Sarchí exit, flames from a raging grass fire leapt into my lane. I was heading right for it, and my options were either to drive through it or hope whoever was in the left lane would kindly let me in. He did, but not without flipping me off. The thing I worried about, in those few seconds I had to decide whether or not to stay the course was, would the car explode?

Traffic was at a standstill on the Thangka-style painted bridge, the main ingress/egress into Sarchí, because a huge flatbed truck carrying blocks of cement couldn't make the curve and got stuck. The other ways to get in and out are on roads so winding and narrow that sometimes even the smallest cars traveling in opposing directions can't be on the road at the same time and, if they are, one driver must back up. A long line of us snaked up one of these roads and the residents came outside to watch, standing on both sides of the road and occupying precious inches of tarmac that we motorists desperately needed.

When I returned to the bongolow, in a rare moment of internet connectivity, I Googled "can you drive a car through flames" and one site said, Yes, but be sure to have a fire extinguisher and a fireproof blanket in your vehicle. I'm pretty sure Avis doesn't offer those add-ons. The good news is that the probability of a car explosion is low. So, if this happens again, I'll drive right through the fire. It'll make a better story.

Sunday, January 16th

In the mornings, a flying insect that looks like a tiny bluish-green jewel appears and hovers in front of the sliding glass door. I like to think that it's admiring its reflection. It looks like a teeny alien spacecraft the way it can hover in one place and then take off in any direction in a fraction of a second. He's my other pet, Marvin.

I drove into Grecia, the next town over, to find Masqsabor, a restaurant recommended on Tripadvisor. Finding any place in Costa Rica is a challenge, even with GPS, because Ticos don't believe in signage. Street signs are rare, and highway signs even rarer. And in Costa Rica, satellite accuracy is sketchy. I knew I was close to the Masqsabor, but the GPS voice got stuck in a continuous loop, repeating over and over "turn on Calle Coyote, turn on Calle Coyote, turn on Calle Coyote, turn on Calle Coyote, turn on Calle Coyote, turn on Calle Coyote, turn on Calle

Coyote, turn on Calle Coyote." I thought I was going to lose my mind.

I passed a gated retirement community in Grecia that was shockingly awful. Like most real estate development projects, the ground is scraped down to the dirt to have a blank canvas to work with. Can't they leave some of the older trees, at least??? I saw a few really big ones, felled, with smaller ones collected around them, as if for a football team homecoming bonfire. What about Costa Rica's ban on deforestation? How could someone buy a home in one of those communities with a clear conscience?

Monday, January 17th

Cost Rica's Costco equivalent is called Maxi Palí, a great place for sugary drinks and snacks, underwear and socks, a twenty-eight-pound bucket of mac and cheese, a chicken coop, or a chandelier if you should need such things. I drove my Jehovah's Witness neighbor there so she could stock up on heavy items like laundry detergent, bulk sugar, and five-gallon bottles of water, things that are difficult to wrangle onto a bus. I wanted to ask why she became a Jehovah's Witness, but that question could catalyze a multihour discussion when all I wanted was the elevator speech.

Since I know nothing about Jehovah's Witnesses, I Googled their Wikipedia page. I discovered some intriguing ideas. They believe the world is run by Satan and that only 144,000 people, called Anointed Ones, both living and not, will make it to heaven. I was curious how the elders know who's in heaven already and wondered what the current count was. They believe in one God: Jehovah, of course, and everyone else is misguided or just plain evil if they practice a different belief system. They also limit contact with non-Witnesses, but this doesn't seem to be my neighbor's MO. I hope I'm not putting her in danger of being excommunicated.

144,000 is an interesting number. 12 x 12 = 144 and times a thousand, you get 144,000. This could suggest that twelve special people from twelve special places have been chosen once a year for a thousand years to be Anointed Ones. Definitely, I'll want to ask about that.

About the last days, something that's on *everyone's* minds, Wikipedia had this to add:

> A central teaching of Jehovah's Witnesses is that the current world era, or "system of things," entered the "last days" in 1914 and faces imminent destruction through intervention by God and Jesus Christ, leading to deliverance for those who worship God acceptably. They consider all other present-day religions to be false, identifying them with "Babylon the Great" or the "harlot," of Revelation 17, and believe that they will soon be destroyed by the United Nations, which they believe is represented in scripture by the scarlet-colored wild beast of Revelation chapter 17. This development will mark the beginning of the "great tribulation." Satan will subsequently use world governments to attack Jehovah's Witnesses, an action that will prompt God to begin the war of Armageddon, during which all forms of government and all people not counted as Christ's "sheep" will be destroyed. After Armageddon, God will extend his heavenly kingdom to include earth, which will be transformed into a paradise similar to the Garden of Eden. Most of those who had died before God's intervention will gradually be resurrected during the thousand year "judgment day" . . . At the end of the thousand years, Christ will hand all authority back to God. Then a final test will take place when Satan is released to mislead perfect mankind. Those who fail will be destroyed, along with Satan and his demons. The result will be a fully tested, glorified human race on earth.[4]

Jehovah's Witnesses believe that Jesus was installed in heaven, in October 1914, as the king of God's realm, and that Satan was exiled to earth, resulting in woe to humanity. I'll definitely want to ask about October 1914. Like, who received this transmission of information about Jesus taking over from God and when in October, exactly? Was it around Columbus Day, Oktoberfest, Diwali, Halloween, National Nachos Day, or Guardian Angels Day? Did Jesus and God collaborate on the month because of the plethora of important causes celebrated in October, e.g., Eczema Awareness, Bullying Prevention, and Selective Mutism Awareness? Since Jesus was a Jew, Yom Kippur would have been the obvious choice, but in 1914, it fell on September 29th, a Tuesday.

I heard a rustle of wings, and a blinding light washed out the image on my computer screen. Ursula the spider scuttled off into a dark corner. "They *did* chose Yom Kippur, not the month of October. The day Satan came back to earth and made my life hell, excuse the pun. And to add insult to injury, September 29th is my special day, the Festival of San Miguel Arcángel—Michaelmas, you know, like Christmas—where I'm venerated all over the Catholic world. Talk about stealing someone's thunder!"

"So the Jehovah's Witnesses' timelines are not to be trusted?"

"Not much. If they stopped to think about it, the Garden of Eden, where Satan was first ousted from heaven, was waaaay before October 1914. Since the beginning, Satan has always chosen to fraternize with mortals even though he still has limited access to heaven. It's more fun here. World War I was a special time for him."

"If Satan can come and go, and obviously you can, too, and we're entrenched in the last days, why do you even bother? We're already in the handbasket going to hell, so what's the point?"

"Angels and demons, we all have expectations about the end of the world, and we want to see how it plays out."

"Does Armageddon have an actual date?"

"The JWs like to think so, but they keep adjusting it forward when all's quiet on the western front."

"You're dodging the question. Will we get to participate?"

The conversation stalled. Michael was formulating an answer.

"Remember my warning back in Uncertain? About avoiding the 'D' word? That goes for the 'S' word, too. It would be a lot easier on me if you took that seriously." His brilliance dimmed a little.

"Okay, D-leted! But with you around, is the world really that vulnerable? You're always depicted as vanquishing the D-guy, standing on his neck and about to thrust your spear into his shoulder."

"Yes, but think about it. It's an ambiguous image. The D-guy—okay if we call him Kevin?—could squirm out from under me and pop back down to the safety of his realm. I'd have to pursue and catch him all over again, we'd end up in the same situation with me standing on a sprawled Kevin, my foot on his neck, spear raised. I wish once, just once, an artist would depict the moment *after* I'd impaled Kevin, his Day-Glo green blood spewing everywhere. Soooo satisfying!"

"But isn't the ambiguity the point?" I added. "If Kevin were vanquished, you, Michael, would be, too. You're two sides of the same coin."

"So I'm stuck in a *Groundhog Day* conundrum like the one you experienced in Guadalajara?"

"Looks that way."

Tuesday, January 18th

Today I drove from Sarchí to Cahuita, a tiny tourist town on the Caribbean, a drive I was dreading and a bit fearful of undertaking. Not knowing what to expect, I didn't drink any water so I wouldn't have to stop and pee, and I did the drive in 5.5 hours just as the GPS, which worked the entire way, predicted. I stayed at a walled, forested compound called the Magellan, which had an excellent pool. Two howler monkeys were on the grounds and an agouti was silently scavenging for food. Mix a tailless squirrel and a Chihuahua, one of those shaky ones with sinewy legs and a back arched in a defensive posture, then supersize it, and you have an agouti. The expression on its rodent-like face suggests shame, or worry about getting caught and scolded.

After dark, I made a recording of a creature with a bizarre voice, probably a frog. It sounded like the monotone voice of a man who's lost his larynx and, in order to vocalize, uses a device that looks like a small electric razor that he holds to his throat. It sounded like the frog was saying, "right, oh right, awright" and "Guillaume Dufay Dufay," and "round and round we go." I wondered what it would sound like to a speaker of Russian, or Choctaw.

Wednesday, January 19th

Today I toured the Jaguar Rescue Center, a no-jaguars-on-the-premises bait and switch. The most fun was seeing a big sloth up close; not a sloth that the center was rehabilitating but an interloper who was looking either for an audience or free snacks, hanging upside down from a low branch right at (my) eye level.[5] Interesting animal facts I learned: possums are immune to venomous snake bite. The loser in an iguana battle, which takes place high in a tree, must let himself free-fall out of the tree. Like the rings of a tree, crocodile bones have rings that reveal the creature's age. Caimans are repelled by salt, so they don't like the taste of humans and will not attack us. So this Brazilian guy I'd seen on TV named Leo Rocha, who mucked around for his adventure show in the Pantanal, the world's largest wetland, wasn't in any real danger from the hundreds of caimans floating around like pool toys.

The macaws at the center taught each other to say *hola* to people passing by. A human taught the first rescue macaw, and when other macaws showed up, the first macaw taught the new arrivals. Interesting, I thought, because what were these new macaws getting out of it? No treats, only positive reinforcement from passersby. Are macaws shameless people pleasers?

Thursday, January 20th

At 5 p.m., I took a dip in the Magellan pool, watched the late afternoon light fade and the birds return to their nests, listened to the chorus of evening bugs, and felt vaguely anxious about the possibility of a coconut falling on my head from the palm tree projecting over the pool. Michael sat at the tiki bar sipping a dragon fruit daiquiri.

"If you ask me, you need to be living in the Western Hemisphere tropics," he offered.

"Well, that narrows things down to somewhere between the Tropic of Cancer and the Tropic of Capricorn. About 3,200 miles top to bottom, and millions of square miles of land mass. You're not being that helpful."

Friday, January 21st

The Sloth Sanctuary is the other big attraction in the Cahuita area. When I arrived at 1 p.m. for a tour, a small group had assembled. A big, burly mansplainer and his timid wife seemed profoundly uncomfortable in the heat and humidity. Because of Covid's continued threat, we were required to be masked, but he wore his under his nose as many refuseniks do. Under normal circumstances, I would be silently criticizing such an individual, but I was delighted to see that he had a nose very much like the animals we were observing. Upturned; a wide base; large, oval, pinkish-beige nostrils; and with a kind of gooey, moist look as if he'd just dipped it in hand sanitizer. His feet, in flip-flops, were intensely pink, like they'd been simmering in hot water. Costa Rica offers ample opportunities to observe people's feet, since flip-flops are the footwear of choice here. At the rescue center, I saw a young woman's feet that made me envious: the big toe and the next two over being the same length, and a vestigial little toe. The Renaissance ideal. There were plenty of feet with skin the color of café au lait, and a slightly lighter color at the tips of the toes, pretty! Occasionally you'd see feet that looked like shoes had not been part of their wardrobe for a good portion of their lives, wide feet with splayed, swollen toes. Calloused.

Back to the Sloth Sanctuary. The place was *really sad*. Its two large rooms housed about a dozen sloths, all who'd suffered horrible, tragic events, one hard-luck story after another. One sloth had survived electrocution when mistaking power lines for tree limbs. Several had missing arms from dog attacks or from getting hit by cars. Another was blind, and another was a paraplegic. I spent a good ten minutes trying to locate one's head on its mangled body. For sure, sloths drew the evolutionary short straw; they have no means for defense, are vulnerable to predators like hawks and wild cats when they're up in the canopy, and when they're down on the ground, which is their toilet of preference, they're vulnerable to everything.

Their tiny cages reminded me of the zoos of the 1950s. No stimulation, no possibility for interaction with others of their species. For a low-maintenance creature that basically eats leaves, sleeps, and poops, the tour guide griped about how difficult it was to take care of them and about the massive amounts of food they eat every day. I imagined the sloths, who live in an entirely different and much slower and constricted space/time continuum, suddenly sprinting to their feed bowls and devouring prodigious quantities of greens, so fast that their keepers can't keep up. I wondered how sloths even perceive time and motion; do we humans look to them like hummingbirds look to us, zipping around, busying ourselves with this and that?

I asked the tour guide if sloths are endangered, and he said, no, they are not. So why all the fuss and expense to house these dozen sloths in assisted living? The only justification for the existence of such a place, that I could think of, was for making money by tapping into tourist empathy and calling it educational. True, I learned things I didn't know about sloths. But there's always Google. You can easily see sloths in the wild, even right in central Cahuita; it's not like they're elusive or difficult to spot. And it's not like they can run and hide when they see you coming. The Sloth Rescue Center was practicing animal abuse, it seemed to me.

I couldn't swim tonight because when I returned to the Magellan, the pool guy was dumping chemicals into the water. And the internet had gone dark, so no emailing or Googling intruiguing animal facts. Sigh.

Have I mentioned that I hate to be sticky? It's the big reason why I don't go into the ocean; it's like being covered in liquid cotton candy. Most surfaces near any beach are coated with this stickiness. When you go to an outdoor restaurant and sit down (facing into the wind to keep your hair from sticking to your forehead and cheeks), and lay your arms on the plastic chair armrests, you risk ripping your forearm skin off. The plastic laminated menu is barely readable for all the sand and salty residue that's adhered to it. When you cross and uncross your legs, the foot on the floor makes a sucking sound when you lift it. The napkin holder is sticky, creating a vicious cycle of napkin use to mediate the sticky. Dunking your fingers in your water glass then rubbing them vigorously with a napkin does no good; the napkin completely disintegrates and some of the sticky bits stay behind, becoming like a second skin. Grabbing another napkin necessitates touching the sticky napkin holder and, thus, more napkins are needed to try to remove the additional coating of sticky. And on and on until your sticky table is covered in used, wadded-up napkins that not even a Caribbean hurricane can dislodge.

Few sensations are as unpleasant as having a sticky face. It makes you want to touch it; then the sticky transfers onto your fingers, and wherever your fingers land next, like on a shin or a shoulder, a new sticky place is created that needs your attention.

Then it's back to the napkin holder and the sticky mediation cycle. Multiply these actions by the thousands of tourists that visit the Caribbean side of Costa Rica every day, month, and year, and this is why restaurateurs are stingy with their napkins and experience occasional napkin shortages. This is also why you don't see outdoor furniture with much decay or rot; the sticky repels water from the daily downpours and preserves the wood.

Another feature of Costa Rican Caribbean oceanside eateries is the packets of ketchup that no one can open, not even the buff surfers who love to exhibit their inguinal folds and depilated bodies. While you're putting all the force you can behind opening these intractable packets of tomatoey sweetness, you observe others having the same issue. You hope there's a waiter present who roams from table to table with a pair of kitchen scissors cutting the serrated tops off the ketchup packets, letting us diners get on with the business of eating our french fries.

Back at the Magellan, I scrubbed my sticky fingers with the excellent soap provided by the management. For the past two days, I've noticed a fine dark brown powder in the sink and on the floor in the bathroom, and I assumed it was me tracking in sand. But today I realized the Magellan has termites, and termite fines were falling from the ceiling. Gosh, I hope they didn't find their way into the bag of ground coffee I'd left open on the counter next to the TV—no way to tell the difference.

Saturday, January 22nd

I need to get on the road to Sarchí, but there's no internet and no Google Maps this morning. I'm trying not to panic. Before I left the States I downloaded an offline map of Costa Rica, but it doesn't show the detail that I need. Is Mercury retrograde? I think it is, but I'll check my handwritten list of all 2022 MRs for sure... Yes, January 13th to February 3rd. Maybe my mouse will start working again on the 3rd; it was *no funciona* as of last night.

Plan A: Get in the car and on the road, stop at the Sloth Sanctuary to see if I have a signal. Plan B: If I don't, prevail on the nice young men employed there to show me why my phone isn't working. Reinstall U.S. SIM card if necessary and see if it works. I'll just have to pay the $10-a-day scalp to Verizon until I figure it out. Plan C: Call Avis at the San José airport and get the nice man to give me directions to the Autopista. From there I can find my way back to Sarchí, no problem.

Crisis averted! Google Maps worked at the Sloth Sanctuary.

Not that much traffic heading west on a Saturday, which is what I anticipated. It would all be going the other way, to the beach. On the road from Limón to San José, you're supposed to slow down to 30 kph in construction zones, which appear every fifty meters or so, and if everyone did this it would add another eight hours to the five-and-a-half-hour trip. Often these construction zones post a large orange sign with black letters announcing the obvious presence of workers in the area, in case you're person-blind. *Trabajando en la carreterra*, working on the road. Kind of like our "Baby on Board!" stickers on the SUVs of anxious U.S. parents. What am I expected to do with that information? I drive cautiously whenever humans are present, newborn or otherwise. Occasionally these Trabajando en la carreterra signs would also be written in simplified Chinese characters. I found out later that Costa Rica's second most spoken language is Mandarin, 45,000 residents are considered Sino-Costa Rican, and the greatest number of tourists come from China. Maybe studying Mandarin back in Houston *did* have a purpose that escaped my understanding. Would I be using it when living in Costa Rica sometime far in the future?

Monday, January 24th

I took my Jehovah's Witness neighbor to lunch and asked about the 144,000 Anointed Ones. She explained that the Book of Revelation says that that specific number of people will appear on the judgment day with the name of Jehovah on their foreheads and were chosen because they were "without stain." I wanted to ask about the stain removal process—because no human is without stain—thinking it might help me deal with my sticky issues. She couldn't explain the meaning of the number itself (12 x 12 x 1,000), and all other difficult questions I posed she answered in an indirect way, often prefacing what she was about to say with "Logically. . .". No information in the sentences that followed the utterance of that word could be called logical. I mentioned pre-biblical sources that had similar creationist stories, like *Gilgamesh*, written c. 2100 BCE, and she politely blew me off. I felt kind of evil, challenging her belief system so aggressively.

If I understood correctly, JWs believe human beings appeared on Earth six thousand years ago. (Cue cuckoo clock sound effect.) I knew it was a lot longer ago than that, but I was fuzzy on exactly when. So I looked it up:

> The oldest known evidence for anatomically modern humans (as of 2021) are fossils found at Jebel Irhoud, Morocco, dated 300,000 years old, making them the oldest known remains categorized as "modern."

Maybe JWs are mathematically challenged. Multiply 6,000 by 50, and the numbers match.

Tuesday, January 25th

My second trip from base camp Sarchí was to the Arenal Volcano. I'd booked a place called the Los Lagos (I know, that's like saying "the the"), and when I pulled up to the guardhouse, at first I thought I'd made a mistake. It was a deluxe resort, and at only $132 per night, the cost of a midrange Amarillo, Texas, chain hotel. The receptionist placed a bright pink, indestructible plasticized band on my right wrist with *Los Lagos* written on it and my room number. Either I was entering Disneyworld Costa Rica or an upscale hospital. The point of the wristband was to let the staff know to which room you are assigned, so they know where to charge the meal or the Pura Vida ball cap you take from the souvenir store. In case you're mute or you only speak Russian or Choctaw.

Next, the receptionist handed me a map of the place, and I'm quite sure they hired the same company that makes theme park maps to make theirs. My lodgings were in the most remote building on the grounds, at the top of a complex of steep, winding, narrow roads made to resemble a labyrinth. It took me twenty minutes to find it, and three or four journeys up and down the hill to be able to drive directly to my room. And I am not directionally challenged.

Wednesday, January 26th

On the drive back to the resort from the volcano, I saw a billboard for an entertainment I didn't expect to see in Costa Rica—it seemed like an activity that would appeal to the Orlando crowd—called Zorbing.[7] The Zorb (z + orb) is a ball within a ball separated by a cushion of air, and the rider inserts him- or herself inside a tunnel that runs through the ball. Imagine pitching this idea to your investors: "A kid gets inside a transparent plastic ball, about ten feet in diameter, and rolls down a hill. He gets super dizzy, throws up, maybe gets banged up a little, and there's a slight possibility of suffocation and death. But the thrill is worth it. Whaddaya say?" The place advertised on the billboard was called Rollcano.

Late afternoon, I examined all eleven of the resort's swimming pools—all varying in temperature and all very beautiful, some with waterfalls and some secluded in hidden gardens. One offered a perfect view of the volcano, and I spent a lot of time in that one just staring at it.[8] Swimming pools offer such fun people watching. A large Japanese family fancied the same pool I did, which is where I learned that this family could out-shout anybody at the resort. They also laughed the heartiest at meals. It makes *you* laugh to hear them enjoying themselves so much.

Thursday, January 27th

I visited the Arenal Hanging Bridges today and got a great photo of one of Costa Rica's deadliest snakes, the eyelash pit viper. In the photo, it looks like it's staring right at me from its perch in a low limb of a tree. That's the thing about the jungle—you can't just scramble up a tree or lie in a pile of leaves and make angels, there's probably at least one deadly snake in that pile and two or three wrapped around those very branches you need to grab onto to climb the tree. Whenever I'm walking through a jungle, I have to remind myself, *Don't touch anything.* You never know what deadly toxin a plant or animal is going to deposit on or in you.

Friday, January 28th

It's 3:40 a.m. The Japanese family in the room to the left are revving up.

It's 5:00 a.m. The Russians in the room to the right have been at it for at least an hour. Talking nonstop, talking at the same time. Banging doors, shouting from the bathroom. In their world, no one else exists. One of the girls is out on the balcony talking loudly on her cell phone. I get it: the time difference. Plus, when I was her age, I probably didn't notice that there were other people in proximity to me, either. Geriatric adults were particularly invisible.

There's a bird that also wakes up around five whose voice sounds like the metal lid of a Mason jar when it drops to the floor and pivots on its edge. The lid rotates faster and faster as gravity flattens out the curve, and the sound speeds up. Although there are no ducks in the area, there are birds that quack and birds that sound like squeeze toys.

Today I drove to Monteverde, in Guanacaste, near the west side of the volcano, the side that's seen all the geologic action over the past twenty years.

The Bella Vista was not the deluxe place that the Los Lagos was. The establishment's name was painted in an awkward, bright blue cursive on a white background. On a boulder. $42 per night was kind of a giveaway, too. My lodging was a simple cabin, basically a box with a wooden pitched roof that reminded me of my childhood summer camp, and as I was putting my things away on the few shelves provided, I was inspired to sing the Camp Fire Girls song.

> Sing around the campfire,
> Join the campfire girls.
> Join the laughter, join the fun,
> It's a wonderful time for everyone.
> It's a busy day and when it's done,
> What fun to sing around the campfire,
> 'Neath the moon above,
> Sing Wo-He-Lo, work-health-love.

Guanacaste is the part of Costa Rica that's the most denuded of its trees, and you can see where all that beautiful hardwood went—into making furniture so heavy you need bodybuilder-strength muscles to pull a chair out from a table that itself is so heavy it makes the floor sag. Lying in bed and looking up at the ceiling, I saw enough wood to build several more ceilings, and it was thick and sagging, too, from its own weight. If this little cabin is ever demolished and the wood repurposed, it could make something four times its size.

Saturday, January 29th

The wind howled all last night. There must be a metal building close by because it sounded like someone was standing next to it throwing pebbles at its walls. It also sounded like someone dropped a bunch of aluminum pie pans in the front yard and was kicking them around for laughs. All night. The little cabin faced the winds head-on, which swept up a cliff a few yards away, and at times it seemed like an angry wind god had taken the cabin in his hands and was shaking it. A couple of times I wouldn't have been surprised if the place splintered into a million pieces. Crazy weather here.

Sunday, January 30th

Today I went to the Curi Cancha tropical cloud forest reserve in Monteverde. Huge strangler figs greet hikers at the entrance to the trails, towering sentinels reminiscent of the columns in basilicas around the world, tall and tapering. The microclimates of the cloud forest have you piling on layers one moment and taking them off down to your T-shirt the next. If you want to experience utter quiet, and an eerie feeling that the forest is full of spirits, goblins, and fairies, this is the place.

    A bird-watching couple I encountered on a trail pointed out two male long-tailed manakins doing their mating dance, trying to impress a disinterested female. Male manakins have a long, curved black tail, a black body with a deep lavender "jacket," red feet, and a little red patch on their crowns, like a yarmulke. The three manakins were balanced on a tree limb lying horizontally a foot above the forest floor, the female facing the two males. While the male closest to the female advanced toward her, the male in the back leapt over him, forcing him to the end of the line. He takes a few steps toward the female while the one in back leaps in front again. They never seem to get any closer to the female, though; it's as if they're approaching the end of a moving walkway at the airport and they're trying to stay in one place. The female has just stepped off, turned around, and is taunting them.

    Farther down the trail, a park guide pointed out a resplendent quetzal, another bird I would have missed seeing if it weren't for his experienced eye. Seeing one in the wild was fantastic, although I was glad I'd also seen one at close range in the Rescate zoo.

Monday, January 31st

I packed up and left the little cabin by 7:30 a.m., and my phone said 3 hours and 40 minutes to Manuel Antonio Park, the rainforest home of the largest and most diverse wildlife population in all of Costa Rica, according to what I'd read. Six hours and 15 minutes later, I was there. I was at a complete standstill for an hour and a half because of a car crash. When that happens in Costa Rica, *nobody moves* until the cops arrive and resolve the situation. This can take a very long time.

Costa Rica prides itself on having the largest automotive support network of all seven Central American countries, boasting a whopping 31 percent of the total repair shops, service stations, and car parts stores. It makes sense, given the condition of the roads, the number of vehicles, and the frequency of accidents. In every little town, places that specialize in mufflers, like the Midases of the U.S., are called mufla shops, as if taught the word by speakers of a south-side Boston dialect.

Manuel Antonio is the place everyone visits on the Pacific coast for a beautiful beach experience;[9] and because of that, its "best kept secret" days are long gone. After arriving in Quepos, the village where I'd made a reservation for the night, I drove straight to the park and arrived there a little before two. Quepos is the most touristy place I've seen so far in Costa Rica, with beachwear and batik bedspread emporiums lining the main road for miles. People near the entrance to the park urge you to buy a coconut with a red straw poking out of it, sometimes pounding on the window of your car and shouting when you don't comply. This shameless commerce put me in an instant bad mood that I carried with me into the forest. Even though Manuel Antonio was touted as one of the best places for viewing wildlife, it distinctly felt like it had been looked at to excess, and all that looking had sapped the life out of it. After twenty minutes, I was done. It was hot, claustrophobic, buggy. I had to get out of there.

The hotel was charming in a midcentury luxury resort way. A plaque in a hallway claimed that at the site of the hotel, Ponce de León landed in 1519 and was chased off by the Amazonian women archers the town of Quepos was named for. On the way to my room, the bellboy and I passed the main feature of the reception area: a fish tank holding a creature much too large for the size of the tank, a three-foot-long piranha named Charlie.

With that name, I would have guessed he was a tuna. I asked the bellboy if they throw him big chunks of beef and when was feeding time? Disappointingly, his diet consisted of fish food from the pet store. But meeting Charlie made me smile.

The rooms were named for the marine creatures and flora of the area: the Flying Fish Room, the Heliconia Room, the Passionflower Room. I wondered if these other rooms were as quirky as mine. All the furniture was painted white; an ornate too-big-for-the-room chandelier combined with a baroque bed looked like they belonged in a guest room at Versailles. Everything in the room was kinda off; there was a short in the dimmer switch for the chandelier, the curtains wouldn't close all the way, a knob came off in my hand when I tried opening a dresser drawer. The latch on the sliding glass doors didn't lock, although I wasn't too worried about someone sneaking into the room in the middle of the night. The bathroom sink water ran intermittently, and the toilet ran all the time. The fact that my accommodation was named the Crappie Room should have been a clue.

I ordered dinner in, thinking I might eat on the balcony and enjoy the fantastic view of the Pacific. The same bellboy arrived at the door with the tray, the price tag still on the woven dome basket (made in Vietnam) that protected my room service dinner from flies and kept it warm. He noticed it first and was embarrassed, and we both laughed nervously about the pretension of it all, or at least that's what I thought we were laughing about. He handed me the faux-leather folio that held the ticket I needed to sign for the dinner, took a step back, folded his arms behind himself, and looked away politely as if I were going to disrobe. I guess bellboys are instructed to do this so the hotel guest doesn't feel under duress when adding the tip. All that posturing was totally unnecessary; I tip people directly so that it's not appropriated by his or her boss or by the accountant. When he accepted the actual paper money, he said *Pura vida*, which is what Ticos say instead of *de nada*. Pura vida means "pure life," and it's an expression of the Costa Rican lifestyle, a relaxed attitude toward life, a reassurance that everything's okay. I think that's beautiful.

Thursday, February 3rd

The Pre-Columbian Gold Museum, right in the middle of downtown San José, is next to a once-elegant but now crumbling and graffitied baroque theater. The museum is beneath a sad plaza, square white tiles covered in food stains, dog poo, trash, and sticky, dirty footprints. I was expecting a multistorey building, and when I asked a policeman where it was, he pointed straight down. The museum was a dazzling surprise, a stark contrast to above-ground San José. A giant bank vault was filled with a fantastic, extensive collection of, as the museum's name suggests, Pre-Columbian gold artifacts: animals (frogs, jaguars, harpy eagles, alligators), jewelry, a life-size gold warrior decked out in even more gold, the artistry a highly sophisticated style I'd never seen anywhere else. The Numismatic Museum is located in the same building and displays Costa Rica's modern paper currency, the colón. Having a wallet-full of colones is like carrying around a stash of beautiful works of graphic design that express political messages you agree with. The people featured on the bills are actual heroes, not slave-owning (and impregnating) ex-presidents, reckless drunks, or creators of forced migration policies aimed at Native Americans. One bill features an important educator, another a woman writer, and the guy who abolished the army in 1949. Costa Rican animals appear on the flip side: a deer on the 1k, a shark on the 2k, a capuchin monkey on the 5k, a sloth on the 10k, a hummingbird on the 20k, and a blue morpho butterfly on the 50k. The 1k and 10k, the 2k and the 20k, and the 5k and 50k bills were designed with complementary color schemes so visually impaired people could recognize them more easily. For example, the 5k-colones bill is yellow and the 50k is purple, hues that are opposites in color theory. It helps the culturally impaired tourist, too.

The neighborhoods surrounding the museums are devoted to the selling of cheap plastics, mostly from China, inexpensive clothing from the sweatshops of the world, and crummy household goods and furniture. Commerce is conducted in stores the size of a walk-in closet and chock-full, from floor to ceiling, with whatever. Some streets are dedicated to selling certain types of goods, as if you were in a Target walking down the kitchen or the Barbie aisle. Sometimes strange juxtapositions of products and services coexist, like the nicely dressed man selling watches out of a kiosk in the garage where I parked. The smell of overripe fruit mixed with car exhaust hung in the air, everywhere.

Except for the baroque theater, the architecture was merely utilitarian. Nothing had a fresh coat of paint; everything was crumbling, moldy, grimy. Dirty windows, water stains cascading down walls; weeds, vines, and trash reclaiming abandoned properties. The sidewalks were packed with frowning pedestrians, and cars sped down streets designed for coffee carts.

Costa Rica's biggest surprise has been the amount of traffic everywhere. Without a car, life here would be challenging, unless you lived next door to the Maxi Palí, a laundry, and a couple of good restaurants. It's also been Costa Rica's biggest disappointment. But emissions here are a tenth of those in the U.S. and by the end of 2021, fewer than two million cars were registered in Costa Rica, compared to 287 million in the U.S.

Plus, access to the best bits of Costa Rica can be expensive, likely excluding many Ticos from enjoying the natural wonders of their own country. I'd read that its enlightened population had made great efforts to preserve its flora and fauna, and restore areas previously exploited, but when you drive through the denuded areas of Guanacaste it's hard to believe. Yet, 60 percent of Costa Rican forests that were decimated during the 1970s and '80s have been restored. In 1996, the Costa Rican government made it illegal to destroy trees without official approval, and farmers were incentivized to rehabilitate their land. The driving force for compliance? Money. The government levied heavy taxes on fossil fuels and distributed over $500 million to landowners over twenty years. In their restoration efforts, Costa Rica is light-years ahead of its other Western Hemisphere neighbors. But it's just not my place.

CHAPTER FOURTEEN

ARENAL

Being within four kilometers of an active volcano was a powerful experience.[1] Colleen couldn't look away from its perfect cone and the mesmerizing plume of smoke or steam or toxic gases, whatever it was escaping from its apex. She just wanted to stare at it, and sometimes it held her gaze for minutes at a time.

The high-end resort where she was staying had eleven pools fed by hot springs, and one of them offered a perfect view of Arenal. In the middle of the pool, a concrete tree with a canopy resembling a large gray pancake, as if the batter had been mixed with volcanic ash, provided shade while she sat on the tile bench underneath the tree. Her limbs floated aimlessly in the water. She thought about the scene in the film *Melancholia* where Kirsten Dunst lies on the grassy bank of a river, nude and receptive, gazing lovingly at a giant planet on a collision course with Earth. In that moment, Colleen understood. The feeling was horrifying but also beautiful and aesthetic and exhilarating and erotic. Knowing that this massive thing looming in the distance could take out everything around it in a matter of minutes, including everyone at the resort, engaged Colleen's reptilian brain. The faint red glow at its peak hinted at the mysterious and terrifying interior of the Earth, but its power felt unrelatable, alien. She nicknamed the volcano Shiva.

In the pool that day, she tried out different poses she might use if she knew she'd be buried in a pyroclastic surge and only had a few seconds left before annihilation. She was thinking of the plaster casts made of victims who were "flash frozen" after Mount Vesuvius erupted at Pompeii. Couples held each other in desperate embraces, others looked like they were still asleep and oblivious, a woman bounced her toddler on her knees, people were killed midscream. Her first thought was she'd want to make the "okay" symbol with one of her hands and make sure she was smiling, just to let people of the future know, were her form to be discovered, that it wasn't all that bad being instantly incinerated in a blanket of superheated ash. It's much much better than the slow decline of old age. Her next thought was, it could be fun to make the gun-pointing-at-her-head gesture with her hand or have a steel cable in the shape of a noose at the ready to slip around her neck and hold as if she had succeeded in doing herself in before the surge arrived. But even if you wanted to, you probably couldn't, because a pyroclastic surge can travel up to three hundred miles per hour.

If she lived near an active volcano, she would go to bed every night with common objects arranged around her that would accompany her into the afterlife and into the terrestrial future; a time capsule for archeologists to discover what life was like back in the early third millennium. It might be fun to play a practical joke on them and have an additional fake head attached to each shoulder, so they'd think there were three-headed humans back in the day. Or have extra arms and legs, like those Hindu gods with multiple limbs. Her hair could be rolled in aluminum curlers, which will make their own spaces to fill with plaster when the time comes, and she could be mistaken for a genetic outlier or an alien life form. For sure, if she wore some outrageous bedroom slippers like Sasquatch feet or velociraptor claws. Or she could wear S&M gear and a chastity belt and, as a nod to the ancient Egyptians, a couple of snake arm cuffs. She'd want to be as culturally confusing as possible. Or simply strike a ballet pose.

Or sit on a toilet and mimic *The Thinker*. Or lie in a crucifixion pose, head bowed, arms outstretched, one foot tucked under the other. There were so many possibilities, Colleen realized it would be hard to choose.

There's an entertainment near Arenal called Zorbing, where you get inside a transparent plastic ball, about ten feet in diameter, and roll down a hill. The Zorb (z + orb) is a ball within a ball separated by a cushion of air, and the rider can either be strapped in, or not, inside a tunnel that runs through the ball. Colleen thought it would be cool to Zorb down a pyroclastic surge, and even cooler to be found entombed in a Zorb a thousand years from now, her remains frozen in a gesture of unambiguous joy.

IMAGES

Image details in the NOTES section at the back of the book.

<u>Chapter 2: São Paulo</u>

1. The Witch House.

2. Beco do Batman (Batman Alley).

3. Pixação. Author: LiaC.

4. The orquidarium in the Parque Villa-Lobos.

5. Museo de Arte de São Paulo. Author: Lucas Oriolo Rodrigues.

6. Osgemeos inflatable and calçada outside the Pinacoteca de São Paulo.

150 · EVA ROME

7. A mesa radiônica and a 1956 TV test pattern/camera registration chart (unattributed graphics).

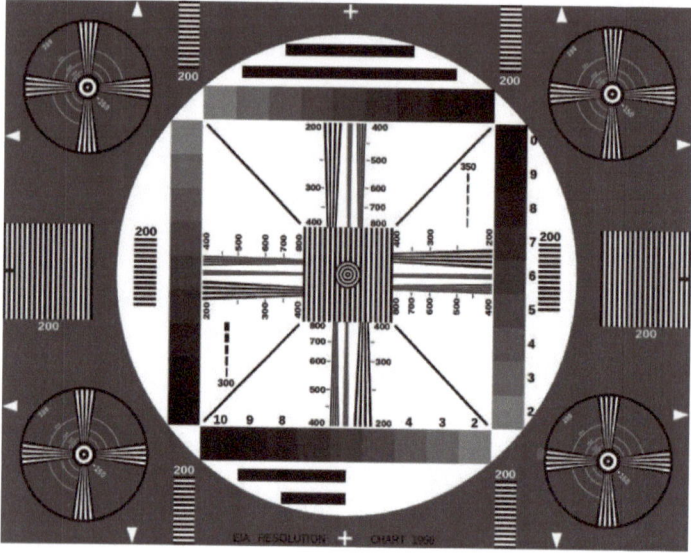

8. Reni, Guido. *Archangel Michael defeats Satan.*

9. Oscar Niemeyer Cathedral and Bell Tower, Brasília.

10. President Jucelino Kubitschek posing with Marlon Brando dressed as Mr. Christian from *Mutiny on the Bounty*.

11. Pirenópolis's friendly Minotaur.

12. Removing scuff marks with a tennis ball on a pole, Shopping Cidade São Paulo.

Chapter 4: México City

1. Immobilized in traffic, on the hop-on-hop-off bus, in a México City tunnel.

2. Palacio de Bellas Artes. Author: Timothy Neesam.

LOCATION X · 155

3. Rivera, Diego. *Man at the Crossroads* or *Man, Controller of the Universe*.

6. Our Lady of Guadalupe. Author: Mike Peel.

The moving walkway, Museo de la Basilica de Guadalupe.

Chapter 7: El Paso, Texas

1. *La Equis* (The X).

2. Starbucks memorial to the U.S. troops killed in Kabul, Afghanistan.

158 · EVA ROME

Chapter 9: Guadalajara

1. The "Riad," Calle San Felipe 39, Guadalajara.

2. Orozco, José Clemente. *El pueblo y sus falsos líderes* (The townspeople and their false idols).

Orozco, José Clemente. *El hombre creador y rebelde* (The creative and rebellious man).

3. Conservation team working on a Jesus figure, the Basilica of Our Lady of Zapopan.

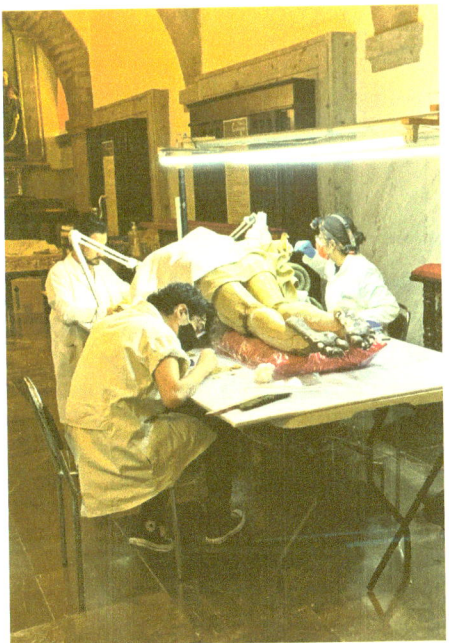

4. Houses designed by Luis Barragán.

LOCATION X · 161

5. Venus glyphs, Chichén Itzá, Yucatán.

7. Querétaro aqueduct Los Arcos. Author unknown.

Chapter 13: Costa Rica

1. The Bongolow, Sarchí.

2. Coffee cart wheel, Sarchí.

3. Resplendent quetzal, Rescate Wildlife Rescue Center.

5. Sloth, Jaguar Rescue Center near Puerto Viejo de Talamanca.

7. Zorbing, near Arenal.

8. Swimming pool at the Los Lagos Hotel, Spa, & Resort.

9. Manuel Antonio beach, Quepos.

Chapter 14: Arenal

1. The Arenal volcano.

Chapter 15: Panamá

1. A mola, handmade textile designed and fabricated by the Guna women of Panamá.

2. Wagua, Orgun. *Guna women drinking chicha and dancing, Ustupa, Guna Yala Region.*

3. The F&F Tower, Panamá City.

4. One of the 350 islands of the San Blas archipelago.

5. Molas and the Guna flag, San Blas Islands.

6. Guna mother and son, Albrook Mall, Panamá City.

7. Young Embera man showing painted tattoos and wearing traditional dress re-created in plastic beads, Embera Village, Gamboa.

Chapter 17: Granada

1. Plastic film toilet seat cover, O'Hare Airport, Chicago. Author: Nskrill.

3. Catedral de Granada, interior painted white, and its two organs.

4. The Alhambra and the Generalife.

5. Street sign, Granada.

6. Muqarnas or "stalactite" vaults, the Alhambra.

Chapter 18: Madrid

1. Angelico, Fra. *The Annunciation*. Close-up of wings.

2. Tintoretto, Domenico. *Portrait of a woman revealing her breasts.*

3. Quellinus, Erasmus. *The Rape of Europa.*

LOCATION X · 175

4. Tintoretto, Jacopo. *Susana y los viejos*.

5. Vecellio, Tiziano (Titian). *Venus and Organist and Little Dog*.

6. Machuca, Pedro. *La Virgen y las ánimas del Purgatorio*, detail.

7. Goya y Lucientes, Francisco de. *La maja desnuda*.

8. Rubens, Peter Paul. *Diana and Callisto*.

Detail of Diana's right foot, or is it a left foot?

9. Rubens, Peter Paul, and workshop. *Achilles discovered by Ulysses among the daughters of Lycomedes,* detail of steaming object and dog.

10. Giordano, Luca. *Capture of a Stronghold*, detail.

11. Rubens, Peter Paul. *The Judgment of Paris*, detail.

12. Goya y Lucientes, Francisco de. *Las floreras o La Primavera.*

13. Goya y Lucientes, Francisco de. *Saturno devorando a su hijo*.

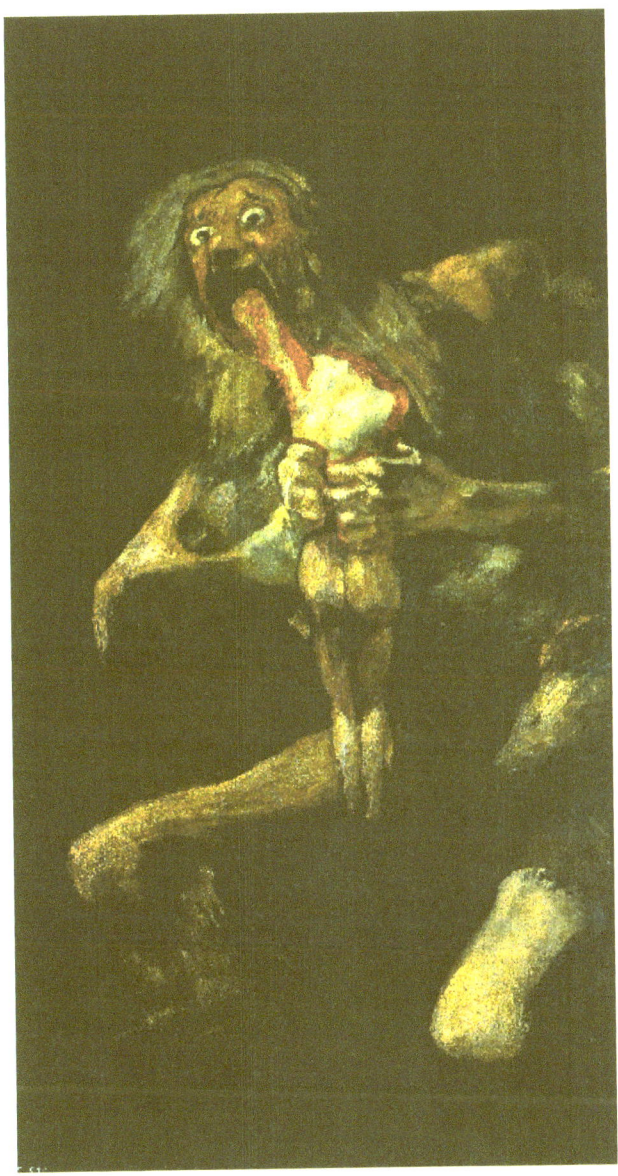

14. Sanzio, Raffaello. *Le Grand Saint Michel.*

15. Young adult mandible and reconstructed model of *Homo georgicus*.

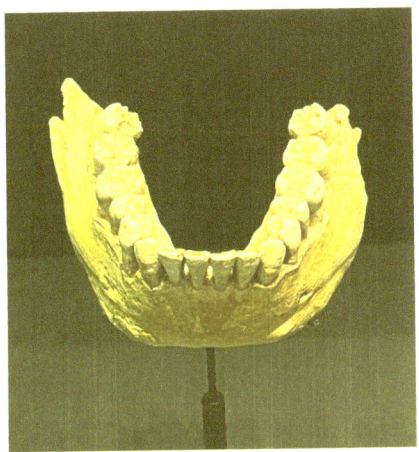

184 · EVA ROME

Chapter 19: Rome

1. Urbino, Raffaello Sanzio da (Raphael). *The School of Athens*, detail.

2. Buonarroti, Michelangelo. *The Last Judgment*, detail.

3. Buonarroti, Michelangelo. *The Creation of Adam.*

4. Realized by Giuseppe Sacconi. Monument to Victor Emmanuel II.

5. Works in the Capitoline Museums.

Equestrian Statue of Marcus Aurelius. Artist unknown. With *Capitoline Wolf*. Artist unknown.

The colossal foot of Constantine. Artist unknown.

Bernini, Gian Lorenzo. *Bust of Medusa.*

The Dying Gaul, copy of a lost sculpture from the Hellenistic period.

Caravaggio, Michelangelo Meresi da. *The Fortune Teller*.

6. Fanelli, Giovanni. *Roma: Portrait of a City*. Eva's doppelgänger, right.

7. Commissioned by Marcus Agrippa. The Pantheon.

8. Plaster casts of figures found at Pompeii.

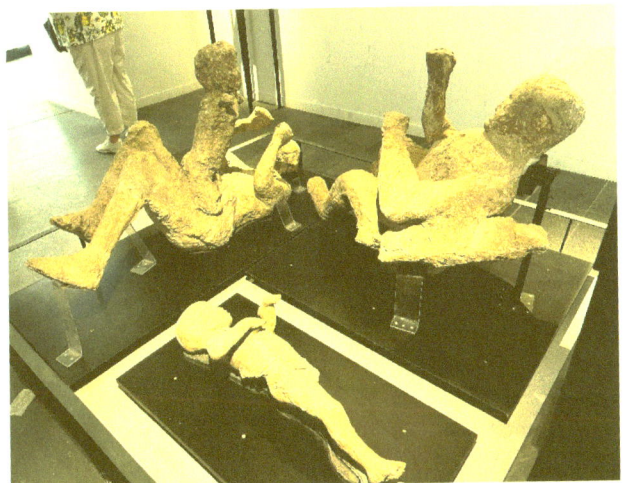

9. Grounds of the Museo Nazionale Romano.

10. Works in the Borghese Gallery and Museum.

Bernini, Gian Lorenzo. *David* and detail, Charlton Heston's face?

Bernini, Gian Lorenzo. *Abduction of Proserpina* (left); *Apollo and Daphne* (right).

From the circle of Leonardo da Vinci, probably Cesare da Sesto. *Leda and the Swan*.

11. Water features and water organ, Villa D'Este, Tivoli.

12. SPQR monogramming, Rome.

Chapter 21: Walking the Camino Trail: the Via Francigena

1. View from the Hotel Miravalle, San Miniato, Italy.

2. Logo representing the Via Francigena.

4. Map of the Via Francigena through Tuscany.

5. San Gimignano.

6. Jesus with skinned knees.

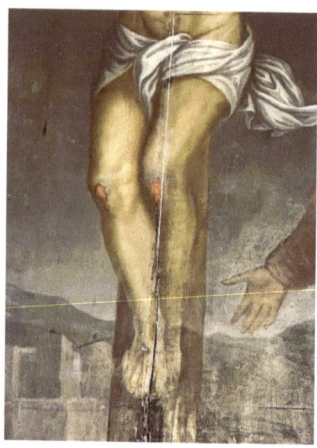

8. Interior of the Siena Cathedral.

9. Caravaggio, Michelangelo Merisi da. *Judith Beheading Holofernes*.

Biondo, Giovanni del. *Triptych of Saint Sebastian*, detail.

Botticelli, Sandro. *Salome with the Head of St. John the Baptist*, detail.

Chapter 22: Florence

1. Botticelli, Sandro. *The Birth of Venus*.

2. Caravaggio, Michelangelo Merisi da. *Medusa*.

3. Francesca, Piero della. *Diptych of Federico da Montefeltro and Battista Sforza*.

4. Caravaggio, Michelangelo Merisi da. *Bacchus*.

5. Cimabue (Cenni di Pepi). *Crucifix*.

Chapter 23: Porto

1. Pasteis de nata.

2. The Sé do Porto.

3. Azulejos, the Sé do Porto.

4. Unknown Italian artist. Archangel Michael and detail showing spear aimed for his foot. Sé do Porto chapter house.

5. A station of the cross and angel, Guimarães.

6. The Capela das Almas (Chapel of Souls) with azulejos, Porto.

7. Majestic Café, Porto.

Chapter 24: Lisbon

1. The prison cell Airbnb accommodation.

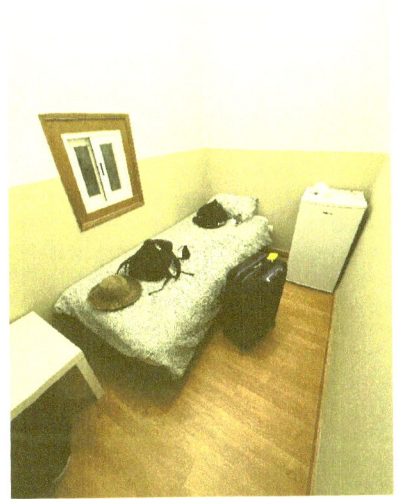

2. Sardine hats and green vegetal wigs.

4. Rossio Square and train station.

5. Photos from the Saint Anthony parade: pincushion float, cell phone marchers, Saint and Baby Jesus in a boat.

6. Quake: Lisbon Earthquake Center.

Chapter 26: Washington. D.C.

1. Faulkner, Barry. *The Charters of Freedom: Declaration of Independence*, and detail showing the Lincoln cloud.

2. Faulkner, Barry. *The Charters of Freedom: Constitution*, and detail showing Washington.

3. Kusama, Yayoi. *Infinity Mirrored Room—One With Eternity.*

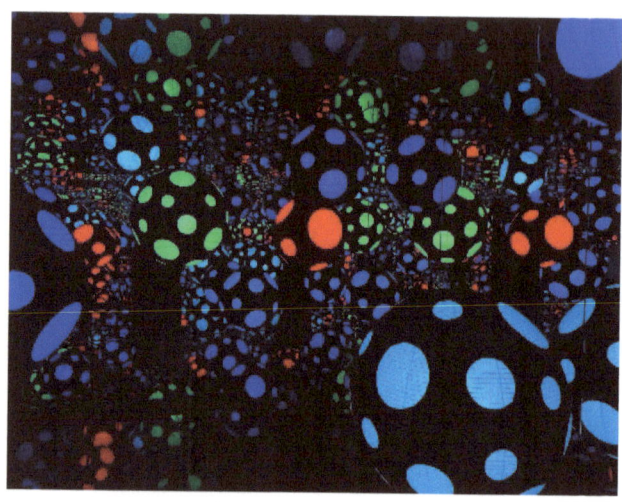

5. Works cited from the National Gallery. Vermeer, Johannes. *Girl With the Red Hat.*

Stuart, Gilbert. *The Skater (Portrait of William Grant)*.

Copley, John Singleton. *Watson and the Shark*.

Vinci, Leonardo da. *Ginevra Benci*.

Chapter 28: San Miguel de Allende

1. The Jardín, Centro.

CHAPTER FIFTEEN

PANAMÁ

Tuesday, February 7th

An uneventful flight to Panamá City was followed by a surprise at the Airbnb. I thought I'd reserved an entire apartment for a two-week stay, but it was only a room. Nice apartment, owned by a handsome young man from Mérida, México, and his off-site husband working in Switzerland. The place has a great view of some of Panamá City's quirky modern glass high-rises: one that's a corkscrew shape, another whose top looks like a flower in the process of unfolding (or an uncircumcised penis, depending on your point of view), and another that looks like a paper straw that's been pinched between someone's thumb and forefinger, in alternating shapes, all the way down the straw.

Panamá City is about as hot and humid as it gets. Even in February, its average temperature is 90 degrees with a relative humidity of 73 percent. How do people who live here deal with being sticky? If you're a gecko or an anteater, I see the advantage. But humans have to scramble from air-conditioned building to air-conditioned car to air-conditioned building merely to stay alive. I just lifted my hands up from the computer keyboard, in my air-conditioned room, and noticed two gooey palm prints were left behind.

Wednesday, February 8th

I Ubered to Casco Viejo, Panamá City's historic neighborhood, and walked around. The area was weirdly vacant and so pristine it looked like a movie set. After visiting the excellent Panamá Canal Museum, I went to the Casa Casco restaurant, highly rated on several travel websites, and I was the only customer. Odd selections of music with bizarre arrangements played on the sound system: soothing, low-energy choral versions of "Another One Bites the Dust" and "Bohemian Rhapsody"; "Sunday Bloody Sunday" sung by a woman who sounded like she was stuck in a hypnagogic state and couldn't transition out of it. The food was delicious, expensive, and a small portion, and the waiters were overly attentive, probably out of boredom, so I was feeling the spotlight effect.

Casco Viejo's Mola Museum was full of exceptional examples of the colorful, handmade, multilayered textiles made by indigenous Guna women.[1] Using a reverse appliqué technique, Molas are created from several layers of complementary colors of cloth, the designs created by cutting away parts of each layer, the process intricate and time consuming. About halfway into the museum, visitors are invited to stand in the middle of an eight-foot-by-eight-foot cube with interior mirrored faces. An animation projected into the cube multiplies the image; the intent is to suggest the trance state and visions that the Guna women experience and manifest in their mola designs. Black-and-white photos of multiple generations of women drinking chicha, laughing and dancing,[2] show that Guna women can rave with the best of us. Chicha is a kind of beer made from maize, and I suspect it may contain some ingredients that enhance the effects of the beer.

Thursday, February 10th

I woke up early, and when I walked past the entryway to the apartment on my way to the kitchen, I saw two pairs of additional shoes that were not my host's, one a leopard print and the other, tennis shoes decorated with Day-Glo colors. Is he cheating on his husband with two other guys? I know they're not his shoes because they're bigger than his dainty feet and differently shaped. What if the threesome doesn't like the idea of someone old enough to be their mother (or grandmother) occupying the room that shares a wall with theirs? To give them their privacy, and to avoid the possibility of having to make uncomfortable small talk, I skipped showering and left.

I spent the next four hours at the Panamá Canal; the first two and a half just waiting for a ship to show up. Maneuvering ships through the canal is an incredibly slow process—lowering the water level in one lock and raising it in the next, opening the lock, then pulling the ship through—but even so, it's thrilling to see how it all works. Midday was as hot and sticky and claustrophobic as a Bikram yoga class and because of the distraction back at the apartment, I'd forgotten to bring water. Thanks to Covid, the canal's concessions were closed.

Friday, February 11th

I took two separate walks today, each a mile and a half, which is all I can do at one time here. One of the walks was to the F&F Tower—the corkscrew glass building[3]—down a busy, noisy, dirty street obviously not designed for pedestrians. Lots of businesses with the *Pana* prefix line the street: Panafoto, Panacredit, Panafiesta, Pana Jam, Pana Kong, Pana Montana.

Monday, February 14th

When faced with the decision to go outside or to stay in, my preference is to sit in the air conditioning and watch the vultures circle at eye level here on the eighteenth floor. And observe the light change on the glass buildings, creating fantastic color effects. At certain times during the day, my host opens two of the windows; a big one in the living room and another big one in the kitchen, for cross-ventilation, I guess. I wonder why the vultures don't just fly in and make themselves comfortable on the dining room table? Build a nest in the limbs of the decorative tree in the living room? Help themselves to the chicken carcass in the trash?

The modern glass architecture, swaying palm trees, and Panamá Bay are the deceptively perfect ingredients that create this photogenic city; if only you could convey the hotness, the noise, the dirt, and the sticky, you'd have a clearer picture of the place.

Wednesday, February 16th

A 5 a.m. pickup to tour the San Blas Islands, an archipelago of over 350 tiny desert islands off Panamá's northeast coast, had me standing in the dark outside the building by 4:45. I'd already been awake for hours, anxious that I'd oversleep, something I've never done in my entire life. The driver was a native Guna—the makers of molas, those layered decorative cloth images—and the Guna occupy the islands. I sat in the passenger seat, an opportunity to besiege him with questions, and either he didn't know the answers or wasn't allowed to share the info with outsiders. Most of my questions, though, were ones that Google could likely provide answers for:

> When the Spaniards arrived in 1519, were the Guna able to defend themselves?
> Were they making molas back then, and if so, how did they get the fabric?
> What did the Guna eat, and did they grow any crops on the mainland?
> How did they get fresh water?
> How did they make their boats and fishing gear?
> Did they ingest hallucinogens?

That last one got a response, and he was adamant that they didn't. When it came to the social hierarchy, customs, and practices, though, he was willing to share, a little. I learned that the Guna are matriarchal, and the women make all the important, life-sustaining decisions for the group. The men are valued as laborers and sperm providers. When a woman decides to marry a man, he must make a small wooden canoe to give to the woman's family. The group makes a big deal out of a girl's first menstrual period, partying for two weeks, and as part of the ceremony, her father paints her entire body black. Not sure the significance of that, but I'm guessing it symbolizes dying to the original family (and to girlhood) and being reborn a woman and available for marriage. I also wanted to ask about clans, and did they exist? But the driver was so frustratingly reticent that after a while, I kept my mouth shut.

Our first stop was a gas station/convenience store about an hour and a half east of Panamá City. It was the last outpost for provisions before reaching the docks where we caught the boat to the islands. We were among the first tourists to arrive, but within a few minutes the parking lot filled with oversized diesel SUVs whose engines were left running, filling the parking lot with fumes and noise. Well-nourished gringos wielding giant ice chests were panic-buying as if they needed to provision for a month; I bought a bag of peanuts and a bottle of water and wondered if they knew something I didn't. Only one young woman worked the cash register, so the line was out the door.

Twenty minutes passed and our driver was MIA. A couple from Germany and I were trying to figure out which vehicle we'd arrived in and who our driver was. Since he'd picked us up in the dark and was masked, none of us had gotten a good look at him. Fortunately, he recognized us.

For the next hour, we traveled the road leading to the docks at Porvenir (meaning "the future" in Spanish), meandering through fantastically dense jungle and dodging huge potholes. We passed a Guna dwelling here and there, usually a pole building with either a corrugated tin roof or a roof made of thick thatch, with hammocks hung underneath. About halfway along this road, and a few meters before reaching the Panamá/Guna border, the driver handed me a Guna flag—a red stripe at the top and bottom and a wider yellow stripe in the middle with a black, counterclockwise-rotating swastika (like the original Hindu version)—identifying us as Guna-sympathetic. He asked me to drape the flag outside the window, then he rolled the window up to hold it in place. When we arrived at the border, the driver handed over our passports and twenty-five dollars he'd collected from each of us to a bunch of scary-looking guys in fatigues, some shouldering AK-47s. He seemed to know everybody, greeting the group with a special hand gesture; even so, there was some kind of issue. He heaved a big sigh, pulled over, jammed the SUV into park, and got out to talk to them. I wondered if I'd ever see my passport again. He was gone for only a few minutes, got back in the van with our passports in hand, said nothing, and we were on our way.

 The wooden docks were improvised and rickety, and trash lined the boundary where land met water. That's where we saw the first large group of indigenous Guna. Both the men and the women were tiny, measuring an average of four feet, ten or eleven inches. Their flawless, smooth skin was the color of coffee with a splash of milk, and their teeth perfectly even and white. Any of them could have been a model for Crest 3D Whitestrips or Invisalign. Some had round faces that westerners associate with the Inuit and others had strikingly prominent cheekbones and long, narrow noses. The women paint a thin, black line down the center of their noses that enhances the length and directs your eye to their traditional dress: blouses with mola inserts; a colorful patterned skirt and scarf; their legs decorated with cloth bands, called *chaquiras*, worn from the knees to the ankles, repeating the geometric designs and colors seen in their molas. Their palette is sophisticated and earthy, complementing and contrasting with the deep blues and turquoises that surround their islands.

 Gringos from all over the world, some with lots of luggage, many with their ice chests and bags of snacks, and most wearing fancy beachwear that provided little sun protection, strutted up and down the docks as if auditioning for *Project Runway*. The wind was strong and seeing the white-capped waves made me queasy and anxious. The Guna's fleet of small fiberglass boats didn't look like they could withstand the violent seas we were about to launch ourselves onto (foolishly?). Each boat had two motors and a canopy, and six rows of bench seats that held three people each. The life jackets provided, had we needed to use them, would have taken us straight to the bottom of the sea.

Yet the Guna have created a thriving business for themselves. They take visitors to three of their islands, all very small and not inhabited by natives, with lots of palm trees and clean, white beaches,[4] where you spend an hour each, swimming or sitting in the sand or, in my case, imagining that we were stranded and looking for a bottle in which to send a message back to the mainland. One of the islands is named Niadup, which is Guna for Diablo Island, and the boat ride from the docks to Niadup was five bumpy, back-crushing miles. Some people panic in airplanes, I panic on boats. But when the Caribbean looks like liquid silver, like it did that day, I understand the appeal of being on an oceangoing vessel for days at a time, feeling the transcendence the seas can inspire.

On each of the three islands, a large, central hut shelters the women who make and sell their crafts—molas and the cloth bands that the women wear around their lower legs[5]—and who provide basics like beach towels and tropical fruit, if you've booked one of the pricier tours. Each island has a primitive bathroom facility. Before reaching the second island, the boat stops at a place the Guna call the ocean's swimming pool, a crystal-clear shallow only a meter deep and around twenty meters in diameter. On all sides, a deep blue hue signaled ominous precipices. The strong currents and choppy waves made it impossible to swim in the pool, so those of us who braved jumping in just kind of stood in place and bobbed up and down. We were told to look for plump, orange starfish that inhabit the pool, but I was glad they were elsewhere today. Certain tourists among us would *need* to take a selfie with a starfish without question. A French photographer and his model girlfriend who'd been posing for pictures the whole trip, her face and scantily clad body getting progressively redder, became animated by the idea. But starfish absorb oxygen from the water through the tiny nodules on their skin, and transferring oil and sunscreen from our fingers to their bodies plugs them up and causes a slow, painful death from suffocation. A moment of drama drew everyone's attention away from hunting starfish when the current nearly swept a young girl under the boat. Her parents and the boat captain grabbed her just in time.

On the third island, the Guna fed us a delicious fish and rice dinner and, loaded up with molas, we returned to the mainland.

We arrived at the outskirts of Panamá City in time to see the sunset reflected in the jumble of glass skyscrapers, notably the JW Marriott Panamá (a former property of our forty-fifth president), the most interesting architectural work in the upscale Punta Pacifica part of the city. Like the Burj al Arab in Dubai, it resembles an inflated spinnaker, designed to look like a gigantic sailboat drifting through downtown.

Thursday, February 17th

The tourist lit says that dining at the Mercado de Mariscos is a must-do Panamá City experience and, when I arrived midday, the only seating available was in full sun. Eating a Panamanian fish means you're brought the whole thing breaded and deep fried—tail, fins, and head intact; its lifeless eyes stare up at you as you dissect and consume its torso down to the spine, flip, and repeat. The process felt raw and barbaric, and when it's sunny, hot, noisy, and you're inhaling fish smell mixed with car exhaust, it's hard to keep your food down. I was desperate for air conditioning.

Friday, February 18th

I got up early to hike an urban rainforest park and arrived right when the ranger was removing the padlock from the gate. From the highest point of the park, an excellent view of the city and glimpses of the canal made the trek worthwhile. I'd seen two toucans up close, huge and colorful, making croaking sounds that resembled the contented grunting of a sated pig. A herd of coatis, raccoons' cute cousins, and I crossed paths. But by then, I'd run out of water and was a little panicky about the walk back in the escalating heat. I was barely functional and my head was pounding, even though I'd walked only a mile and a half. I wished I could be airlifted out of the park and dropped into a rooftop pool filled with crushed ice.

Back at the ranger station, I ignored the No Entry sign, stormed the building, and went straight for the reach-in refrigerator for a cold bottle of water, pausing to let the condensation escaping the fridge cool my face. The angry ranger threatened to call out the Panamanian army. I've been giving Panamá my best shot, and so far it's been incompatible with the activities I enjoy, like cordial interactions with fellow human beings and avoiding heat exhaustion and collapse. At least in Panamá, there's no danger of hypothermia.

Saturday, February 19th

It's 1 p.m. and I haven't been able to make myself go outside. I've been watching a pair of pigeons that selected the eighteenth-floor window ledge as their favorite mating place. I hope they don't fly around to the other side of the building where the windows are open and decide to avail themselves of the living room sofa.

I'm going to try to leave the apartment now...

I walked the half-mile round trip to the local convenience store, and I'm dripping wet. I gave in to the temptation to buy an ice cream sandwich and sat on a low wall just outside the store to enjoy it. But by the time I got the wrapper off, it was an undifferentiated goo that coated my hands and sizzled as it hit the pavement. I'd forgotten that the water in the apartment had been mysteriously turned off all afternoon and I wouldn't be able to wash up. I'm sure I deposited ice cream sticky on all the door handles of the building and the elevator buttons.

In the three elevators I've been in, in Panamá City, the button for the lobby level floor says PB. I haven't been able to figure out what it stands for, but here are some guesses: panic button, pneumatic brake (in case of emergency), or the perfect description of the elevator experience: penalty box. Oh, wait, it's probably something in Spanish. Googled it: *planta baja*, low level.

At 5:30 I walked down the hill to the Coffee Max and ate a delicious dinner. This isn't the first time that a waiter or waitress or Uber driver has kindly offered to speak English to me, and then when I take them up on it, it turns out that the most they know is "hello" and "where is the bathroom?" Gringos do this, too, and it becomes immediately clear that our proficiency in Spanish is limited to two or three phrases. At 6 p.m., the temperature became tolerable; a stiff breeze helped and so did the food. My mood improved one hundred percent and I actually felt happy. Then the mosquitoes arrived, flying in a combat chevron, carrying an arsenal of malaria, dengue, and chikungunya.

Tomorrow is my last day in Panamá City, and I'm determined to explore as much as I can tolerate, hopping from air-conditioned Uber to air-conditioned place back to air-conditioned Uber and the air-conditioned Airbnb.

Sunday, February 20th

According to Google, one of the fourteen largest malls on the planet is here in Panamá City, the Albrook Mall. I Ubered there, thinking that it's likely to be 80 degrees or cooler inside, and I could walk my usual three to four miles. Plus, it would give me the opportunity to examine a sampling of Panamá City's capitalist establishments all in one place. Half of Panamá City had the same idea, trying to escape the heat like I was, no doubt.

The mall was celebrating Valentine's Day as if it hadn't happened yet. Kids' stores offered bright pink and purple backpacks with shoes and toys to match, and Panamá's Ross and T.J.

Maxx equivalents were packed with off-price merchandise. Dozens of stores offered identical cell phone accessories, and a single kiosk sold pellet guns and spy cameras. I snapped a photo of an indigenous Guna woman, wearing traditional dress, snapping a photo of her son in the grip of a life-size, ferocious King Kong, as if he were about to drag the boy into his gaping mouth.[6] Only the upper half of his massive body was above floor level, so I took the escalator down to the floor below to see if the rest was there.

That was the extent of my exploring the city. The remaining museums I wanted to see were either closed permanently or closed on the weekend, and I had leftovers, so I didn't need to find a restaurant. What kinds of air-conditioned spaces did that leave to visit? I was so hot I couldn't think.

Monday, February 21st

Forty minutes had passed, and Uber drivers kept bailing. One guy texted, lamely, "My car is too *decrépito* (worn out)." After four tries, someone was finally willing to drive to the Gamboa Rainforest Reserve, a fancyish resort I thought I should include in my Panamá experience. Google Maps said it was a half hour away, but it was closer to an hour. I told the driver that he was getting a big tip, and when I handed him a ten USD at the end of the journey, he looked shocked and pleased.

Part of the road to the reserve parallels the Panamá Canal and at one point you're close to the ships. And they are huge, like floating cities. I wanted the driver to pull over for a longer look, but I was already pushing it.

Like in Manuel Antonio in Costa Rica, my room at the Gamboa Rainforest Reserve wasn't quite right. Both the sliding glass shower door and the light-blocking curtains were off their tracks and wouldn't close. Tiny spiders were living inside the electrical socket at the base of the bedside table lamp, and they came pouring out when I plugged in my phone charger. No instant coffee packets were available. It made me wonder if hotels save their faulty or not quite fully functional rooms, or the ones in an old wing that the staff forgets to service, for the discounted rates you find sometimes on the internet (which I had nabbed for this place). These were minor inconveniences, but if the teeny spiders don't return to their home inside the electrical socket, I may ask for other accommodations.

Tuesday, February 22nd

My leather handbag has attained a permanent state of stickiness.

The people indigenous to Gamboa are called the Embera, and early in the day an Embera woman set up shop in the resort lobby to sell their handicrafts. She wore her traditional garb, which barely covered her plus-size body, while her young son lay on the floor next to her, in western dress, playing video games on his iPad. One of their signature handicrafts, woven from local plant fibers and painted in exquisite detail, suggested little nesting canoes. I couldn't resist and bought two. These unconventional souvenirs of Panamá made more sense than a vegetable peeler from México.

Midday I sat outside on the balcony reading and listening to the palm trees swaying in the wind, their stiff fronds scraping against each other in a way that, if you closed your eyes, sounded like the beginnings of a powerful rainstorm. Which made me realize that I need to love not only the stories, but also the sounds of a place.

And the currency. I need to feel like it's real money, not poker chips. Panamá's currency, the balboa, falls into this category. If you have a pocketful of balboas, you hardly notice the weight they're so flimsy. My guess is that they're made from coconut shells painted silver. The more substantial one-dollar coins resemble México's ten-peso coin, a stainless-steel rim surrounding an embossed, bronze-ish center. Some of the one-dollar balboas have a scene of a Spanish ship, or figure holding a flag with the Spanish cross, painted in color in the center field of the coin. Of course, the paint wears off quickly, knocking around in people's pockets and being passed from one cash register to another, so it's hard to find one in perfect condition.

A friend who envies my peripatetic lifestyle texted today, writing, "Please keep living as though you will never grow older." Peter Pan syndrome—isn't that one of the things we Baby Boomers are criticized for? Although it doesn't sound like a bad idea to ignore the aging process and just drop dead in your tracks somewhere sometime. It doesn't really matter where, does it? Better on a steamy hiking trail in Panamá than a bed in a depressing nursing home.

Wednesday, February 23rd

This morning, teeny spiders were pouring out of the electrical socket again; I wonder what spiders get out of hanging around electrical currents. Warmth? A buzz? Does electricity smell good to them? I hope they're not planning on colonizing my computer; all those portals leading into it must look enticing. At least I don't have to worry about them invading the bed—no electric blanket.

Yesterday's Embera woman and her handicrafts piqued my curiosity about their village, a short boat ride from the resort, so I signed up for the tour. I thought this might be a mistake that would plunge me into the foulest of moods, but it was so transparently contrived that it was fun. Two young men greeted us at the resort's boat dock, wearing plastic beaded loincloths, and ferried us over to their village of seventeen houses. When we disembarked, an ad hoc band of instrumentalists greeted us: a drummer, a guy with maracas, another with a small hand drum, and a flutist playing a tune that sounded vaguely like "I Left My Heart in San Francisco." At that moment, I knew I was right: Disneyfied gringo tourism. We were led into a large hut, a circular pole building covered in a conical thatch roof, and were herded toward plastic folding tables covered in the Embera's superb handicrafts. Next, an elder—the master of ceremonies—led us to benches lining the perimeter of the hut where he explained a few basic things about the Embera, their indigenous clothing (the plastic beads and fabric that constitute their loincloths and skirts, aisle three, Joann's), tried teaching us some Embera words (nobody could pronounce them correctly), and made us guess what some of the local natural materials were used for, like red seeds, still in their pods, that a young woman passed around. (Dye and mosquito repellent.) The young men's arms were painted in dark geometric patterns with another natural dye, stunning on their perfect skin.[7] The women wore bodices that in the past might have been made of gold pieces, shells, and animal teeth; now they're layered in imitation coins, the kind used on cheap belly dancing costumes. Red passionflowers and heliconia formerly harvested from the forest to make headpieces were likely culled from the flower aisles of Panamá's version of Hobby Lobby.

After this rudimentary introduction to their culture, we were entertained by Embera dances, basically a simple step ball change performed in a circle accompanied by monotone singing—something about monkeys—while we ate a delicious snack of breaded tilapia and fried plantain discs served in a banana leaf. People were selected from the audience to join the dancers, and a tiny girl, probably age four or less, bravely approached the oldest guy in our group and extended her hand. A teenage boy selected me, and I flashed back to junior high school ballroom dance class c. 1966. My hand was covered in tilapia grease, and I tried to figure out how not to transfer the grease to my partner's hand, but I had to let that go.

When the entertainment was over, we were herded to the souvenir tables for a second time. I bought another canoe-shaped handicraft; again, I couldn't resist. When I reached for my wallet, it occurred to me that the Embera guys might be interested in seeing some Costa Rican colones. They seemed really enthused by the idea. When I handed the emcee a two-thousand-colón bill, he examined it and announced, "It's plastic!" Everyone started laughing, which I thought said something about the whole "authentic" Embera village ruse. Were the Embera accepting of the absurdity of their tourism-driven livelihoods, signified in this piece of plastic bearing an image of an apex predator, the hammerhead shark? I wondered if they suffered from the same existential difficulties that I do around money, our own Federal Reserve notes mere pieces of a cotton-and-linen-blend paper, with tiny red and blue synthetic fibers distributed throughout, their meanings conferred by important cultural symbols. The absurd system that forces all members of the same economic alliance to agree that their bank notes have specific values so they can be exchanged for things like food or diamonds or special favors. Someone asked how much two thousand colones was worth in U.S. currency. I said, *Mas o menos tres dólares* (Three dollars, more or less). They thought that was hilarious.

Both the Guna and the Embera hide everyone away who's over forty. Like the Buddha's father, curating his life so he wasn't exposed to sickness, old age, and death, the Guna and the Embera didn't want us to see those things either. The Embera demographic skewed young, and as far as we tourists knew, all the elders, except for the keeper of the tribe's oral history—the master of ceremonies—were launched into the river in leaky boats to die.

Back at the hotel, I Googled the Embera and discovered that the village we visited was indeed a gringo tourist trap. The real villages are at least a two-hour boat ride up the Chagres River from Gamboa. If these are the ways in which the Embera and the Guna have adapted in order to sustain themselves in a capitalist economy, then so be it.

I've been crushing teeny spiders running around on my computer while writing this.

Friday, February 25th

Relief from the heat was a mere two-and-a-half-hours' drive west of Panamá City, in the highlands where it's ten degrees cooler, so I rented a car and drove to El Valle de Anton, a town built in the caldera of a huge dormant volcano. I'd read about the El Valle zoo and thought it was worth a visit and discovered, confusingly, that it was populated with acres and acres of potted plants. Then I started to smell its zoo-ness, and the first exhibit of fauna I encountered was a cage full of chickens. Not a coop, a cage. Ducks were running around unconfined, and I hoped there were no geese also wandering at will, keen on protecting their territory. Cages of rabbits dotted the landscape, and anyone could have easily absconded with one and a potted plant to take home. The cages were too small for *all* the animals, which consisted mostly of birds you'd commonly see in the wild, like toucans. A single caiman lay in a dirty pool whose diameter was only a few inches more than the caiman's length head to tail. I wished I'd had my heavy-duty tin snips with me (I really do own this tool), so I could liberate the tapir and his friend who were placed in separate cages and obviously desperate to have the barrier between them removed.

The zoo's standouts were a flock of silver pheasants from China, a species of bird I never would have seen otherwise. The male was doing his mate-attracting display, which in his case meant extending his huge, pure white wings and flapping them vigorously; the contrast with his black body and bright red comb was positively exciting. Even so, after a few minutes I'd seen enough.

"Square" trees (to be explained) and a golden frog exhibit were two additional not-to-be-missed El Valle attractions that the Airbnb host had encouraged me to see. They were on the grounds of a fancy hotel where a parking lot attendant guarded visitors' cars. I asked him the whereabouts of the frogs and trees, and I *know* I put my sentences together correctly, although I didn't know the word for "square" (*cuadradas*; if I'd thought about it for a few seconds, I might have guessed correctly), so I said, *los árboles especiales*. He pretended that he didn't understand and told me to go to the zoo. If only I'd looked past him another fifty yards, I would have seen the flashing neon signs for both things.

I guess he liked being mean to befuddled tourists. My experience has been that only the French did this.

Near the signs I noticed a huge sloth hanging by his arms from a branch of a cecropia tree, swaying in the stiff wind with a silly grin on his face; I think I witnessed what play means for a sloth.

Earlier in the day I'd gone to a snake exhibit, another place specializing in animal abuse, where some of the snakes' homes were no more than a few paper towels on the floor of a filthy exhibit and a dish of cloudy water, a snake sensory deprivation tank. I wanted to see, and memorize, what a fer-de-lance looked like, and as I suspected, their triangular-shaped heads are larger than what seems proportional to their bodies, the better to bite you with, I guess. It's uncanny how much their camo looks like a pile of fallen leaves.

At the golden frog and square trees attractions, a woman collected an exorbitant entrance fee for a glimpse at a single male frog barely visible through an algae-covered glass aquarium. She explained that Chinese visitors had brought special trees with square bases from their homeland, some decades ago, to plant in Panamá. Which also could have accounted for the silver pheasants at the zoo. She led me to a rusty, padlocked gate that she opened and then locked behind me, explaining that the exit was a thirty-minute walk away, just follow the trail. I wondered if she'd greet me at the other end to let me out. It was already late in the day and the light was fading, and as I started out on the path, I saw that it was largely covered in fallen, decayed leaves. Exactly the colors of the fer-de-lance. Several Costa Ricans had told me the fer-de-lance population was "exploding" in their country, and I wondered if it were also the case in Panamá. I questioned my decision, but I was on a one-way street and there was no turning back. Another metaphor for something.

I bent at the waist to have a closer look at the ground ahead of me, and every single step I took was measured. Having crushed, with bare feet, something both crunchy and squishy the night before in my room, I was reminded to always have plenty of light and enhanced vision when venturing into unknown territory, be it across the tile floor from the bed to the bathroom or through a dark rainforest overrun with venomous snakes. I didn't see a single tree on that walk, not to mention trees with square bases, but I made it to the exit without seeing any snakes either. The gate was unlocked.

I bought three bananas from a fruit stand for a dime. This same quantity of bananas had once set me back five dollars in Miami.

Saturday, February 26th

While I was in town eating ice cream at an outdoor table, a cute ginger-haired dog walked up to me, looked me right in the eye and said, telepathically, *I'm your best friend, right? Well give me some of that ice cream!* Obediently, I put it down on the ground and with a few strokes of her tongue, it was gone.

Sunday, February 27th

I decided I'd be kicking myself when I returned to the States if I hadn't visited the tiny mountain town of Boquete, a place that frequently receives the highest praise in *International Living, Condé Nast,* and the *AARP Magazine*, the relocation guides for geezers. Chiriquí Province is lush and gorgeous, but I didn't understand what all the fuss was about when it came to Boquete. It's full of impatient gringos in their giant vehicles clogging up narrow roads, the centro area like any other in small-town Panamá. The natives looked unhappy; I would be, too, if a bunch of norteamericanos showed up and appropriated my land and created an economy that I had to adjust my lifestyle to and ended up depending on it.

But I had another reason to visit Boquete: to add the green Panamanian quetzal to my bird list. The list already numbered over fifty species, mostly from Anton Valley, and I was on a quest-zal. I left El Valle at 7:30 a.m. and arrived at 1:30 p.m. at the Finca Lérida, a coffee plantation on the outskirts of Boquete, quetzal territory. The thought that I may see one kept me going during the six-hour drive. The Pan-American Highway speed limit is mostly 60 kph (about 37 mph), infrequently 80 (about 50 mph), and there's one longish stretch in Chiriquí Province that's a whopping 100 kph (about 62 mph). Yesterday was the start of Carnival, and motocops were stationed every thirty kilometers or so with speed traps. Only a few people had been stopped along the way, so I wondered if their radar measured your speed and automatically issued tickets that arrived in your email a few days later. If so, I never heard about it from Avis.

The Finca Lérida is a huge operation with thousands of coffee trees planted on the steep slopes of Boquete. The plantation owners left stands of dense rainforest here and there, and I scrambled up a hillside to explore one of those areas. The forest was populated with huge, first-growth trees that created a thick canopy, and the metallic sound of a black-faced solitaire echoed eerily through the space. Like the path to the Chinese square trees, the path here was littered with a variety of earth-colored leaves, and I wasn't nearly as vigilant looking for snakes since they're usually lethargic at high elevation. The forest smelled of rot and decay, a chthonic smell I love. I was on the clock; I had only thirty minutes to find a quetzal because I also had to find the Airbnb before dark—sometimes even more of a challenge—and I was losing light fast. I identified an area with several avocado trees (quetzals *love* baby avocados) and a few rotted trees with holes (quetzals prefer to leave the building of a suitable, predator-proof house to the woodpeckers), and waited. I wish I could write that a quetzal materialized but, sadly, that was not the case.

I found the Airbnb and survived the experience. Here's the review I posted:

> By all means, stay here if you like the creepy dilapidated shack-in-the-woods experience. And bring a nose clip or an early-stage cold if you want to block the heady smell of disinfectant emanating from the linoleum floor and bathroom.

You won't want to open the windows to let the fumes escape unless you don't mind being covered in welts from mosquito bites. No hot water, but what did I expect? Around dusk, one tiny glitch happened—a couple from France showed up to inhabit my room. The owner had double-booked it (oops!), and we weren't able to contact her to sort it out. Since I arrived first, I had squatter's rights. A disinfectant-induced headache prevented me from sleeping, but I wouldn't have had the pleasure of hearing all the creatures of the night, like roaming packs of snarling dogs and feral hogs rooting around. Then, at about three, the local roosters. This being Airbnb, I was expecting a little more comfort, but I'm a seasoned camper so I just switched into rustic mode.

Monday, February 28th

The moon was an upside-down crescent and dazzling Venus was directly overhead when, at 6 a.m., I left the Airbnb. As the sky brightened and the moon and Venus faded, I thought about the *Odyssey* and how Homer began several chapters describing sunrise—the "rosy fingers of dawn"—at whose tweeness I would roll my eyes, but this dawn was the meaning of rosy-fingered. They were huge, fat, splayed fingers, but I could see where Homer was coming from. The drive back to El Valle was going to be an even bigger slog than the drive to Boquete. Did I mention that *boquete* means "blow job" in Portuguese?

Deliriously tired, by seven I was famished and feeling another layer of headache from coffee deprivation. At 9:30, a McDonald's appeared shimmering on the horizon, an oasis in the rural Panamanian food desert. I pulled into the parking lot, right in front of a grinning Ronald McDonald statue sitting casually on a bench in a tastefully designed little garden. This magical scene was an unexpected and delightful change from the empty plastic bottles and bags, discarded food wrappers, cardboard, and shredded tires collected against the walls of the rural establishments along the Pan-American Highway, deposited there by the constant winds of Chiriquí Province. Inside, the facility was *really nice*, the bathroom clean and modern, and the food ordering and delivery system smooth and efficient thanks to cheerful workers in spotless uniforms. Neither a blob of ketchup or mustard nor puddle of sticky, dried Coke lay on any surface, not even on the swinging door of the *basura* container. McDonald's is known, internationally, for its good coffee, and Panamanian McDonald's coffee was spectacular. After three sips of the super-heated delicious stuff, my headache of the last fourteen hours vanished, and the Egg McQueso was pure deliverance. I was fortified for another two and a half hours of driving at the ungodly speed of 37 mph, up to 50, if I was lucky.

Wednesday, March 2nd

While I waited for an Uber to take me to the Crowne Plaza Hotel by the airport for tomorrow's departure, a septic truck painted with a graphic of a smiling cartoon toucan drove past. The name of the company: Portucan. Another bird for the list!

Is Panamá a relocation possibility? Only if the next ice age arrives sooner than expected.

CHAPTER SIXTEEN

PORTLAND, OREGON
A Housesit

Another housesit took me to Portland in the early spring of 2022. Again, my charges were three dogs: a miniature schnauzer, a Havanese, and the third one a last-minute add-on, a plus-size dachshund. The house was in the Hollywood neighborhood, an upper-middle-class enclave of 1920s craftsman homes occupied by doctors, lawyers, and businesspeople: proponents of the replacement theory of human reproduction (one child per parent). This was a neighborhood of and for the liberal left: yoga devotees, fine wine collectors, cannabis growers, baby-on-boarders, Black Lives Matter adherents, their properties decorated with fanciful yard art and blanketed with daffodils and tulips. Little libraries sprinkled throughout the neighborhood were populated with self-help books, the works of Michel Foucault, well-worn copies of *The Rights of Others: Aliens, Residents, and Citizens*, and were occasionally used for the transfer of certain pharmaceuticals. Electric cars traveled silently through the neighborhood, sharing the road with bicyclists going to work.

After I'd been in the house for a few days and had developed something of a routine, dictated mostly by the dogs, just after dawn one morning I stood at the kitchen window while the dachshund whined for food. I'd been told that he was twice his girth at some time in the recent past, and one of my jobs was to keep him from overeating. He'd had his breakfast only thirty minutes earlier and was ready for seconds, expecting the all-you-can-eat buffet he'd been accustomed to for most of his life, but he was going to stick to a healthier regimen on my watch. While trying to background his whining, I saw a homeless Black man walking the street, wearing a pink jacket over a bright red shirt, and a sky blue cap and gloves protecting his dark head and hands from the damp cold. He walked back and forth along our street and the one perpendicular to it, scanning people's yards and looking into their cars. A woman dressed for work had just left her house and locked the front door when she noticed him and ran to her car for safety. A well-heeled man with a briefcase and a travel French press pretended not to see him when the homeless man tried to get his attention. An older couple on their morning constitutional picked up the pace and crossed the street as a precaution. The homeless man's incursion into the neighborhood had made it a dangerous place. These were the folks for whom Black lives mattered. But whose Black lives, I wondered?

Portland is full of homeless people, some of them given one-way bus tickets back in their hometowns and told to go west. When it comes to zoning rules and homeowners' association covenants, the homeless are lawless. They set up encampments next to children's playgrounds, claim the spaces between sidewalks and streets with their tents and improvised lean-tos, occupy entire downtown parks with their tent cities. Throughout Portland, abandoned vehicles are transformed into domiciles and augmented with tarps and cardboard, and all kinds of urban detritus attaches itself to them like iron filings to a magnet. The homeless lack essential city services, so they eat, defecate, and wash wherever they can. It's common to see rows of moss-and-mildew-covered beater RVs lining a road for blocks and blocks, as if queued to enter a national park that closed long ago and nobody bothered to pass the news along. Throughout the city, their refuse cascades down the slopes of highway embankments, originally the provenance of Keep America Beautiful's flower campaigns of the '60s and '70s. The City of White Guilt, Portland lets them live their lives with little fear of retribution but not as citizens needing protection. To the well-off, they're a problem to be solved; a blight to be scraped off the sidewalks and deposited elsewhere. Do Homeless Lives Matter?

A week into my housesit, the adorable, also-obese Havanese that I nicknamed Tubby began scooting around the oak living room floor on her rear end and trying unsuccessfully to lick her behind. Earlier in the day, she'd also been scooting around on the dirt at the dog park, grinding whatever pathogens and parasites contained therein into the delicate tissue around her anus. I had no idea what this behavior meant, but I feared worms of some kind. I didn't want the responsibility of diagnosing and deworming Tubby myself, especially since she's a creature with sharp canines who would possibly be uncooperative, so I loaded her into the car and drove to the vet's office. She liked riding in the car. We arrived and checked in; everyone made a fuss over her because she's just so darn cute and friendly. The vet's assistant led us into an examination room; Tubby liked that, too. Tubby liked everything and everybody. When I was told she was going to have her anal glands expressed, clogged anal glands being the main cause of her discomfort, I thought, Okay, finally I'm going to see Tubby get upset about something. But she seemed to like that just as much as anything else. Next lifetime I'm going to request that I come back as a Havanese. This lifetime, I don't intend to return to Portland.

CHAPTER SEVENTEEN

GRANADA, SPAIN

Wednesday, May 4th

The flight to Granada left from Dallas-Fort Worth and continued via Chicago and Madrid. Well known among travelers for its bathroom innovations, way back in 1993 O'Hare installed the first of several versions of "hygienic" toilet seat protectors designed to automatically replace the Saran Wrap-like cover after each use.[1] Wave your hand over a sensor, and a mechanism produces a new piece of wrap that enfolds the seat, drawing the soiled cover into a slot in the back of the toilet. For the benefit of the next patron, a digital display reads, in big red letters, "New cover, ready to use." But in 2013, the *Chicago Sun-Times* reported that the gizmo "drags up liquid from the rim of toilet bowls and leaves drops of that liquid atop seats, on the clear plastic film,"[2] and the nearly $100 million contract with the toilet seat cover company was investigated. Before this reveal, it kinda grossed me out that I had no say in whether I had a choice to sit on the plastic wrap (was it the cling variety?) or on a bare toilet seat. At least on the seat, you could see someone else's pee and wipe it away; plastic wrap and its reflectivity made that much more difficult. I also wondered where all those used seat covers disappeared to, and whose job it was to clean them out and replace the plastic wrap. Did this person also replenish the paper towel dispensers? Did they change their hygienic protective gloves between tasks?

O'Hare continues to innovate. The bathrooms have cylindrical red and green lights protruding from their ceilings, like traffic lights, indicating which stalls are occupied and which ones are available, precluding the nagging question, *Is someone in there or not?* No more bending over, your backpack or purse slamming into the dirty floor in the process, to look for carefully aligned feet, toes pointing toward you. No more pushing on a door to see if it's open and being embarrassed to discover the current occupant forgot to lock it. Thank you, O'Hare!

Madrid's airport has a graceful, undulating ceiling made of thin bamboo slats, like air currents visualized. The floors are kept spotless by a fleet of what looks like highly maneuverable snowplows with eight-foot-long dry mops attached to their fronts. Mostly middle-aged women pilot these machines and zip around, cleaning up our messes as fast as we can make them.

After a long flight, one of the most stressful parts of travel is arriving at the door to your Airbnb and not being able to get past it. Hosts often don't make it perfectly clear how to operate the lock or whether the mechanism works reliably. I've had this exasperating experience now in four cities: Mérida and Guanajuato, México, on a previous trip to Lisbon, and now Granada. These days, owners are seldom available in person and communicate through Airbnb messaging only. When questioned, they will breezily respond that the lock is quirky and will send photos of the succession of special hand gestures and incantations you must successfully master, and for someone who is lock-and-key-challenged to begin with, no amount of jiggling the lock or chanting Open Sesame helps. But when I messaged the owner of the Granada rental that I was having trouble with the lock and key, the indifferent reply was, *Sorry, you'll need to look for another place.* Ten minutes later, as I sat on the staircase searching the Airbnb and VRBO sites on my phone, exhausted from traveling for over fourteen hours and wanting to take an ax to the door, a nice young man materialized, showed me how to double-unlock it and, while giving the key another quarter turn counterclockwise, how to apply a sharp, upward pulling movement that may someday dislocate my shoulder. Adding a little kick to the bottom of the door, it worked, and I was in.

Thursday, May 5th

Fried my hot rollers this morning when I forgot to flip the switch to change to European 240 voltage. I set out to do a Rick Steves self-guided walking tour and once I reached the imposing Granada Cathedral, I threw the tour out the window and decided to wander aimlessly and see what came up. The cathedral has not one, but two pipe organs that rival everything else in the interior in their ornateness.[3] Would love to hear the baseball "Charge!" theme played by dueling organists in that cavernous space. The cathedral is a mishmash of plateresque (silversmith-like, with ornamentation that suggests fine jewelry), Renaissance, and baroque styles. Sparing the organs, an eighteenth-century bishop ordered all interior surfaces painted with lime to ward off disease. Church officials should have considered applying a new coat in 2020.

A small square near the church featured a fountain with a circle of hideous human/simian hybrids bent over and spewing liquid from their mouths, as if hurling pitchers of beer they had for lunch. A tiny Poseidon topped the fountain, holding his trident aloft in his left hand, his right hand amputated at the wrist. I suspect that humans have always been avid souvenir collectors, and before there were purveyors of refrigerator magnets, T-shirts, scale models of iconic monuments, and Disney merch, people cut off the heads, hands, and penises of statues, and sometimes the feet (see Juan de Oñate, page 75). Every house, ancient or modern, can use a paperweight, a doorstop, or a penis pestle, so these souvenirs also had utility. Granada is full of vandalized, life-size stone figures standing on top of arched doorways and precariously balanced on narrow ledges high above the streets, and when silhouetted by the setting sun, they look like the mutilated victims of the Spanish Civil War returning home from battle.

After an hour-and-a-half siesta, I walked up the hill to the Mirador de San Nicolas, a popular overlook, to watch the sunset reflected on the Alhambra,[4] the fantastic Islamic palace-fortress complex begun in 1248 and repurposed many times over the centuries. The snow-covered Sierra Nevada was a striking backdrop to the landscape created by the buildings, a contrast to the hot air of late afternoon Granada. Street musicians played their songs of desperate longing, music that, for me, asked the question, *Where is Location X?* On the way back, I passed a street sign installed next to a cobblestone driveway that read Physically Impossible Entry.[5]

Friday, May 6th

The Alhambra! A World Heritage bucket list destination that half the population of Europe was visiting along with my small tour group. Exploring this architectural masterpiece fulfilled a dream many decades long, and our excellent guide was full of enthusiasm and knowledge and referred to the Alhambra as his office. Visitors are not allowed to linger anywhere except in the Generalife gardens*, but the privilege of experiencing the palaces and imagining what transpired in those places was like being inserted directly into the orientalist lit I'd read as a kid: *The Thousand and One Nights*, "Ali Baba and the Forty Thieves," Tennyson and Kipling. Even though no words or images can ever do justice to the Alhambra, consider reading Washington Irving's *Tales of the Alhambra*. It's both exhilarating and mystical, but Irving himself wrote, "How unworthy is my scribbling of the place."

I wish we could have taken the tour at a slower pace, but like the immigration queue at the airport, visitors were processed as expeditiously as possible. We were told to stay in a straight line and walk in the middle of all pathways. Like in a museum, we weren't allowed to touch anything; with eight thousand visitors a day, how else could they maintain the integrity of the place? The geometric tile work, slender columns holding substantial arches, and intricate stucco carvings gave the place a feel of grace and ethereality. Palace ceilings covered with muqarnas or "stalactite" vaults looked like giant colonies of snoozing bats.[6] The jumble of buildings, their various shapes and sizes, was intended to confuse invaders and protect the secrets of the place, and if I were there unescorted, I could see the value of dropping breadcrumbs to find my way out.

The brick floors showed the signs of relentless human trodding and shuffling, day in and day out for over seven hundred years, each individual brick sagging toward the middle and the mortar between the bricks worn away. I was surprised that we were not required to remove our floor-scratching shoes or, at least, were not provided with protective shoe covers to prevent further damage to the floors and walkways. Plus, the Alhambra was built and occupied for centuries by Muslims, and considered one of the world's most important works of Islamic architecture, so wasn't entering its former mosque, shod, being disrespectful?

The water for the Alhambra comes from the nearby Darro River and flows throughout the compound without the use of pumps—it's all gravity fed—powering fountains, channels, filling reflecting pools; they even had flush toilets back in the day. Our guide explained that the quiet fountains were built by the Moors and noisy fountains were built by the Christians. For centuries, both groups struggled for control of the Alhambra, adjusting the compound to their specific physical and aesthetic needs and, for once, the Muslims came out on top.

The Alhambra offers great views of Granada from its towers. The residential parts of the old city are composed of whitewashed buildings called carmens, from the Arabic word for vine (karm). Carmens are surrounded by high walls and have interior gardens that are both ornamental and food producing. When you walk the neighborhoods composed of carmens, bougainvillea bursts over these high, white walls, and jasmine, orange blossoms, and roses encircle you with their aromas. During one of those walks, the Rumi poem "What Was Said to the Rose" sprung to mind.

> What was said to the rose that made it open
> was said to me here in my chest.
>
> What was told to the cypress that made it strong
> and straight, what was whispered to the jasmine
>
> so it is what it is, whatever made sugarcane
> sweet; whatever was said to the inhabitants
>
> of the town of Chigil in Turkestan that makes
> them so handsome, whatever lets the pomegranate
>
> flower blush like a human face, that is being
> said to me now. . .[7]

Maybe if I listen closely enough, what is being said to me in Granada will lead to Location X.

---

*The word is pronounced hen-er-a-LEAF-aye, not General Life, like the insurance company. It comes from the Arabic جَنَّة الْعَرِيف, Jannat-al-'Arīf, which means "garden of the architect."

CHAPTER EIGHTEEN

MADRID

Sunday, May 8th

The high-speed train from Granada to Madrid took three and a half hours and arrived in Madrid at 4 p.m. Because of its proximity to the Prado, I'd booked the Hostel Aguilar, located among a cluster of hostels in a repurposed multistorey building. The key and lock weren't an issue, and when I opened the door, I was pleased to see that it wasn't a cavernous mixed-gender room full of bunk beds; the spotlessly clean room with a single bed and a nice bathroom looked like a typical Comfort Inn. I wheeled in my suitcase, locked up, and headed down the hill to the Prado, a five-minute walk away, excited to see Goya's work in person and, like every other Prado visitor, Hieronymus Bosch's *Garden of Earthly Delights*.

The museum is free on Sundays from 5 to 7 p.m., and it was packed. As I entered room 056B, seeing Fra Angelico's *The Annunciation*[1] slackened my jaw and made me forget to breathe. The technique used to paint the wings on Archangel Gabriel, delivering the message to Mary that she's going to be impregnated by the Holy Spirit, defies understanding. Each barb of each feather is perfectly and meticulously incised and gold-leafed, using the refractive quality of gold to create a shimmering effect as you walk the length of the painting. A set of disembodied hands delivers a dove, whose wings mirror the shape of Gabriel's, to Mary via perfectly straight lines of gold emanating from a sliver of sun painted in the upper left corner. Angelico must have used brushes with only two or three hairs to paint these gold features, including Gabriel's curly locks, and he must have fallen somewhere on the obsessive-compulsive spectrum. Jackson Pollock or Willem de Kooning wouldn't have been artists during the early Renaissance, they would have been the guys who scrubbed stone floors or tossed slop to the hogs. Howard Hughes? Maybe.

Although *The Annunciation* is a notable exception, many programmatic religious paintings don't divulge much of the artist's own mind, and I guess that's part of the point. They painted what they were told to paint to create religious devotion in the viewer's mind, or to tell a story, or to convey allegory through religious symbolism, and to sublimate themselves, a concept lost on contemporary artists.

Monday, May 9th

The number of works in the Prado with religious and mythological themes is staggering. Many repeat the same composition or are copies of other earlier works showing slight differences. After five hours of exhausting art-viewing, a theme had emerged: men have always been obsessed with women's breasts. Whenever they can justify displaying them in an artwork, they will. If there's just no getting around it—the woman must be clothed, like in paintings of the Virgin—often the painter will expose only one breast, as if it were an important identifying feature, like an aquiline nose or green eyes. An identifier that, if the woman's face were covered, would signal yes, without a doubt, that's Eve, or Mary Mother of Jesus, or St. Cecilia, or Catherine of Aragon. Or as if to say, *I wanted to make sure that you, the viewer, understand that this person is a woman.* But everybody's breasts are painted pretty much the same according to the accepted ideal—rounded, full, with nipples the size and shape of a Hershey's Kiss and the color of pink bubble gum[2]—suggesting they're depicted gratuitously.

Everyone knows that women come in all shapes and sizes and with great variations among breasts, but not at the Prado.

Conversely, these same painters rarely (never?) rendered their mature male subjects' penises, conveniently covering the sensitive area with a fig leaf or a mist or a strategically draped mantle. Why the modesty? Confusingly, in paintings where women are being raped by satyrs or soldiers or bulls or whatever, you never see an erect penis or penetration[3], and you can be sure the men are fully clothed while the women are not. Often a mischievous, lecherous old man will be standing off to one side looking at us viewers, and he might as well be winking with approval or giving the thumbs-up. Or he's getting some action himself, grabbing a woman's breast.[4] Scopophilia, the aesthetic pleasure experienced from looking at a woman that today we call the "male gaze," is evident throughout the Prado. Trace the sightline of the (clothed) male organist in Titian's painting *Venus and Organist and Little Dog,* and he's looking right at Venus's crotch.[5] IMO, scopophilia motivated the acquisition of much of the Prado's (dare I use the word pornographic?) collection.

Just because a painting has a religious theme, it's not okay to be breast obsessed. In a special genre all its own, Baby Jesus either has his mouth clamped down on one of Mary's nipples or he's squeezing one of her breasts, priming it for feeding time. Or she's squeezing it herself, offering it to his open mouth while he's giving us the side eye, and maybe has a little baby erection, proud of and excited by what's exclusively his to enjoy.[6] He would be pissed if he knew that there were occasions when she expressed her milk into the mouths of lecherous old men (we the viewers are told they are saints, so that makes it okay). The milk's projectile is rendered in thin, perfectly straight lines, and sometime travels a great distance, into greedy, open gullets, and we are told the purpose is for purification of sin.

King Philip IV of Spain, a member of the malocclusioned Hapsburg dynasty, had his wife painted bare chested. Was he trying to inspire envy by flaunting one of the many perks he enjoyed as king? Or is this a fourteenth-century version of revenge porn? In *The Beheading of Saint John the Baptist and Herod's Banquet* (1630–1633, by Strobel the Younger), not only is Salome offering up John's head on a silver platter, but her breasts, popping out of the top of her gown, are part of the deal, too. Most of the dozens of other figures in the painting are modestly clothed. I'm not one hundred percent sure, but I think breast implants weren't available until a couple centuries after Goya's *Nude Maja* was completed. Her painfully pert, baseball-sized breasts, installed high up on her chest, look like they may collapse onto her neck and suffocate her any minute.[7]

The Prado is replete with church- and emperor-sponsored artworks, conveying the idea that pre-Renaissance, career artists painted dark and stiff-looking portraits and gruesome scenes from Jesus's life and little more. Wouldn't you be tempted to add some subtle visual humor to the works, here and there? What about an extra finger on one of the Magis, or a stain or two on Mary's mantle where some of her breakfast ended up, crumbs in Jesus's beard? To keep yourself from dying of boredom. "Oh, look, Andrea, we got another commission from the pope for a crucified Jesus. Excuse me while I go outside and crucify *myself.*"

I started looking more closely at the works, and sure enough, by the 1630s painters had had enough. Philip IV (the Hapsburg king) commissioned Peter Paul Rubens to paint a Diana and Callisto to hang over the couch in his hunting lodge, replete with fat naked women. (In Greek mythology, Callisto was a member of Diana the huntress's clique of virgins, but when Diana found out that Callisto was pregnant by Zeus, she kicked her out of the group.) Painted c. 1635, it's a copy of a Titian, also called *Diana and Callisto*, wherein Callisto reveals her pregnancy to Diana. The nine female figures in the painting are nude; some have a thin gold band encircling one arm or are depicted partially covered with flowing, genitalia-concealing cloth. Each figure has ample, squishy breasts. Diana sits with her back to the viewer—she is the most important figure, so she is the fattest—her ample butt spilling over the edge of a rock. Her right leg is crossed over her left knee, exposing the sole of her right foot. But wait, isn't that a left foot attached to a right leg? The toes are in the correct order, big toe to little, but the sole of the foot is clearly a left sole with a faint bulge of an outside ankle bone. I'm pretty sure I'm right about this.[8]

I wondered if Rubens painted in these little jokes as a relief from the boredom of painting yet another saint, nobleperson, or scene from mythology. So I started looking for clues in his other paintings. *St. Thomas* (1610–1612) pensively and painfully looks down at his Bible, his cranium having been presciently disfigured when caught under the wheel of a cart in *The Triumph of the Church* (1625). In *Achilles discovered among the Daughters of Lycomedes* (1630–1635), a little dog barking at the intruder stands close to a mysterious steaming pile sitting on an elaborate claw-foot stool (pun intended?).[9] The steaming pile and the stool are exactly in the middle foreground of the painting, and a *putto* at the top looks down and points at it. Paris's sightline goes straight to Venus's front-and-center boobs in *The Judgment of Paris* (1606–1608), and she wins the beauty contest.

In the 1600s, some painters seemed committed to rebelling against the fantasy of idealized human form. What a relief to find a few paintings that, along with idealized humans, have a realistic (that is to say, not with an airbrushed-looking skin wrapper over rippling muscles) face of a wrinkled and tanned grinning man with a few missing teeth looking directly at us, the viewer.

In banquet and battle scenes, I've been searching for someone who's rolling their eyes or holding their fingers up in a V-shape behind another soldier's head. Here's another major pet peeve. Many battle scene figures are so obviously carefully posed and painted in a studio with proper northern light that they don't translate well at all outside of that environment. Especially because of the use of certain predictable, pat gestures: graceful, upturned hands often with an upraised index finger; fingers relaxed as if anticipating receiving a chocolate delicacy,[10] even as they're being riven with a sword or pinned to a wooden cross with huge iron nails. Don't get me started on feet, with the longer second toe and vestigial little toe, the foot balanced on its ball.[11] Nobody's going to be that blasé when their head's getting chopped off.

Zurbarán's delightful *Labors of Hercules* paintings (1634) all feature figures of Hercules that are comically out of proportion, with short torsos, long legs and arms, and huge feet, squished into the same-size square canvases, imprisoned within the frame. It was as if Zurbarán had gone to Michael's and that was the only canvas they had on hand, and he was facing a tight deadline.

I was hoping to find a still life with lascivious goings-on reflected in the grapes or in the beveled edges of a mirror, or an elegant lady in the act of sitting down on a seventeenth-century whoopee cushion, but five hours was not enough time for this kind of detailed research.

One of the most fascinating discoveries to make at the Prado concerns Goya. There, in the Prado's sparse upper floor, are Goya's idealized, pastoral paintings (*La Primavera*,[12] *The Parasol*) from the 1780s, so twee and cutesy, pre-*Maja*. It's hard to believe they're his and not Thomas Kincade's. Two floors beneath, in a darkened gallery, are Goya's so-called Black Paintings, the ones depicting the horrors of the Napoleonic Wars, his fear of insanity, and his bleak view of humanity. It's where his famous mural of Saturn devouring one of his male offspring[13] hangs. During this period, he painted on the walls of his home, his subjects wide eyed and feral, a visual trope signaling the fear and horror caused by the famine, brutality, and poverty Goya himself experienced. Around 1874, the paintings were removed and transferred to canvas. Thank you, Goya, et al., for your thoughtful consideration of subjects other than women's breasts! As Goya matured as an artist, he made painting honest.

The Prado owns at least five paintings of Archangel Michael, but my fave of all time, *Le Grand Saint Michel*[14] by Raphael, is in the Louvre.

Tuesday, May 10th

As I packed up to leave the Aguilar, I started obsessing about where to leave a ten-euro tip intended for housekeeping. I assumed that after checkout, hotel staff would search the room to see if anything's left behind or missing, like the coveted Aguilar bath mat or the batteries from the TV remote, prior to allowing the housekeeper access to the room. So, the question was, Where to hide the ten euros so only she would find it? Definitely not sitting on one of the end tables on each side of the bed or in a drawer. I thought about hiding it in a folded-up hand towel, but it could go straight into the wash without being detected. I settled on this: on the side of the bed I'd obviously chosen to sleep on, with the top sheet and blanket folded down into a crisp triangle as if someone had entered the room to prepare it for my evening arrival. Under this triangle. I imagined her delight as she stripped the bed and saw the ten-euro note, its peachy-orange color and contrasting number *10*, rendered in green, the color we in the U.S. associate with money, lying on the bright white bottom sheet. But what if, in her haste to clean the room and get on to the next one, she yanked the sheets off all at once, balled them up with the towels, and threw the whole muddle into the wash? Would the ten euros survive the hot water and cheap, perfumed detergent and all that agitation? Surely someone would find it before it came to that. I had to stop thinking about it and make my way to the hop-on-hop-off bus.

    I rode the bus most of the day, admiring Madrid's amazing architecture, thanks to the Hapsburgs, the Bourbons, the neo-plateresques, and the modernists. Installed on the tops of buildings near the Prado, a Diana figure with bow drawn and Apollo driving his team of four horses were silhouetted against the afternoon sky. We were stuck in traffic, and it was hot; didn't I learn my lesson in México City? I hopped off the bus at the National Archeological Museum to see the re-creation of the Altamira Cave; the exhibit was closed but other parts of the museum were accessible and worth visiting. Several ancient skulls with perfect dentition were on display, and a reconstruction of an early human, *Homo georgicus*, based on these skulls loomed in a case nearby, wild eyed and with spear in hand. I was jealous of their straight teeth and perfect bite, but I wouldn't want the face to go with it.[15] I'll take *Homo sapiens*' small jaw, crowded teeth, and Invisalign any day.

CHAPTER NINETEEN

ROME

Thursday, May 12th

For several days I've been stressing about how to arrange transport to the Granada airport for the early morning flight to Rome. I realized no Uber or taxi driver would be willing to pick me up at the corner of Horno del Vidrio and the Avenida de los Tristes, cobblestone streets built in the eleventh century for donkey traffic, at *any* time of day. So, at six this morning, while Granada was still pitch black, I schlepped my suitcase and backpack the half mile to the Plaza Nueva where I assumed there would be abundant taxis, since whenever I've walked through the plaza, day or night, there have been. I kept thinking, If I were a thief, I would hang out in these crazy narrow streets surrounding the plaza and wait to ambush vulnerable tourists, easy targets!

In the distance, a blonde gringa and a local were headed for the plaza, too. She was pulling two large suitcases and he wasn't helping. I wondered why until I got within earshot and heard her saying, not very convincingly, "Stop." She kept saying "Stop, stop, stop." Then her *stops* got more intense, but he wouldn't leave her side. He wasn't trying to steal her stuff, he was pleading with her, like a spurned lover. Since she wasn't asking for help, nobody (me and two others in the plaza) intervened. Six taxis were lined up to accommodate early morning travelers, their welcoming bright green roof signs, signaling availability, aglow; she made it into one, leaving the pleading guy behind, and I was next in line. What was I stressing so much about?

When you enter Italy from Spain, because it's a member of the Schengen Area, they just let you in. No going through customs, no surprise QR code to produce. Granted, back in Granada, my entry point into Europe, I had to show the document that provided a detailed account of my whereabouts while in the EU and my vaccination card, but that was it. But let the buyer beware: never fly Spain's Vueling Airlines, you'll be charged $115 to check a 15-kilo (33-pound) bag.

The owner of the Airbnb said his neighborhood was one of the most ancient in Rome, so I guess that made it over 2,200 years old. I was glad to see that the locks and keys were contemporary. As soon as he finished his orientation and left, I rushed to the window to check out the view. Rome had first entered my relocation radar thanks to a website called WindowSwap, a concept that allows participants to "fill that deep void in our wanderlust hearts by allowing us to look through someone else's window, somewhere in the world." WindowSwap is profoundly addictive and satisfyingly voyeuristic, and after a few hours of gazing out other people's windows, I lingered on one in Rome. It was the light. The way it fell on the buildings across the street, the old woman watering her potted lilies crowding the tiny balcony, and how it created deep relief in the cobblestones, as if the light itself had manifested into existence everything that it touched, like a fairy's magic wand. I hadn't seen anything else quite like it in the hundreds of other windows I'd looked through, and I was desperate to experience Rome's light firsthand.

Friday, May 13th

In preparation for visiting the Colosseum and the Forum, I'd read that the Catholic Church had stripped much of the marble facings of Rome's ancient buildings, most notably from the Colosseum, to use for their own purposes, and it's kind of shocking to see in person and imagine what the defiled buildings must have looked like in their glory. Tomorrow, I have a hugely expensive skip-the-line ticket to see where all that beautiful marble ended up.

Reading some wall text at the Colosseum, I learned an excellent Latin word: vomitorium. It's not what people usually think it is, a room where gluttonous Romans purged their stomachs to indulge in the uninterrupted pleasures of eating. Vomitoria are entrances and exits found in ancient Roman public spaces like the Colosseum, so the vomiting that's happening is of people from a building through a rather confined, esophageal space. After I vomited myself from the Colosseum, along with an insane number of other tourists, I hiked up to the Forum and the Palatine Hill, not nearly the mob scene I'd just been a part of. Giant columns and pieces of pediment and other ancient detritus were strewn all over the place, resembling an undisturbed battlefield littered with the body parts of a defeated army. Very little of the original structures remain.

Saturday, May 14th

The pilfered marble that built St. Peter's Basilica and the Vatican Museums underscored how magnificent the Colosseum must have looked in its glory. Standing in St. Peter's Square, by 9 a.m. the temperature was already uncomfortably hot, and another group was trying to cut in line ahead of ours. During the two days I've been in Rome, I've noticed that people have an interesting way of queueing: a *let's all crowd together at the entrance and see who gives in and lets us through* strategy, and some of us visitors react negatively, and sometimes violently, to this behavior, including our very own tour guide. I observed several people getting new assholes chewed for themselves by irate single-file-is-the-rule followers, authoritarian people for whom rules are *not* made to be broken. Even with "V.I.P." tickets, and a take-no-prisoners tour guide, it took our group an hour to get inside.

Seeing the Raphael rooms (*The School of Athens*, forgetting to breathe again)[1] and the Sistine Chapel was to realize another decades-old dream, even though I was just catching glimpses of these works in the spaces between peoples' heads. The chapel and its famous ceiling is the Mecca of the Christian world and equally as crowded, and to observe the masses craning their necks to see the work, their eyes cast heavenward and their bodies bumping into each other, was an added entertainment I wasn't expecting. It was a miracle that no children were trampled as the crowd shuffled through the room. Since they couldn't see beyond all the adults' heads, some of them lay on the floor to claim more space to be able to view the ceiling. I was tempted to do the same.

I love that Michelangelo painted himself into *The Last Judgment*, his fresco of the second coming of Christ and the judgment of all humanity, as the flayed skin of the martyr St. Bartholomew with a long, droopy face.[2] How could one person, in his sixties, create such a work, plus all the other sculpture and architecture he contributed to Rome, deal with the dispiriting politics that undoubtedly went along with that, and not be utterly exhausted? Michelangelo himself was an artist-martyr, and that was his message.

He also had to endure the jealousy and competitiveness of his rival Leonardo da Vinci. Leonardo could be exceedingly cruel, comparing Michelangelo's renderings of the musculature of human bodies to "bags of nuts." You have to admit he was sort of right, in Michelangelo's paintings and drawings at least. If you examine his most famous fresco from the Sistine Chapel, *The Creation of Adam*, where God reaches out from what looks like a giant uterus to touch (almost, but not quite) Adam's finger, there's clearly a bag of nuts installed in Adam's inner left thigh.[3] Michelangelo never considered himself a painter and complained about the label; to his mind he was a sculptor. But in my opinion, his *David* has bigger problems than any of the Sistine Chapel frescoes, problems that were fixable. I'm talking about the giant head, hands, and feet, way out of proportion to the rest of his body. I'm not even planning to see it when I visit Florence; the Accademia Gallery charges twenty euros for fifteen minutes of time with the big guy, what a scam! Why spend that money when you can see an exact replica of *David* outside in the Piazza della Signoria and a bronze replica in the Piazzale Michelangelo, all three *David*s in Florence, two of them viewable for free?

Since the Sistine Chapel is a sacred space, no talking is allowed, and since no one honors that request, every few minutes a guard ceremoniously approaches a PA system and says "SHHHHHH" in a loud whisper into the microphone. Visitors respect the silence for a few moments, then the volume rises to a dull roar again. I think visitors shouldn't be allowed even to *breathe* in the Sistine Chapel; I couldn't help but think of all the moisturized air that was being expelled into the space, day in and day out, the fine aerosols of spit that shoot out of our mouths when we talk, and how that must affect the frescoes. Cave frescoes in Spain, France, India, and elsewhere have survived wars, earthquakes, and even vandals, but when visitors are allowed in, their breath corrodes the paint in no time. I hope the Vatican is putting away some of the heaps of cash they collect every day for future restoration. Or is considering providing full-face respirators to visitors, or at least a mandatory swish of bacteria-killing mouthwash at its entrance.

The Castel Sant'Angelo, with its statue of Archangel Michael on top, was only 750 meters from the Vatican, but I was just too exhausted to drag myself over to pay my respects. I hope he wasn't offended.

Sunday, May 15th

There's no monopoly on heads of state who are imbecilic liars and whose time in office was ruinous for their countries. Before there was Mussolini there was Victor Emmanuel, the first king of

Italy, the perfect subject for an ostentatious tribute: the Victor Emmanuel II National Monument, also known as the Altar of the Fatherland. Despite all his bad press, the unification of Italy is attributed to him.

I've noticed that the more art and architecture I see in Rome, the greedier I am for the hits of dopamine they trigger, and the Victor Emmanuel II Monument[4] intensified that desire. I wondered what it was about the design that made me feel greed and if Victor himself intended for the monument to evoke this feeling of insatiability. The curvature of the colonnade suggests both the enveloping arms of the Vatican's double colonnade and the unification of Italy, but there's also something avaricious about it, as if Victor's arms are encircling and dragging the chips from a successful poker game toward himself and is feeding on the misery of his crushed opponents. Was I mistaking Italian nationalistic pride for ostentatious excess, or could I trust my instincts on this?

At 5 p.m., when the afternoon heat had lifted, I walked to the Capitoline Museums, right behind the monument, the best collection of works representing Rome's antiquity, IMO. The original bronze equestrian statue of Marcus Aurelius is in the Capitoline, and so is the earliest known sculpture of Romulus and Remus suckled by the she-wolf. The colossal head, hand, and foot of Constantine are there, too; Bernini's *Bust of Medusa*, the *Dying Gaul*, and Caravaggio's *Fortune Teller*[5] are among the other great works housed in the Capitoline.

On the way, I saw a large flock of vultures in a spiraling flight pattern, slowly descending to their target. I set an intention and started counting. Twelve vultures, auspicious if you're an ancient Roman looking for guidance from the gods. Romulus counted twelve, Remus six, and Romulus got to choose the hill on which Rome was founded. My intention was far more modest. I just wanted to know if I'd be settled somewhere within six months. The answer was, yes.

The works in the Capitoline were largely pilfered from ancient ruins and installed in the collections of various popes when Pope Sixtus IV (pope from 1471 to 1484) "donated" the work to the museums. Open to the public in 1734, the museums house what we might consider the eighteenth century's version of Washington, D.C.'s portrait gallery, only the portraits are rendered in marble. Entering a room of these busts lined up on shelves, at your eye level, is like attending your fiftieth high school reunion and being overwhelmed by people you vaguely remember but can't quite put the name to the face. You see a visage, rendered in marble, that reminds you of the jock you had a crush on or the mysterious, dreamy poet who was never heard from again after graduation. As I left one of these galleries, I crossed paths with a young man and his girlfriend just as he passed his own ninth-century effigy. When I was back on the streets, I searched the crowd for faces I'd seen in the museums, and they were everywhere: two young women talking earnestly, a handsome young man sitting on his motorcycle smoking a cigarette, and a man with a noble, patrician profile. It's a funny illusion.

Back at the Airbnb, I sat on the couch to rest my feet and look through a coffee table book, a photographic history of Rome, *and there I was*, in black and white, on page 133.[6] The occasion was the Day of the Italian Flag, in 1915, and two girl scouts stood smiling at a handsome officer. A younger version of me held a box of small bouquets, while my companion pinned one of the bouquets on the officer's lapel. I texted the photo to a few friends for confirmation, and they all said, Yes, this is your doppelgänger. One person wrote, "She looks *exactly* like you!!"

Monday, May 16th

Why does eating have to be such a challenge? I'm starting to worry that all Rome has to offer is pizza and salad. Mid-afternoon yesterday I went to a restaurant on Via Urbana, highly recommended by my host and, in addition to pizza and salad, a few pasta selections heaped with olives were on the menu, and I detest olives. I ordered bottled water, and the waiter brought a carafe. The owner of the Airbnb had assured me that Roman water was safe to drink, so I poured half a glass and took a teeny sip, as if my taste buds could detect bacteria and parasites. A few minutes later, a waitress came by and substituted my carafe with a fresh one, making an utterance that signaled utter frustration. I wondered, What was wrong with the first one? I drank a little from carafe number two and decided I was pushing my luck. Ate half the pizza, half the salad, and asked for a to-go box. The waiter whisked the plates away, returned a few minutes later, and thwacked the table with my leftovers wrapped in aluminum foil, punctuating the action with a smirk and a dramatic folding of his arms. I've come to expect this kind of behavior in Rome: when you want to eat in a restaurant/enter a museum/get into a cab, supreme annoyance from the person you're inconveniencing. When buying provisions at the local grocery, and you're next in the queue, instead of greeting you the checkout person emits a big sigh, then does you a *huge* favor and rings up your items, and if they're packaged in a flat container (e.g., cold cuts and sliced cheese), he slaps them down on the counter as if he were swatting flies. When bagging your stuff, you must keep pace with the lightning speed at which he's checking you out because after he throws the receipt at you, he's already on to the next person. You worry that he's going to call security to escort you out. Plus, if you can't keep up, the shopper behind you gets annoyed, and you can just hear his thoughts: *Che idiota!*

While exiting the grocery, I remembered a painting in the Capitoline Museum of a single, human-size angel looking up to the heavens and doing a perfect Italian shrug.

Leaving the apartment two hours later than I'd intended, after successfully managing the fallout from yesterday's sketchy water, pizza, and salad, I walked to the Pantheon,[7] expecting a mob scene like at the Colosseum. But Rome's tourists weren't out in force yet, and although no one was particularly interested in creating a proper queue, I got in quickly. The Pantheon's current iteration is almost two thousand years old, and it's in amazing condition considering the accumulation of smoke and grime deposits and 130+ years of pollutants emitted since the invention of the internal combustion engine. Most of its Corinthian capitals still look crisp and well defined, and the arches of bricks constructed within its exterior walls are still doing their job of holding it all together. Those crafty Romans outsourced the Pantheon's sixteen forty-foot-tall columns to the Egyptians, and after being hewn and polished, they floated them up the Nile, across the Mediterranean, and up the Tiber River. At sixty tons each, they were dragged to the construction site about a mile away from the river. How is it that the ancients built all these great structures without the use of computers, forklifts, cranes, not even a jackhammer? We've got all this technology, and we build mega malls and roads that have potholes within a few years. Are we that lazy and stupid?

Tuesday, May 17th

The Amalfi Coast and Pompeii were today's destinations, and a large group of people congregated in the Piazza del Popolo, the piazza that fronts the Pantheon, at 7 a.m. for the guided tour. Its central feature is one of Rome's many Egyptian obelisks, sitting in the middle of a fountain surrounded by lions with jets of water issuing from their mouths. I read that the Romans had stolen the obelisk from Egypt, but maybe the Egyptians threw it in as a client appreciation gift after making delivery of the Pantheon's sixteen columns. While we awaited the tour guide, a seagull flew overhead and left a deposit on my hat and purse, a good reason to wear a hat when outdoors and carry a purse you don't care about particularly.

The Amalfi part of the journey took waaaay too long—how much time does a person need to spend exploring shops full of overpriced lemon-themed tablecloths, ceramic lemon napkin rings, soaps, linen clothing, underwear, flip-flops, whatever you could slap a lemon on, the town's trademark? Pompeii was waaaay too short and we were whisked through the main attractions, including a room with small, pornographic frescoes, a Kama Sutra of ancient Italy. In certain places, and from certain viewpoints, Pompeii has the eerie feel of a contemporary Roman city, and Vesuvius looks ominous in the distance. If I did the math correctly, I think the townspeople might have had two minutes to do their estate planning before being covered by the pyroclastic surge that came barreling down the mountain. When you see the plaster casts of the people recovered from Pompeii, the poses often suggest they were caught completely off-guard. One man clearly was asleep, lying on his side with his head resting on his hands, another leaning on an elbow, and a woman in a sitting fetal position, with her hands covering her face, distraught.[8] Seeing Pompeii and these figures, not just imagining the event as I did while lounging in the shadow of Arenal in Costa Rica, conveys the horror of that day with a visceral directness.

Wednesday, May 18th

I think I understand Rome as "the eternal city" in a slightly different way than, yeah, it's a really really old place. Guadalajara produced a *Groundhog Day* trapped-in-a-time-loop experience, repeating in its quotidian details, and Rome is the opposite of this. Rome is infinitely varied.

Because of this, Rome creates a particular set of anxieties. When I open the front door of the building and take those first steps out into the world, I wonder, *What will I need to do to survive the day's unknowns?* Rome is dense and detailed in every way, down to the small, thin bricks the ancient Romans used to build their colossal structures and the tiny tesserae used in the pictorial works in St. Peter's Basilica. Sensory overload is almost a continuous condition, much more than your brain can sort through and process. You could never really apprehend it all; you could roam Rome eternally and see the city in new ways every day.

Inserting yourself into the Roman mystery also has the effect of suspending your sense of the passage of time. Time feels like an unbroken cycle of day and night, containers of experience that are also part of a larger continuum. While in Rome, I've noticed that the best way the passage of time gets my attention is with the pragmatic demands of the body, like the need to cut my fingernails. It's a sudden awareness that even though the brain may not be experiencing time in its usual ways, the body is still engaged in its time-based process of change, discarding that which isn't useful to its functioning, decaying and disintegrating. Experiencing the feeling of suspension of time is a welcome sensation, substituting a different set of anxieties for these more *existential* worries. Living in a place that performs this function for a person feels judicious and rational!

I visited the Museo Nazionale Romano and the Barberini today. I tried to visit the Domus Aurea, Nero's over-the-top opulent palace, but when I tried breaching the locked gate, an old guard told me it was open only three days a week: Saturday and Sunday. When I asked him what the third day was, he held up three fingers and repeated: three days, Saturday and Sunday.

Thursday, May 19th

Rome has a patina. It's on everything. Even on the cherries I wanted to buy at the local market. When I touched one of them to test its firmness, it felt like it was coated in Sticky Tack. I bet I could have written my name in cherries on the wall outside, a wall patinated by decades of acidic drips from plants watered on the balconies above and, where the wall meets the sidewalk, glazed with urine and vomit stains. Like most huge cities, Rome has a trash problem, and trash containers are so infrequent you have to consult Google Maps to find one. Rome's cobblestones don't even look like stone anymore. After centuries of the city's grime being ground into the cobbles by horses and carts and cars and trucks and trod by millions of pedestrians, they have a burnished, pewter look that no amount of scrubbing could ever remove. Ancient statues, when they've been left outside, have a fine coating of particulates that have settled on the tops of their heads and shoulders and other surfaces of high relief. Pollution pocks their once-smooth skin and faces. If only they could step off their pedestals and into a shower.

I walked to the Museo Nazionale Romano, on the site of the Baths of Diocletian, which was what I wanted to see, but either you're not allowed to visit the baths, or they don't exist anymore. Of all the museums I've been to, this one was the least interesting. It's full of statues with their heads and hands cut off, and sometimes just the feet are left, attached to their pedestals, with the entire body missing.[9] A lot of real estate is given to terra-cotta pots dug up at sites around Rome, and their unsophisticated craftsmanship was surprising. When it comes to utilitarian objects, the ancient Romans don't have anything on the ancient Maya. I couldn't help but compare.

Friday, May 20th

Rick Steves cleared up the Baths of Diocletian mystery—it was repurposed, originally by Michelangelo, as the Basilica Santa Maria Degli Angeli. It still retains its impressive original structure, the interior at least a football field long, to use a contemporary reference, and one of its most majestic features are huge granite columns, five feet in diameter and twenty-four feet tall, that flank the transept. The entrance has a mini, Pantheon-like dome with a stained-glass oculus. In ancient times it was the tepidarium (the place where you cool off after steaming yourself in the caldarium) part of the baths. In the pocket edition of his travel book *Rome,* Steves writes that when in these ancient places, you should try either to imagine everyone walking around in togas or try to undress them and watch them bathing, doing jumping jacks, or wrestling. I'd really rather not do that, Rick, especially the jumping jacks part. What I'm sometimes inspired to do, usually in the sculpture galleries of a museum, is to drain people's faces, hair, and skin of color and imagine their eyes completely white and non-seeing, so they look like the marble statues I'm wandering among. It's surprising how many people actually look like what's been immortalized all around them.

Entrance to the Villa Borghese, the opulent art galleries constructed to house the family's collection, is by timed visit. The museum limits the number of people in the galleries and kicks out the previous group when their time is up, but if you hang out after the first hour of your two-hour time slot, the galleries mostly clear on their own and you have the place to yourself. The Borghese is where some of the most famous Bernini sculptures ended up: his version of *David*, whose face resembles Charlton Heston's, the abduction of Persephone by Hades, and a related sculpture, Apollo grabbing Daphne as she's turning into a laurel tree. A copy of Leonardo da Vinci's lost painting *Leda and the Swan*[10], executed by a member of Leonardo's workshop, hangs in the Borghese, not behind bulletproof glass and not monitored in any significant way. Weird, I thought, but maybe what's more weird is how we've fetishized the *Mona Lisa* and because of that, since the early 1800s it *has* been behind glass and is closely monitored. In the early 1950s, someone poured acid on her, she's had a rock thrown at her, and several attempts have been made to paint the canvas black. In 1911, it was stolen right off the wall at the Louvre and squirreled away in a trunk for over two years. What is it about Lisa that inspires such disrespect and actual violence? She's just sitting there, looking mysterious and passive, and maybe that's it, she's an easy target, a scapegoat. Let's throw Lisa under the bus for all the other art we despise or don't understand. On the other hand, Leda articulates our naughty, repressed shadow selves. The swan's encircling her (nude) right side with his wing and hissing in her ear, and she's got a knowing smirk on her face. It's interesting that this salacious image has never inspired a thief or an attacker and has never been censored from the public eye by the Catholic morality police. Is rape by swan just not that controversial?

Saturday, May 21ˢᵗ

Hadrian's Villa and the Villa d'Este on the agenda today. See Chapter Twenty, "Grace," for context.

Outside in the Villa d'Este's expansive gardens, among five hundred water features, is its showpiece: an over-the-top baroque structure, its domed space flanked by four grumpy male caryatids with folded arms.[11] Who could blame them, when large Doric scrolls are pressing down on their heads? Above them, four female caryatids clutch their distended stomachs, as if to say, Where's the Tums? Bizarrely, their legs twist into corkscrew shapes that drill into their pedestals. In the middle of this grouping is an elaborately carved shrine, called an aedicule, and inside is a special surprise. At 2:30 p.m., a door opens, like a cuckoo clock, and reveals a small pipe organ. A powerful cascade of water falls behind the organ and operates a pump that forces air into the pipes, driving the turning of a cylinder with protruding pins on its surface. Like a music box or a player piano, the water organ plays set melodies, mostly Renaissance-era madrigals, and the pitches are amazingly accurate. I thought it might be fun to do an update: change out the cylinder with one that plays the restless ostinato of "In-A-Gadda-Da-Vida" and reengineer the five hundred fountains to pulse their jets of water to the beat. The water organ probably couldn't handle the arpeggios, though.

On the bus back to Rome, I overheard the man sitting behind me say, "I squeeze my nose too much." Later, his wife said, "Where ARE we?" He replied, "Who cares?"

Rome's urban planners consider it imperative to put SPQR on as many things public as they can get away with, like someone who obsessively monograms her stuff: sheets and towels, notepads and stationery, a favorite tote, a tissue box cover, her hubcaps. SPQR means *Senatus Populusque Romanus*, the Senate and Roman people, and was first used when Rome became a republic around 80 BCE. We've all seen it in Roman-themed movies, like *Ben-Hur*, *Spartacus*, *Fellini Satyricon*, and *Gladiator*, emblazoned on legionnaires' protective gear and on Roman banners. Today you see it on metal garbage containers[12] (when you can find them), on grates in the street, on streetlights, on many public buildings and, thanks to Mussolini, on manhole covers, thinking it made an effective propaganda tool to promote his dictatorship. He was counting on people looking down at the sidewalk as much as I do. I learned that the popular meaning of SPQR had evolved: *Sono pazzi, questi Romani*. They're crazy, these Romans.

CHAPTER TWENTY

GRACE

Colleen pulled the heavy wooden door shut, double-checked the license plate number on her phone's Uber app, and breathed a sigh of relief when she saw the same number on the car waiting in front of the Airbnb. She was in Rome, an unfamiliar city, and had signed up for a tour headed to Hadrian's Villa and the Villa d'Este, about an hour's drive northeast of the city. The Uber conveyed her to the tour group's meeting point, a poorly marked bus stop in a neighborhood close by, where she arrived forty-five minutes early. Her anxiety about being the annoying person who is late and holds everybody up or, worse, the one who gets left behind, had kept her awake since 4 a.m., and now she stood on a nearly deserted street wondering if anyone else would show up. The meeting point was near a stairway leading to a permanently closed subway station, and anyone who lives in a city with an underground knows these places are magnets for trash and other quotidian discardables. The station was close to a McDonald's, and there lay the evidence of a supersized Rome, mixed in with dirty T-shirts and scuffed shoes and plastic bottles and Styrofoam food containers, although she didn't think the subway station was intended to be repurposed as a municipal solid waste facility or a Goodwill. Looking into this pit of despair raised her misanthropic hackles while, simultaneously, something was tickling her nose. She hated sneezing into her N95; all those little droplets of mucus had nowhere else to go but back into her face, so she tried suppressing the sneeze. But that rarely works. A small Ziploc in the depths of her purse held some tissues and an emergency supply of toilet paper and, as she extracted a tissue, two wads of TP came flying out and landed at her feet. The toilet paper's pristine whiteness contrasted with the gray griminess of the sidewalk and looked nothing like the other seasoned trash lying around. In an instant, Colleen found herself facing a moral dilemma: *Do I pick it up and stuff it back into my purse or a pocket, or do I leave it on the ground and pretend it's not mine?* Clearly, she had been the litterer, contributing to Rome's trash problem immediately after having so bitterly scorned *the others* who had littered before her.

Ignoring the evidence of her carelessness, she checked WhatsApp for new messages while considering the options. She wasn't proud of her decision, but she stepped over the wads of TP and approached the group that had begun to assemble for the excursion. She talked to a woman from Peru for ten minutes or so, their friendly chatter erasing the memory of the petty crime she had committed only a few moments earlier. Suddenly, another woman came rushing across the street, and Colleen panicked. Was she about to be busted? The woman dropped to her knees close to where Colleen stood and began gathering rose petals that had collected where the street met the curb. She was careful to pick up every single one and, task completed, she stood up and happily announced to the group that the petals were for Saint Gemma, the patron saint of those seeking purity of heart, whose effigy was in a church around the corner. Clutching her offering, she sprinted off in that direction, blissful and beaming.

The woman's example made Colleen consider her own negative response to trash. What if she could think of trash as rose petals and not be so repulsed by it? Then she could forgive everyone, including herself, who had littered, and focus her attention on the astonishing beauty that, if she would shift her focus away from the sidewalk, was everywhere around her.

CHAPTER TWENTY-ONE

WALKING THE CAMINO:
THE VIA FRANCIGENA

Sunday, May 22nd

For my last day in Rome, I'd rented a place close to the Roma Termini train station. The idea was to minimize the schlep to the train I'd booked to Florence, connecting to San Miniato, the starting point for the Via Francigena. Pre-schlep, I walked the route, much longer than it looked on the map, but I told myself, I've walked farther in airports with heavy bags before, so I can do this, too. On the actual schlep, I left midmorning and walked on the shady sides of the streets and where the cobblestones weren't too bumpy. I'd seen some street repair guys cementing in the gaps between the stones the day before. The process was like grouting a mosaic—you mix up the cement, squeegee it into the cracks, and wipe the higher stone surfaces clean. During the walk, the difficulty was the backpack, not the heavy suitcase, unbalanced and too flimsy for what was inside. No padded straps. Maybe somewhere along the camino route, REI will have set up a table of pre-used hiking gear to sell to underprovisioned pilgrims.

The train from Rome to Florence was at nearly 100 percent capacity; challenging, because 70 to 80 percent of us had big suitcases that needed seats of their own. Like a typical long-distance bus, an angled, metal shelf installed over the seats ran the length of the train car and held airplane regulation-size carry-ons and backpacks, so people with oversized suitcases had to improvise. All passengers had assigned seats, and mine was part of a foursome: two seats facing two other seats with an unanticipated space-hogging table in between. I had a window seat. If need be, I'd planned on hoisting my suitcase into the seat and sitting on top of it—not terribly comfortable, and I'd have to sit in a fetal position so my head would fit under the rack—but the volume of real estate I'd rented on the train didn't entitle me to space beyond the armrest. But no way could I maneuver my suitcase past the table and into the seat, so I sat in the aisle hoping no one was going to complete the foursome. Two video game-playing young men wearing earbuds were already seated across from me and didn't seem to mind that I'd slid my suitcase under the table, appropriating valuable foot room. And I got lucky. The doors closed, and no one claimed the aisle seat. Lesson learned: when traveling on a potentially packed train, like Rome to Florence, and you're schlepping more than a small backpack and a purse, buy two seats together. It won't set you back that many euros and you'll have plenty of space. Well, maybe not plenty, but sufficient.

Each time the train approached a station, a recorded announcement reminded passengers that, in Italy, the trains are punctual. For example: "We are now arriving, ON TIME, at Poggibonsi, at 13:52." I wondered, Was the insertion of the phrase "on time" a nod to Mussolini?

In Florence, I caught the train to our camino starting point, San Miniato. The train had an abundance of space and was a short ride to its destination. The San Miniato train station was a little larger than a bus transit shelter and no queue of taxis was waiting to pick up disembarked passengers. In fact, there were no taxis at all, only a few tumbleweeds blowing through the parking lot and the cawing of a European crow, the sound effect used in

Italian movies to signal sadness and desolation. One of my camino companions had WhatsApped me a few minutes before arriving at the station to warn that taxis and buses weren't running because of a town holiday. She'd arrived several hours earlier but didn't share by what means she was transported to the hotel and, after sending that single helpful message, she'd either put her phone on airplane mode or was laughing at my panicked replies and ghosting me.

Google Maps calculated the walk from the train station to the hotel: fifty minutes with an all-uphill elevation gain of five hundred feet. I dialed the hotel. A friendly, English-speaking man picked up and said he'd send a taxi. One thing I remember to tell myself when assuming I can rely on other people's information is never to assume I can rely on other people's information, and never to believe in absolutes.

The hotel was indeed at the top of a winding, steep road and built close to the town tower: an architectural feature that is the norm in Tuscany. My room was at the top of a winding, steep staircase, and when I flung open the window to enjoy the view, disturbing some mating pigeons, a landscape of unanticipated verdant beauty lay before me.[1] Puccini's aria "O mio babbino caro," the (overused) theme music from the film *A Room With a View*, flooded my brain. I tried thinking of a good descriptor to express what I saw, "stunning" coming closest because, for me, stunning implies a kind of shock that halts your breathing and takes a few moments to recover from (think: stun gun). But "stunning" is also overused and has never really done the job. Actually, none of these descriptors are adequate. "Magnificent" comes close. Amazeballs, really?

"O mio" became an earworm I couldn't shake. I headed out to climb the tower. A guy wanting four euros sat in a glass booth that blocked the entrance, and I didn't need to part with the money to gain forty more feet of elevation when I was already five hundred feet higher than where I'd started out. So I took a pass.

How was walking the Via Francigena² leading me closer to deciding where to live? Wasn't this merely a diversion? Yes and no. After being alone for three weeks, it was going to be great to have the company of two friends, Anatha and Laurie, who had flown in from the Pacific Northwest. I knew that neither of them would make huge conversational demands because they were both hoping to have a spiritual experience, which is the number one reason why people walk the caminos, and a lot of yakking about this and that does not usually lead to transcendence. But there was another reason why I was walking the camino. I'd run across a couple of helpful bits of wisdom that I thought could inform my quest for place. According to filmmaker Werner Herzog, "The world reveals itself to those who travel on foot." Predating and uncredited by Herzog, St. Augustine wrote, *Solvitur ambulando*, it is solved by walking. I was hoping they were right and after walking the Via Francigena, I'd know for sure where I should live.

Monday, May 23rd

People have traveled the camino for centuries, and these days it's become a cliché, but in the Middle Ages, pilgrims believed their exertions would reduce the punishment they'd receive in the afterlife for their sins. They started in Canterbury, England, walked through France and Switzerland and Italy to Rome, then caught a boat that sailed through the Mediterranean to the Holy Land. More than two thousand miles. Today, we're doing good if we make it from San Miniato to Siena, a journey of around eighty kilometers, or fifty miles, that takes an hour to drive.

Here's a brief history of the Via Francigena, first walked by Sigeric the Serious, the Archbishop of Canterbury *(cousin of Philip the Flippant?)*, whose writer forgot to proof his work:

> In 990, he traveled from Canterbury in England to Rome to receive his palladium and for Pope John XV to ordain him as a Cardinal. *(I think the writer meant* pallium, *which is a special vestment bestowed by a pope; palladium is an element that was discovered in 1803 and is highly toxic.)* On his return to Canterbury, Sigeric documented the places he stayed in a journal. The walk took him 80 days to complete and covered a total of about 1,700 km.[3]

Sigeric, the first traveler of the Via Francigena, walked an average of twenty-one kilometers per day, about thirteen miles, to become a cardinal. Our trek, considered easy, averaged eleven miles a day, and we had no expectation of receiving an ordination from the pope. This was the schedule:

> First day: San Miniato to Gambassi Terme, 23 kilometers (14.29 miles), estimated eight hours of walking.
> Second day: Gambassi Terme to San Gimignano, 17 kilometers (10.5 miles), estimated six hours of walking.

Third day: San G to Colle di Val d'Elsa, 13 kilometers (8 miles), estimated six hours of walking.
Fourth day: Colle di Val d'Elsa to Monteriggioni, 14 kilometers (8.7 miles), estimated six hours of walking.
Fifth day: Monteriggioni to Siena, 23 kilometers (another 14.29 miles), estimated eight hours of walking.[4]

The company with which we arranged the trek ferried our bags to and from each of our nightly accommodations, and I had to decide what were essentials—the things I would have a hard time replacing if lost—and carry those things with me. Just in case. This included: my wallet, passport, immunization record, itinerary, the U.S. SIM card removed from my phone, Calcet for leg cramps, Advil, Valium for a potential panic attack, Imodium, electrolyte replacement drops, phone charger, an umbrella, sunglasses, an extra pair of reading glasses. And of course, plenty of water: four 600-milliliter bottles, weighing about five and a half pounds total, and a Grayl water purifier. We weren't sure we'd be able to buy or even find water anywhere.

At 8:15 a.m. we were conveyed, by car, five kilometers to a place on the trail that got us out of town and into the countryside. I was nervous. My big fear was getting stuck out on the trail somewhere, needing assistance, and no one answers the emergency line. It was too early in the game to start relying on Valium.

The cool weather lasted until 10:30 and by then we were walking through endless tracts of wheat fields. I was already getting hungry, and my rations included a small piece of cake from breakfast and a few cashews. Because of the holiday, there'd been no place in San Miniato to provision ourselves the night before. I tried to keep happy music playing in my head, mainly Beethoven's *Pastoral* Symphony, and the images of Kewpie doll centaurs gamboling in an idyllic meadow from *Fantasia*. After I ran through the *Pastoral* a few times, I switched to the scene from *Monty Python and the Holy Grail* where King Arthur (Graham Chapman) rides a fictitious horse and Patsy, his aide-de-camp

(Terry Gilliam), uses a pair of coconut shells to make the sound of a horse cantering on cobblestone. I had to play these games with myself to keep going, but I would often default to thoughts about the Bataan Death March from World War II, where eighty thousand American and Filipino soldiers were forcibly marched sixty miles from one POW camp to another, and many didn't survive. Our march was only ten miles short of theirs.

I contemplated the term *pilgrim*—which is what we walkers of the caminos are called—and the idea of pilgrimage, journeying to a holy place or shrine to venerate relics or other special objects, or the place itself. Since that was not my intent, I felt, vaguely, like a fraud, an imposter. I had my reasons, other than to help identify Location X, all ego driven:

> Because it's not something most people do.
> To wring the last little bit of youthful energy from my body before I enter a state of complete decrepitude.
> To say that I had done it.

Fun was officially off the table.

By 2 p.m. the temperature had risen to ninety-one degrees, and we'd been walking nearly six grueling hours. My water had reached a slow simmer, and I wanted to rip off my clothes and finish the walk in only my hat and shoes. I resisted looking at my phone to see how close we were to our destination. Soon enough, a sign appeared that said six kilometers to Gambassi Terme, a surprise and a relief. Six kilometers is a little less than four miles, and I'd been thinking we were still six miles away. That last stretch, though, included a one-thousand-foot elevation gain, a diabolical penance imposed on exhausted pilgrims.

I tried the emergency phone number to see if it worked, and nobody picked up.

Tuesday, May 24th

Only ten blessèd miles from Gambassi Terme to San Gimignano,[5] four miles fewer than yesterday's trek. A beautiful Tuscan landscape unfolded, carpeted with electric orange poppies and ancient, gnarly grapevines, dotted with farms with stone houses and barns, and green hills—requiring lots of slogging up and down—cut with rocky paths occasionally shaded by ancient cypress trees. We stopped at the Sanctuary at Pancole, an obscure holy site, because we'd heard it housed an important fifteenth-century Madonna and Child painting, but I was more interested in a black-and-white photo mounted on a wall of two kids, a girl and an older boy. The boy may have been lame in one leg—he was leaning on a crude wooden crutch—or maybe he had blisters from walking up and down hills day in and day out. The girl had a ferocious scowl and a penetrating gaze. The wall text explained that she was a deaf-mute and had seen a vision of the Blessed Virgin Mary, who cured her of her deficiencies and provided her family with provisions like flour, oil, and wine. The sanctuary had been built, in 1670, because of the deaf-mute girl's vision. Something was off about the timeline, though. The world's first photograph was taken in 1826. A miracle, indeed.

I was also intrigued by a smaller-than-life-size crucifix that featured a Jesus with skinned knees,[6] as if he'd been in a roller-skating accident right before being nailed to the cross.

After yesterday's thousand-foot ascent to Gambassi Terme, I understood. These medieval Tuscan towns were built on the highest hills available and fortified with sky-scraping stone walls—no moats needed here—not to torture pilgrims walking the camino but for protection from marauding neighbors. In the third millennium, now that this is no longer an issue, you'd think these towns would be more tourist friendly since their economies rely so heavily on us. A funicular or two would be nice, some rent-a-donkeys to convey weary passengers to the town gate, or at least a sturdy rope we could hold onto, to help our ascent, would be a welcoming gesture. I pitied anyone without at least an inch-deep tread on the soles of their shoes. One false step in loose gravel could send you tumbling down the path and into a Sisyphean loop to attain the top.

San Gimignano had not one but two torture museums, as if we pilgrims needed educating on the subject of torture. Where you could see such things as the Iron Maiden, a metal coffin shaped like a person that when closed, penetrated a body with sharp spikes; the Inquisitorial Chair, also covered in spikes, where a naked person was seated and if not forthcoming with whatever the inquisitor wanted to know, the chair could be heated, rocked, or in more contemporary times, electrified. It gets even more gruesome than this, but let's stop right here.

Wednesday, May 25th

I started today's walk with two sizeable blisters, one each at the base of the big toes, which I learned is called the metatarsophalangeal (MTP) joint. After completing nine miles, I was a wreck. We were expecting to walk 11 km (6.8 miles), a nominally insignificant difference, but when every single step of the 25,000+ ones I took delivered an agonizing jab, this extra distance became the podiatrical equivalent of a Penitente slapping himself on the back with a flagellant while wearing a hair shirt. Was mortification of the flesh a common practice while walking the camino? I asked Google to help me dig a little deeper and, yes, this is something you do in solidarity with Jesus. Since our fleshly bodies crave comfort and pleasure, it follows that the more you punish yourself physically in this life, the lighter your sentence will be in the next, so I *think* walking with blisters is an activity that qualifies. Perhaps I missed an opportunity back at the torture museum. I could have flung myself into the Inquisitorial Chair and taken care of a lot of sin all at once instead of doing it one painful step at a time. I tried thinking of it in those terms, that I was expiating my sins with each step, but really what I wanted was some analgesic cream, a place to put my feet up, and an ice-cold Mexican Coke.

Arriving in the medieval town of Colle di Val d'Elsa was the cruelest joke of all. After climbing climbing climbing in hot hot hot afternoon temperatures, we descended an endless spiraling hill into town, mimicking Virgil's descent into the Inferno. I thought my throbbing big toes were going to burst through their shoes from the relentless ramming ramming ramming, but they did not, a testament to the (questionable?) quality of Hokas, my expensive and blister-fostering hiking shoes.

When walking the camino was just too much, and nothing else helped, my thoughts turned to Cabeza de Vaca. Álvar Núñez Cabeza de Vaca (head of the cow) was one of several Spanish explorers we learned about in elementary school, maybe in part because of his name, which was funny and memorable to a seven-year-old. Even though the Spanish colonial period officially started with Christopher Columbus in 1492, Cabeza and his men were credited with being the first Europeans to explore the interior of Florida, Texas, New Mexico, Arizona, and northern México. He walked from Galveston, Texas, to México City, a camino of over 2,400 miles, without anyone to carry his luggage to the next stopover or to provide food and wine at the end of the day. He was a competent, engaging writer, and his report to the king of Spain reveals what a harrowing ten-year odyssey, between 1527 and 1537, that walk was. Hurricanes, shipwrecks, hostile natives, dysentery, malaria, starvation, no GPS, you name it, they experienced it. Only four out of three hundred men survived the expedition, and Cabeza de Vaca's ability to endure rested largely on his talent for adapting to the people and situations, in a superhuman kind of way, that he encountered on his journey and on his facility for identifying with Native Americans. He was resourceful and levelheaded. After losing his clothes when a barge capsized in the Gulf of México, he wandered naked and shoeless, his hairy body and bearded face frightening and intimidating the natives he encountered, and he used this to his advantage. He became widely known as a healer; often his remedy consisted of first blowing on his patient and then making the sign of the cross (what we might call the placebo effect), and he treated thousands of Indians successfully. He amassed what is considered in modern times an amazing amount of anthropological information on tribes and places, no doubt helpful to Spain's future explorations of the "new world."

I carried his narrative with me, entitled *La Relación* (The Relating of the Tale)[7], in case I needed perspective.

From Chapter 10, "Our departure from Aute"

(Aute is a short distance from the mouth of the Apalachicola River, which forms at the state line of Georgia and Florida and flows to the Gulf of México between Panama City and Tallahassee. It was from there that Cabeza and his men embarked to cross the Gulf of México, which they called the North Sea, haha!)

> . . . it was painfully clear to all that we were unprepared to go further. Had we been prepared, we still did not know where to go; and the men could not move, most of them lying prone and those able to stand to duty very few. I will not prolong this unpleasantness; but you could imagine what it would be like in a strange, remote land, destitute of means either to remain or get out.

From Chapter 11, "The Building of our Barges and Our Departure from the Bay"

> . . . the sides of the barges remained hardly a half a foot above water; and we were jammed in too tight to move. Such is the power of necessity that we should thus hazard a turbulent sea, none of us knowing anything about navigation.

From Chapter 17, "A Sinking and a Landing"

> It was winter and bitterly cold, and we had suffered hunger and the beating of waves for many days. Next day, the men began to collapse. By sunset, all in my barge had fallen over

on one another, close to death. Few were any longer conscious. Not five could stand. When night fell, only the navigator and I remained able to tend the barge. Two hours after dark he told me I must take over; he believed he was going to die that night.

From Chapter 19, "The Indians' Hospitality Before and After a New Calamity" (This is how Cabeza lost his clothes)

> Being provided with what we needed (by the Indians), we thought to embark again. It was a struggle to dig our barge out of the sand it had sunk in, and another struggle to launch her. For the work in the water while launching, we stripped and stowed our clothes in the craft.
>
> Quickly clambering in and grabbing our oars, we had rowed two crossbow shots from the shore when a wave inundated us. Being naked and the cold intense, we let our oars go. The next big wave capsized the barge. . . We lost only those the barge took down; but the survivors escaped as naked as they were born, with the loss of everything we had. That was not much, but valuable to us in that bitter November cold, our bodies so emaciated we could easily count every bone and looked the very picture of death. I can say for myself that from the month of May I had eaten nothing but corn, and that sometimes raw. I could never bring myself to eat any of the horse-meat at the time our beasts were slaughtered; and fish I did not taste ten times. On top of everything else, a cruel north wind commenced to complete our killing.

From Chapter 26, "The Coming of the Indians with Dorantes, Castillo, and Estevánico" (The other three men who survived the trip; Estevánico was a Black African slave Cabeza brought with him.)

> . . . the Indians who had Alonso del Castillo and Andrés Dorantes reached the place we had been told of, to eat pe-

cans. These are ground with a kind of small grain and furnish the sole subsistence of the people for two months of the year . . . The prickly pear [or tuna, the fruit of the Opuntia cactus] is the size of a hen's egg, bright red and black in color, and good-tasting. The natives live solely on it three months of the year.

From Chapter 30, "The Life of the Mariames and Yguaces"

I can declare from sad experience that there is no torment in the world equal to it. (hunger)

From Chapter 33, "Our Success with Some of the Afflicted and My Narrow Escape"

I would go into the low woods by the river before sunset to prepare myself for the night. First I hollowed out a hole in the ground and threw in fuel, of which there was plenty from the fallen, dry trees in the woods. Then I built four fires around the hole in the form of a cross, and slept in this hole with my fuel supply, covering myself with bundles of the coarse grass which grows thick in those parts. Thus I managed to shelter from the cold of night.

From Chapter 44, "Rabbit Hunts and Processions of Thousands"

Every Indian brought his portion to us to be breathed on and blessed before he would dare touch it. When you consider that we were frequently accompanied by three or four thousand Indians and were obliged to sanctify the food and drink of each one, as well as grant permission for the many things they asked to do, you can appreciate our inconvenience. The women would bring us prickly pears, spiders, worms—whatever they might gather—strictly forgoing even these until we had made the sign of the cross over them, though the women might have been starving at the time.[6]

So, you see, I really had very little to complain about or be bothered by. At those times I wanted to rid myself of my clothes (but not shoes, hat, and water) and just get the damn walk over with, I would think of Cabeza. Endurance and acceptance, and their larger meanings, was what the camino was teaching me.

Thursday, May 26th

A fire raged inside my shoes, distracting me from the sweetness of a partly cloudy sky, cool temps, and a shaded walk through a riparian area. We wouldn't have known about this four-kilometer route if the woman at the front desk of the Colle de Val d'Elsa hotel hadn't mentioned it, because the official camino path led pilgrims through a dry, treeless field overlooking the river, no doubt to inflict more torture. The river path eventually did connect with the camino and led us through an expansive agricultural area, with a great view of the walled medieval town of Monteriggioni in the distance. If it had been painted green, it could have been Oz. Whenever we found ourselves on a flat, treeless expanse of land, with our hiking goal visible in the distance, I noticed an interesting illusion. No matter how close we got, the horizon seemed to be receding, as if we were on an airport people-mover walking backward. When the terrain transitioned to hilly and forested, it felt like we were covering ground more quickly. It must be related somehow to the moon illusion, where our brain's size-distance mechanism needs to see the moon in relation to other familiar objects to make sense of its magnitude. While it looks huge when it first rises—because we see it in relation to the horizon, buildings, and trees—when no objects are nearby for context, the higher it is in the sky, the smaller it seems.

In order to take a photo of my companions at Monteriggioni's magnificent entry gate, I had to stand on a hill angled at forty-five degrees, leaning into it to keep my footing. Despite having blisters on top of blisters, I scrambled all over Monteriggioni and climbed to the top of its windswept walls, in two different places, for views of the countryside we'd recently traversed.

A man driving a red beater Jeep arrived to take us to our accommodation, the Colombaio, a beautiful ancient farmhouse with its own wine production facility. Tuscany is full of what they call agritourism places, a fancy name for a hotel stay in the midst of a vineyard. The Colombaio was our best accommodation so far: classic Tuscan, friendly people, great food and wine, great shower, comfy bed. "O mio babbino caro" was stuck in my head again. If I could choose theme music for this book, it would be "O mio" sung by Renée Fleming, "This Time Tomorrow" by the Kinks, "Road to Nowhere" by the Talking Heads, and specifically for this chapter, the last line of "These Boots Are Made for Walking," the Nancy Sinatra version ("Are you ready, boots? Start walkin.'") If you're curious, visit the Internet for lyrics.

Friday, May 27th

Anatha and I took the bus to Siena while Laurie walked the remaining twenty kilometers of the trail. I might have attempted it, painful feet and all, but I wanted to see Siena and hadn't budgeted time into my itinerary for doing that. The bus took us right up to the gate of the old part of the city.

The Siena Duomo and its alternating bands of white and black stone reminded me of the U.S.'s black-and-white-striped prison uniforms of the nineteenth century. The Duomo's interior was visually busy and dizzying.[8] Scenes from the Bible were created in cut marble, like a child's giant jigsaw puzzle, and installed in the floor; King Herod's genocidal massacre of Bethlehem's infants was a standout. Now that I've seen lots and lots of Renaissance-era art in Italy, I've noted that several biblical themes make their appearance again and again. Here's the list: the Madonna and Childs and crucifixes that are everywhere, Judith beheading Holofernes, St. Sebastian's torso as target practice, St. John's head on a platter.[9] Human sacrifice and incest, abduction and rape. The six o'clock news of the

Renaissance, no doubt designed to terrify its viewers and keep them close to home and subservient to church and state.

Italy's restaurant schedules seldom align with demanding American appetites, and it's a challenge to find places open when you want to eat. Don't even think about dinner before 7:30 p.m., and if you sit outside at one of their tables, waiting for the restaurant to open, the waiters chase you off as if scattering pigeons. Anatha and I were hungry for an early lunch and, after lots of wandering, found an inexpensive pasta place run by two young women clearly suffering from whatever the Italian version of ennui is called. Anatha wears Invisalign teeth realignment retainers and, true to their name, they are practically invisible. So when she removed them, placed them in their special box, dropped the box on the floor, and the box popped open, they vanished. It didn't help that the floor was a dark gray terrazzo speckled with white. We both got down on our hands and knees looking for them, rearranging tables and chairs and sweeping the dirty floor with the sides of our hands, providing amusement for the other diners. Anatha found the lowers but neither of us could find the uppers. In the meantime, the bored young women were walking back and forth across the floor delivering food and drink and possibly stepping on the uppers or getting them stuck in the deep grooves of their tennis shoes. A group of young men, also suffering ennui Italian-style, entered the restaurant to drink espresso and flirt with the young women, so I crept to the back of the restaurant and found a broom. Before any of the staff noticed, I had swept the entire dining area, around the tables and under the chairs, and finally, in a substantial pile of dirt, the Invisalign upper became visible. Not the nicest medium in which to find something that you will place inside your mouth, but mothers do this all the time with dropped pacifiers thinking it will activate their babies' immune systems.

Total walking over the past four days came to 67 kilometers, which sounds a lot more impressive than its equivalent in miles, 41.6. Thirteen miles short of my goal, but my feet were grateful for the reprieve. My assessment of the benefits of walking the camino? In Tuscany, you experience one of the world's most beautiful walkable landscapes. When you have blisters on your feet, your attention is unwaveringly in the present, and every step is meaningful. Like a successful meditation session, walking with blisters creates both a razor-sharp focus on a single pursuit, in this case, putting one foot in front of the other; and a suspended sense of time, reminiscent of what I experienced in Rome. I didn't see a vision of the Blessèd Virgin, and I didn't feel that I had reduced my sins by any significant number, but I did gain a certain sense of satisfaction for having put those miles behind me.

What I also realized from our perambulations is that walking the Via Francigena was a metaphor for my quest for permanency, and that taking one's time, step by step, to discover that place was the way to arrive. Even though ten to twelve miles a day was an awfully slow way to get closer to that place, *solvitur ambulando*.

CHAPTER TWENTY-TWO

FLORENCE

Monday, May 30th

It's high time I expand on a topic I've largely been ignoring but that has been on my mind, a minimum of three times a day, for the entire trip. That should be enough of a hint to know what I'm talking about. It's food. I don't have the best relationship with it, and not only when I'm traveling. I can enter a Whole Foods, survey the store, and think, There's nothing to eat in here. Those are the days when I've waited too long to eat plus I'm thinking about the narrative leading up to the beef lasagna I'm staring at, that poor, processed cow layered between noodles and two types of cheese, encased in a plastic container. Or when I peruse the salad bar, I think about the droplets of sneeze and drool that have slid down the plexiglass splash guard onto the sliced hard-boiled eggs. I think about all the unwashed hands of customers who have squeezed the bread to determine its freshness, and who have opened berry containers, popped a few in their mouths, and replaced the container if the berries were lacking in a certain tartness or cellular integrity. The soups with their multiple and varied ingredients look suspicious, and should I find something in one of them—a fingernail, for example—a loss of appetite for at least a few days may follow. Once, while eating a high school cafeteria lunch, I found a staple in my portion of meatloaf and, up to then, meatloaf had been one of the cow-based foods I could force down because of the "loaf" part of its name. Loaf meant bread, right? And meatloaf was crustless, a plus. I hated crust as a kid and made my mom cut it off or I wouldn't eat the (Wonder Bread) sandwich she put in front of me. When she introduced me to olive loaf, I realized that "loaf" was a euphemism employed to distract consumers from its horrors. Olive loaf consists of cow and pig parts rendered into a rubbery, pink gel, embedded with pimento-stuffed green olives, compressed into a bread loaf pan, and thinly sliced. It looks exactly like a human tissue sample with multiple, gangrenous tumors as seen through a microscope. If you survive eating this without developing a lifelong aversion to olives and meat, congratulations! On a related subject, blood, tongue, head, and cheese are four things that just do not belong together either in a sentence or in a sausage casing.

If I found a bug in the lemonade that accompanied my crustless Wonder Bread sandwich, my dad would say, "Don't worry, he didn't drink that much." I've tried to adopt that carefree attitude as an adult, but when your inner voice is constantly second-guessing what you're about to put in your mouth, and that voice tends to be squeamish and skeptical, a bug in your glass of lemonade is grounds for discarding the entire pitcher.

Those are just a few of the challenges of eating domestically, but what about travel? Travel introduces additional eating unknowns into the mix that you might take for granted at home. The two main ones are: you don't know if the person(s) who prepared your food followed good hygiene practices, and you don't know the freshness or cleanliness of the ingredients. If either one is not up to the standard your gut microbiota expect, they may rebel. Sometimes you don't know what a new food in a new country is supposed to taste or smell like, and that's an additional complication. For example, today I ate a mini-quiche, tomato and cheese, and it had an unpleasant smell I couldn't quite nail and a flavor I didn't like. Halfway into the quiche I realized it was the cheese, not that someone had vomited into the whisked eggs before popping the quiche into the oven. When it comes to digestive issues, traveling leaves no room for error. And anesthetizing your gut with Imodium, so you can carry on, may have unintended consequences.

I was so delighted to find that here in Italy, even at last-resort food places at the train stations, you can buy a crustless, white bread sandwich. It's thrilling to be in a place where the people understand the crustless sandwich aesthetic. Italy gets points for this.

On the way to Florence's iconic Duomo Cathedral, at around 9:30 a.m., a female figure was prostrated on the street between two parked cars, her backside facing up and her head lying on folded arms on the sidewalk. She was covered head to toe with a dirty brown mantle, and the only part of her anatomy that was visible was a supplicating, upturned hand that emerged from the cloth. A flimsy plastic cup, like the kind wrapped in cellophane in cheap motel bathrooms, sat next to her hand to receive donations. How could anyone not respond to such a submissive posture and desperate plea for funds?

Jesus got his revenge today for the snarky remark I wrote about his skinned knees. On the way to the Piazzale Michelangelo, just as I was stepping into the street that parallels the Arno, my left ankle collapsed, and I went down right in front of a nice British family walking toward me. My first impulse was to apologize to them saying, *I hope I didn't frighten you.* I managed to get up immediately and gracefully and was surprised by how painless the experience was. They were asking if I was all right in their blubbering English way, and I assured them that I was. I thanked them profusely for taking interest in a clumsy old Yank who had taken a tumble on the cobblestones and, as we went our separate ways, the family unit's little girl turned around and asked again, sweetly, if I was all right. Maybe I reminded her of her granny. Within a few moments I began to bleed through my pants, and when I got to the Piazzale, at the top of yet another impossible hill, I bought a bottle of cold water, doused the knee, and kept going. Back at the apartment, I saw that I'd given myself a formidable gash in the fleshy part just under the kneecap, the optimal place in which to inflict injury to a knee. I may need a stitch or two.

Tuesday, May 31st

Today, the Uffizi, and like the Alhambra, a place I've dreamed of visiting for decades. Seeing Botticelli's work in person made me cry. Seeing hordes of young men and women lining up to take selfies using *The Birth of Venus*[1] as a background made me want to scream. Practiced smiles, puckered lips, come-hither looks, gang gestures. I wanted to look at Venus close-up, so I dared to penetrate their picture-taking space. I took my time. No one else was curious about Botticelli's brushstroke or compelled to look at individual passages of painting unmediated by their phones. Their photo-obsessed behavior felt like greed, a contest to accumulate the most images a prestige activity, like the collecting of baseball cards or vinyl records. Would they even look at their hoard of images, ever? The room was full of people with bowed heads, not in reverence to the work but to gaze at glowing screens.

Sometimes the decibel levels in the galleries were like what you'd expect at an ice hockey game, and I wished the Uffizi had followed the example of the Sistine Chapel, installing a sound system in each of the rooms with a guard who whispers "SHHHHHH" into a microphone every few minutes. People rushed to crowd in front of the more famous works, like Caravaggio's *Head of Medusa*[2] and the *Diptych of Federico da Montefeltro and Battista Sforza*[3] (portraits of the Duke and Duchess of Urbino by Piero della Francesca) to take photos; again, not bothering to look at the work unless there was a phone inserted between his or her face and the painting. If sociologists wanted to study their subjects' preferences for looking at an image on a screen v. looking at the same image in the three-dimensional analog world, to support the idea that viewing glowing screens is an addiction, the Uffizi would be a perfect place to conduct the study and to collect a lot of supporting data in a short amount of time. With its small rooms full of people taking photos and not looking at the art, the conclusion is obvious. However, at least one person looked at the *Diptych*; I heard a guy asking his guide whether Battista Sforza's elaborately decorated sleeve was in fact a fifteenth-century tattoo. Uh, no?

Unexpectedly, I entered the gallery where Caravaggio's youthful *Bacchus*[4] is installed, the image I used for the "Peanut Butter and Jelly" essay in my book *What It Means: Myth, Symbol, and Archetype in the Third Millennium, Vol. 1.* For the illustration, I Photoshopped a PB & J sandwich into Bacchus's right hand, erasing what was there in the painting. Finally, I could see what it was he held, something I couldn't parse in reproductions of the image. It's a black ribbon.

Wednesday, June 1st

I couldn't leave Italy without seeing the Leaning Tower of Pisa, and it was only an hour's train ride away. The LTOP was an icon of my childhood; whenever we learned about Italy in elementary school, the Pizza (as we called it), along with the Colosseum, were the main architectural go-tos. That gravity-defying cylinder with its Archimedean corkscrew of columns was an enigma we loved to ponder. *How come it hasn't fallen over?* was the question on every second grader's mind. Interestingly, the architects knew by floor three that it had a serious lean to one side, because of the soft foundation underneath, but they kept going anyway. They stopped at floor eight, 55.86 meters (183.27 feet), 294 steps. I wonder if they were kicking themselves for not fixing the problem when they could have, or did they realize they had a tourist gold mine on their hands? Something that would put Pisa on the map globally? In 2022 it costs twenty euros to enter the tower and climb to the top, and the line was as long as if the pope were lying in state. Various guidebooks warn that it's claustrophobic and dark in there, and even though you can't see out most of the way up, the lean makes you dizzy. I wondered if prepubescent boys waited inside to feel you up as you passed, like I'd experienced in the windowless minarets of the Jama Masjid Mosque in Old Delhi nearly thirty years ago. I was fine with admiring it at a distance and augmenting my souvenir refrigerator magnet collection.

I arrived back in Florence in time to see the Dante Museum. The museum is housed in a cluster of buildings that belonged to the Alighieri family, but no one is sure where he lived exactly and no personal possessions of his are extant, not even one line of poetry written in his hand. Given those circumstances, it's kinda hard to make a museum, but they did have a few interesting exhibits. One of them was a rotating hologram bust of Dante created from images of him recorded in the media of the day, paint and stone. The other was an excerpt from *Purgatory* in which he wrote about the Battle of Campaldino, a skirmish between two rival gangs, the Ghibellines and the Guelphs. Dante himself had participated in the battle, and the excerpt describes the last few minutes of the life of Bonconte da Montefeltro, a Ghibelline general, who had received a mortal wound to the throat. Animated from a series of drawings, with a soundtrack read by an Italian actor, it was a compelling watch. I never read the *Purgatory*, but the *Inferno* made a lasting impression, grabbing my attention immediately from its opening lines:

> Midway upon the journey of this life,
> I found myself alone and in a dark wood,
> For the straight path had been lost.

Had I lost the straight path, wandering around the way I was?

The *Inferno*, of course, is full of stories of sin and suffering and punishments that fit the crime. Maybe that's where that expression comes from. Fourteenth-century Florence must have been a challenging, lawless, smelly place, and if Dante could see it now, he may never have written *The Divine Comedy* in the first place. He'd be shocked by its clean, vermin-free streets, its beautiful shops and repurposed medieval buildings, and the hordes of eager tourists visiting the Duomo, only just completed when Dante was thirty-one years old. He'd also be delighted, but perhaps confused, to learn that Italy's government and the Catholic Church were BFFs, and that Italy has been at peace for over seventy years. Politician Silvio Berlusconi and his infamous bunga bunga sex parties would definitely land him in the second circle of hell, but contemporary Italy was pretty tame otherwise. What is a compelling story with no conflict?

Thursday, June 2nd

Today I visited the Duomo Museum and Baptistery, and the Basilica di Santa Croce. Neither of these places was crowded. On my way back to the Airbnb I passed the Uffizi, and that's where everyone was. Rick Steves should tell tourists that when the Uffizi crush becomes too much to bear, they can see works by Cimabue, Donatello, and Michelangelo in situ in Florence's churches, the places they were created for. The otherworldly, astonishing Cimabue crucifix[5] (fourteen by twelve feet, created between 1268 and 1271 and badly damaged in the 1966 Arno River flood) is in the Santa Maria Novella, along with a black-and-white photo of it being carried out of the church to higher ground, the water having reached Christ's halo. Several Donatellos are in the Santa Croce. Five of Michelangelo's sculptures can be seen in the Medici Chapels, and his crucifix with a controversial, and anatomically precise, naked Christ hangs in the Basilica di Santo Spirito, thankfully lacking a postmortem erection.

The Duomo museum is home to many relics, why do I find these amusing? They invite sniggers and eye rolls from those of us who think they're proof of the gullibility of the church fathers. After all these centuries, it's a stretch to believe that a specific bone was previously one of St. Peter's digits, or that these socks, bled on by Jesus at his crucifixion, were worn by Mary Magdalene. Just because a cardinal or bishop says they're authentic, should we believe that? I'd like to see proof of their provenance or a DNA analysis. I wondered if you could buy a relic, so I Googled "relics eBay," and yes you can! Listed were a strand of Mother Teresa's hair paired with a strand of Pope John Paul II's for $79.99; reliquary soil from St. Francis of Assisi's tomb for $455; and a tiny swatch of garment worn by Pedro Gonzales encased in a small glass tube for $130. Who was Pedro Gonzales? Facebook lists fifty men, more or less, by that name, and you can be sure thousands more have walked the earth. Two standouts were a Pedro Gonzales who was the patron saint of Spanish and Portuguese sailors and the other a character actor who appeared in John Wayne movies. On both eBay and Amazon, you can even buy your own ornate brass reliquary in which to place a relic of your choice, in case you lose a finger in a woodworking accident or want a fancy container for your child's baby teeth.

When tourists are out en masse, you must negotiate annoying and sometimes dangerous behaviors. The flow of people through confining spaces, such as doorways between museum galleries, is like the flow of water that accumulates behind a dam. Clusters of people entering a passageway from one room to another often stop, forming one of these human dams. This phenomenon also occurs when riders of escalators disembark at the top and stop, when people exit any form of public transportation, and at exits from buildings. Maybe our brains aren't well designed to handle transitions between spaces or to negotiate sudden changes in forward momentum.

Families of three or more walk shoulder-to-shoulder down the street allowing no one else to pass. Glassy-eyed young women, looking in any direction other than the one in which they are walking, slam right into you or sometimes turn in a complete, confused circle, knocking you aside with their backpacks. Persons on the sidewalk directly in front of you stop suddenly to consult their phones, so that you almost plow into them. I don't think any of these behaviors are deliberate, I just wish other people would remember that everyone strolling through buildings and walking the streets has similar intentions to yours, and space is at a premium. Does this sound like the ravings of a cantankerous, not quite seventy-year-old?

Would Italy be livable for a medigan?* Unless Italy is a bureaucratic nightmare for immigrants, I think yes. It's shocking how many people speak English, so if you don't have an ear for Italian, communication wouldn't be so problematic. Fresh fruits and vegetables are readily available, and as long as your feet and knees hold up, you wouldn't need a car and you may not even miss having one. The trains are *always* on time, buses go everywhere, and whatever your destination, unless it's a major holiday, clusters of gleaming taxis are at the ready. There is beauty everywhere you turn. I learned how to navigate Italian cities in no time—two or three passes—and I knew where I was and how to get back to my quarters. Confusing Santa Fe took me a good three years. I've only scratched Italy's surface, and I want to know more. But who doesn't love Italy?

---

*Medigan is a contraction of *merde de cannes*, dog poop. Its meaning: anyone who isn't Italian.

CHAPTER TWENTY-THREE

PORTO

Friday, June 3rd

Sometimes in an airport bag-drop line, especially when there's only one airline employee checking travelers in to their flights, the people around you become your temporary best friends. Waiting to divest ourselves of our luggage, the woman in front of me and I passed the time by talking about our 1970s art school experiences. She'd studied oil painting in Florence, and for a return trip to the U.S., packed a can of gesso in her suitcase. Gesso, Italian for "plaster," is used to prime a canvas for painting, and traditional oil gesso contains rabbit glue, chalk, and white pigment. When she reached her destination and opened the suitcase, somewhere in transit the can had exploded and covered everything in white goo.

"Next in line!"

She was called to the counter, leaving me wondering what the contents of her suitcase looked like and thinking about the shock that must have delivered. Because gesso dries quickly, her makeup bag was probably glued shut, maybe preserving a tube of expensive lipstick; a pair of shoes facing one another stuck to the bottom of the suitcase; T-shirts, socks, and underwear an indistinguishable blob. An unintentional artwork, the white suitcase a nod to the Roberts Rauschenberg and Ryman, known for their white paintings. I wondered if TSA had chosen her bag to examine.

I made it to the gate with only a few moments to spare and presented my boarding pass and passport for the final pre-board check. A white smear covered the passport's upper left corner. I knew I didn't have any Liquid Paper, white nail polish, or a half-used cream cheese packet in my purse, where the passport had most recently been, and I tried scraping the substance off with a fingernail. But like gesso, it was tenacious. Besides me, only two airport personnel had touched it that day, neither with hands coated in Elmer's glue, meringue, or toothpaste. I just uploaded the story to *Unsolved Mysteries*'s submit page.

Porto has an excellent train system that conveys passengers from the airport directly to the São Bento neighborhood where I'd booked an Airbnb. If only Google Maps were so efficient. Often it can't locate you in a place with lots of hills and narrow, twisting roads, a place like Porto, for example. I dragged my luggage all over creation trying to find the Airbnb and was hot, sweaty, and impatient when I arrived. The people who owned the place were welcoming and wanted to chat, but I was desperate to unload my stuff and find a place to buy provisions. Am I getting too old for this???

The Airbnb had a strong, perfumed smell, and tracking down its source took several minutes. Little bowls of potpourri were placed around the apartment, so I figured it was one of them. But it wasn't. The smell seemed more intense in the hallway so, following my nose, I left the apartment, looked up, and the offenders were sitting on narrow ledges above the doors. Two pots of scented oil and incense sticks per the three apartments, out of reach but not impossible to remove with the help of a wobbly barstool. I stowed the pots in a cleaning cabinet inside the apartment, removed the sticks, and placed espresso saucers over the pots' openings. A spare towel blocked the gap between the cabinet door and the door above it, trapping any escaping scent inside. Problem solved!

Saturday, June 4th

Heavy rain fell for thirty minutes in the morning followed by partly sunny skies for the rest of the day. Shuffling carefully downhill on the slick pavement, I toured the neoclassical Stock Exchange building, walked the Gustave Eiffel-designed metal arch bridge that crosses the Douro River, ate a fantastic lunch (a white fish, truffles, mushrooms, small potatoes, and cherry tomatoes) at an Italian restaurant, and found a grocery store that sold blueberries. After seven days, the gash on the knee is finally getting better.

Sunday, June 5th

Maybe it's unfair to compare Porto to a place in Italy, like Rome or Florence, but I've been doing that a lot since I've been here. I walked to a Rick Steves-recommended tourist destination, the Crystal Palace and gardens, and wondered how they made the must-see list. Entrance to the palace wasn't allowed, the gardens were neglected, water in a large pond was dirty, and debris and trash had collected around its perimeter. I've also been comparing the art. In Porto, did no one come up with the idea of painting in plaster? Murals painted on ceilings of churches sometimes were executed on wide slats of wood, looking more like a floor than a ceiling, with no attempt to fill in and sand the cracks first to create a uniform surface. The painting often looked kind of slapdash. Wooden sculptures of saints have huge heads, hands, and feet compared to their bodies, their eyes wide and staring, giving the figures a comical appearance, as if they were repurposed Punch and Judy marionettes. Maybe the superior painting and sculpting techniques of Renaissance Italy and points north didn't make it into little Portugal, isolated as it is on the far southwest coast of Europe.

Around the corner from the Airbnb, the Rua das Flores is a lively pedestrian street lined with chic boutiques and alfresco eateries. Hoping for a repeat of yesterday's excellent lunch, I chose a place and sat down. A trio of twenty-something diners next to me had just been served their food when a seagull with a wingspan as wide as the table swooped down and stole the young woman's thinly sliced salmon. The gull landed only a few feet away and devoured his catch while everyone else at the restaurant bent over their food in a protective posture and froze in place. The waiter appeared immediately, with a squirt gun, and laid it solemnly on their table. "Use this if you need to," he said.

After lunch I walked down the hill to the riverfront. A large double-decker boat full of inebriated tourists, all talking at once and trying to out-party each other, was docking. Some of them stood perilously close to the upper deck railing, and shoremen on the dock kept shooing them away from the edge. The handsome boat captain, joining his passengers on the upper deck, began serenading two bikini-clad young women sunning themselves on the dock below. When he finished, he was generously applauded, even by the young women he was clearly hitting on.

I thought of Lewis Hine's early twentieth-century photos of immigrants arriving at Ellis Island and the implied solemnity and reserve of the people. I wondered if they'd be able to relate to this scene in any way. A video clip viewed by future inhabitants of Porto may also be enigmatic, in the same way photos and films from a hundred years ago aren't that easy for us to connect with. What would they think of ball caps worn backward, low-slung trousers with exposed underwear and visible butt cracks, women with cartoonishly long eyelashes and fingernails crafted to look like diamond-studded talons?

If you've ever lived in a place with a large Portuguese expat community, like southern Massachusetts or Providence, Rhode Island, you recognize the old-country aesthetic embraced by these places. But why, in the 1970s when I lived in Providence, hadn't *pasteis de nata*,[1] the excellent Portuguese custard tart, become a huge hit stateside? You were hard-pressed to find a Portuguese bakery, much less pasteis. It's not like the ingredients were exotic; they're made from flour, sugar, milk, a little vanilla, and eggs. Maybe the bakers and homemakers, who made dozens of the little tarts day in and day out back in the Old Country, were in desperate need of a break from the tyranny of that tradition and, on the journey over, conspired to pretend to forget about them.

Monday, June 6th

Google Maps continued to direct me in ridiculously circuitous routes and added minutes/hills to my daily walks, but now that I know the city pretty well, I'm fine with it. I walked to the Sé do Porto,[2] not realizing it was the brooding building to which Google directed me when I first arrived at the São Bento train station, dragging my suitcase uphill in the opposite direction of the Airbnb. Narrative panels made of azulejos,[3] Portuguese ornamental blue tiles, are the Sé's main tourist draw; otherwise, it's a grim medieval granite building, the exterior pockmarked from centuries of rain and pollution and with weeds sprouting from cracks in its crumbling walls, beautiful in its own way. Inside is an excellent collection of crucifixes depicting Jesus with skinned knees. And Archangel Michael made a surprise appearance.

"Look up."

There on the ceiling was his image, sword raised, his foot on the Devil's right temple,[4] a plaque on the wall explaining Michael's significance to Porto.

Puffing up his chest and spreading his wings, he said, "I'm the patron saint of the Sé's chapter house, and people worshiped me at an altar near the entrance to the church, third pillar on the right. Until, that is, the altar was removed during renovations in the eighteenth century. At least they left my painting alone."

"It's the work of an Italian, right?"

"Yep, how can you tell?"

I dodged the question. "It looks like you're about to stab yourself in the foot." But he knew what I was thinking.

"This little painting is actually one of my favorites," he said. "But the Italians didn't always get it right, either."

Tuesday, June 7th

A popular tour from Porto takes tourists to the medieval towns of Guimarães and Braga. Guimarães is fastidiously maintained, with rose gardens, hip restaurants and coffee shops, and not a scrap of trash anywhere. The tour guide took us to an unremarkable castle, the building a cube shape and made of big, chunky granite blocks, with more blocks hewn into pyramid shapes lining the ramparts. Either their architects had no imagination, or the townsfolk were in a hurry to protect themselves and aesthetic considerations were out the window.

In the historic center of Guimarães, shadow box window displays that house dioramas illustrating the stations of the cross are built into granite walls.[5] In one of these scenes, rendered in carved and painted wood, Jesus had tumbled to the ground under the weight of the cross and was staring, wide eyed, at passersby. To those of us accustomed to seeing featureless mannequins wearing the latest fashions in commercial window displays, it was shocking. In the large main plaza, a woman in whiteface and dressed as an angel stood unmoving and mute on a pedestal.[5] I gave her a euro and she let me take her photo. I wanted to ask her to shrug for the photo, but I didn't know how to say that in Portuguese.

Wednesday, June 8th

Porto is a contradiction of both dark, filthy, narrow streets and boulevards with magnificent public buildings and churches. The cobblestone is different from Rome's and Florence's (comparing again), and it's not as well maintained. Big gaps between the stones trap your tennis shoes as you cross streets that often resemble a riverbed more than a thoroughfare. The sound of car tires on Porto cobblestone is pleasing, though. How horses and carriages managed to navigate Porto's many hills, especially on rain-slicked streets, is a mystery. There must have been lots of accidents and mishaps.

I walked the neighborhood around the Rua de Santa Catarina, a commercial district, and saw a little chapel, called the Capela das Almas (Chapel of Souls), that dates from the early eighteenth century. Its exterior is completely tiled with azulejos[6] and looks oddly out of place among the United Colors of Benettons and Starbucks and gelato shops. The Majestic Café, with its loopy art nouveau façade,[7] is in the same neighborhood. The first *Harry Potter* book was partially written inside its gloomy belle époque interior—decorated in ancient mirrors, plaster nudes, dark varnished wood, and creepy grinning putti—and made the Majestic world famous. They charge a lot for the privilege to dine there.

Friday, June 10th

A train strike today threatened my travel plans to Lisbon. I left the Airbnb in a state of hand-wringing panic and was dropped at the train station, anticipating having to drag my belongings, which I was considering abandoning, through an unknown neighborhood to look for lodging and wait out the strike. I expected the station to be packed with other panicking vacationers, but it wasn't particularly, and I queued up to ask about the train to Lisbon. No problem, the ticket seller said. The train arrived in an hour, so I had time to calm down and get a sandwich (not crustless like in Italy). I headed out to the platform, and to my delight, an escalator, a lift, and a long staircase were all options. Following the crowd, I stepped onto the escalator and as the descending stairs began to separate, I lost control of my luggage and the backpack that was balanced on top of it. While trying to grab my things before they slammed into two young Indian women in front of me, my left ankle twisted, and I landed on my rear. They helped stabilize my bags, and I didn't seem to have suffered any serious injuries but with ankles you can't always tell immediately. As soon as I could I took three Advil, forced my way onto the packed-like-sardines (I can write this, it's Portugal) train, and sat for three hours barely moving, wondering what was going on down there in ankle territory. To distract myself, I continued reading a story from Washington Irving's *Tales of the Alhambra* that I'd started earlier in the day. The story was about a Muslim prince who was raised in isolation, away from girls, so that he wouldn't understand love and be tempted by it. A Christian princess was raised in the same fashion. Guess who got together?

CHAPTER TWENTY-FOUR

LISBON

Friday, June 10th

In 2017, I visited Lisbon for three days on a leg of an around-the-world trip and was kicking myself for not scheduling more time in this friendly, culturally rich city. I'd done all the "what to see in Lisbon in three days" activities: Belém Tower, the Castelo de São Jorge, the Praça do Comércio, Sintra and Cascais, etc., and wanted to have a more immersive, less touristy experience. In 2022, Lisbon landed in fourth place on the InterNations Expat City Ranking list, so it seemed worth reconsidering.

Getting to—and inside—the Airbnb was as easy as could be expected, but the place bore little resemblance to the owner's description and photos. It reminded me of the monastery stays that are plentiful in Italy—a spartan room, six feet by eight at the most, about the size of a prison cell, no AC, no screen on the single (tiny) window to keep out mosquitoes.[1] At least there weren't any feng shui issues; there wasn't much choice when it came to arranging the child-size bed and the mini-fridge. I rented the room knowing that I may be sharing two bathrooms with at least two other people, and two bathrooms for three people was okay with me. What I didn't know was that there were six other rooms in the apartment, and two of those were large rooms with three beds each. If I've added this correctly, by tonight there could be up to ten more people.

The room was stuffy and smelly, and I traced the bad odor to the pillow. No one else was around so I switched it with one from a vacant room. The other pillow was a bit of an improvement, but I began to notice that all rooms emitted an unpleasant, sweaty smell, suggesting that the bedding also functioned as a nutrient medium for growing various bacteria. Mosquitoes weren't the only bugs I was concerned about.

I left and walked around the King Eduardo VII monument, one of Lisbon's many beautiful public spaces, bought some provisions, ate dinner, and took a shower before the place started to fill up at 9:15. I hope there's not going to be a lot of partying until two or three in the morning.

Saturday, June 11th

At 3:37 a.m. I was still wide awake, sitting on the bed writing Flavio, the owner of the Airbnb, to tell him that the prison cell wasn't working for me. In the 85-degree (30 degrees Celsius) heat, there was no hope of cooling down in the stagnant, humid air, and as I wrote Flavio, a mosquito pursued me relentlessly. For hours I'd been listening to doors banging and hearing the steady, thumping patter of desperate feet heading to one of the two bathrooms. People in this part of the world don't flush their tissue, and I agree with this practice and the idea of fouling our water as little as possible, but the growing mound of used tissue in an open, 55-gallon drum was beyond disgusting. I was forced to listen to the conversations of others who must assume all people in my demographic are deaf insomniacs. I reread the listing to make sure I hadn't missed any important disclosures, such as: "no amenities; no vented air or fans; eat in the kitchen at your own risk; lights are on 24/7 for your safety; no guarantee of sleep and no earplugs provided." I packed up and was on the streets by 8:30 a.m., heading for a conventional hotel.

Sunday, June 12th

To cool off, I rode the hop-on-hop-off bus to Cascais, a beautiful beach town north of Lisbon, and late in the day visited the Museo Nacional do Azulejo, everything about it so well done. Outstanding examples from the 1500s on and good explanations of the tile-making process.

At 7 p.m. I walked down Liberdade, Lisbon's exclusive avenue modeled after the Champs-Elysées, toward Rossio Square, where Lisboetas* were celebrating the Festas da Sto. Antonio (Saint Anthony), also known as the Sardine Festival. Bleachers and sardine-grilling stations were set up along Liberdade; everyone wore either sardine hats with long, floppy tails or wigs that looked like bright green Afros.[2] The wigs represent a local plant that's considered both good luck and a love token. Women sell the plant from card tables, and each little pot had a toothpick stuck into the dirt with a card attached. One of the cards read:

> Minha carvalhinha verde
> Do verito es combater
> Anda espero acabar
> Nos teus braços, a minha vida.

> My green oak tree
> The truth is to fight
> Come on, I hope to finish
> In your arms, my life.

There was something vaguely sexual about the message of the poem, the implication of *le petit mort*, the little death. I wasn't sure about the context of the plants and their messages, so I looked it up later:

> There is another cute tradition that surrounds St. Anthony's feast. This one involves a small plant, which the locals refer to as *manjerico*. It is a type of basil with tiny leaves and a strong, lovely, sweet smell. The small potted plants of man-

jerico are given as gifts to loved ones . . . it symbolizes newly sprouted love. Traditionally, men give a manjerico plant to their object of affection on St. Anthony's Day, June 13th. Each plant carries a piece of paper. . . with four verses or a love message. The girls who receive the plant are supposed to take care of it so that it thrives.[3]

Girls, to assume responsibility for a newly sprouted love via this symbolic tradition could inform your relationship in unintended ways. Since your love is "new," you probably hardly know the guy, yet as the recipient of the plant, like it or not, you accept the role of caregiver, investing your time, affection, and emotions, and if the manjerico thrives, expectations for the relationship to thrive are created. What if, regardless of the attention and care it receives, it withers and dies, does it follow that you neglect the relationship until it goes down the tubes? What if you receive plants from several suitors, and what if you already have a sizeable stash of manjerico lining the windowsills of a sunny back room? This tradition sounds confusing, triggering, and potentially heartbreaking. Make a nice pesto with it and focus on the relationship, not its signifier.

The Rossio Square train station is one of the great examples of Portugal's flamboyant Manueline architecture, a blending of Gothic, Renaissance, and Moorish styles from the late sixteenth century.[4] The square, also called Mar Largo (wide sea), is covered in waves of white and black *calçadas* (sidewalks) that create a dizzying optical illusion of actual waves. A man with a huge multiple-headed soap-bubble wand entertained the Rossio Square crowd, filling the sky with hundreds of bubbles per swoop of his arm. After an hour and a half, the parade hadn't materialized, so I walked back to the hotel and discovered it was starting at that end. The parade route was packed with Lisboetas wearing costumes symbolizing neighborhood identities, and prizes were awarded for the most colorfully and thematically outrageous. One group dressed in bright yellow, with larger-than-life measuring tape stripes on their pant legs, maneuvered a huge, dome-shaped pink pincushion stuck with sewing needles the size of swords. Buttons that could double as hubcaps and giant spools of thread decorated its circumference. Another group carried Styrofoam cell phones the size of doors; the women wore sashes made of emojis and cell phone hats tilted at an angle, a Portuguese fascinator. And what would a Catholic nation's parade be without saints? One saint held a baby Jesus in one hand and a Bible in the other, the crisp folds of his polyester pajama set suggesting they'd recently been removed from their packaging. Their bodies were painted a macabre dark purple, offset by a shimmering gold fabric background, and the grouping stood upright in what was intended to be a small, white fishing boat that looked more like a coffin.[5] Surreal, baroque, nonsensical, heretical, Felliniesque. All it lacked was a soundtrack composed by Nino Rota.

Saint Anthony is the patron saint of Lisbon. When you lose something, he gets involved. This includes people (with a specialty in lost spouses) and one's soul. He's the patron saint of amputees (lost limbs) and once reattached a severed foot, but the day the Acoma Indians lost their right feet, his schedule was already packed. Other categories of loss assigned to St. Anthony include elderly people (lost youth), shipwrecks (loss of cargo), runts of litters (loss of size, status among sibs, and often nutrition). Fishermen and sailors are also within his purview, hence the connection to Lisbon and sardine hats. When the earthquake and tsunami struck Lisbon on November 1, 1755, coincidentally the Feast of All Saints, he was MIA again and thirty thousand people lost their lives. After that catastrophe, you'd think Lisboetas would designate a different saint as their patron, for example, Genevieve, the patron saint of calamities. But she was already taken by Paris.

Tuesday, June 14th

It was my last day in Lisbon and there were still sixty-plus (!) museums I hadn't visited. I decided on the excellent Quake: Lisbon Earthquake Center, a multimedia environment that imagines and simulates the catastrophic earthquake and tsunami that wiped out most of Lisbon in 1755.[6] Quake is a labyrinth of installations that are intended to convey visitors on an emotional and experiential journey of the day before, during, and after the earthquake.

The first room is a re-creation of a historian's study. Borrowing from the film *Back to the Future*, a professorial voice explains that he's built a time machine to travel back to that day, and we're his guests. Next, the group entered a second room—all surfaces mirrored—where images projected on the walls and an earsplitting soundtrack instilled the right amount of dread for what was to come. Colored lights cascaded in vertical stripes down the walls, and on the ceiling, dates and images of corresponding events were shown in reverse order, with accelerating rapidity, until we arrived at November 1, 1755, All Saints' Day. The Quake experience so far: Disneyfied and nauseating. After we arrived in 1755, we were herded into various rooms made to look like Lisbon's streets from the eighteenth century, but then, without reentering the time machine, we were inside someone's apartment in San Francisco and it's 1906. A narration explained the lead-up to that earthquake, and the floor started tilting and vibrating. It felt exactly like riding the Lisbon metro.

The centerpiece of Quake is a room made to simulate the Lisbon Cathedral, and we are worshippers sitting in its pews. Again, projections cover all walls and the ceiling, and a video of a priest conducting mass with several boys in attendance plays directly in front of us. Suddenly, we feel a bump. In the video, a thin stream of dust descends from the ceiling of the cathedral. The priest ignores it and continues with the ritual, but one of the boys looks frightened. More bumps and a few shakes. Now some major debris starts to fall. The boys take off, but the priest continues to ignore what's happening, like he's got some kind of ecclesiastical immunity. The anticipation was fantastic. Would the cathedral collapse around the priest, sparing him, like the scene in the Buster Keaton movie where the façade of a house falls forward, but he survives because he's standing in the location of an open window? Our seats began to vibrate in earnest and the priest finally takes off, no longer willing to go down with the ship, the cathedral collapses, and we're all engulfed in digital flames. We're told that the twenty-foot-high tsunami arrived forty-five minutes later and slammed into Lisbon but didn't extinguish the fires; all the flammable debris it brought ashore provided even more fuel. There were no open windows to escape being crushed. The event must have also crushed Lisboetas' faith in Catholicism, it being All Saints' Day.

For the Uber trips there and back, a Pakistani and an Indian driver, respectively, picked me up. They both agreed that Portugal was a great place to live. They even gave the same reasons, the most important being that it's easy to get papers (residency). They gushed about the beauty of the place, the weather, nice people, great food, low crime, and no racism. The Indian guy even invited me to his home to meet his family.

As I lay in bed tonight, the Feast of St. Anthony continued, loud thumping music and cheering filtering through the windows and vibrating the glass. When's curfew, I wondered?

Portugal is definitely on the short list for relocation. The Archangel Michael-Porto connection a plus.

---

*People from Lisbon are called Lisboetas. They're also called Alfacinhas, which means "little lettuce." Nobody knows why exactly, but my hunch is that it may have been borrowed from the French term of endearment, *mon petit chou*, meaning "my little cabbage" and altered to the more distinguished "lettuce."

CHAPTER TWENTY-FIVE

A WILD GOOSE CHASE

On Monday, June 27th, I was back in the U.S. and driving on I-295 near Woonsocket, Rhode Island. An official State of Rhode Island vehicle passed me, and painted on its sides and back bumper were the words Wild Goose Control. I had no idea wild geese were so intractable that an office had been established and vehicles deployed to keep these creatures in check. I was tempted to abort my journey and follow him to the site of the problem geese, but I'm deathly afraid of them, having been chased by (domestic) geese both as a child and an adult. Wild geese are probably even more ferocious.

I Googled the etymology of the Wild Goose Chase:

> The idiom *wild goose chase* goes back at least to the 1500s. . . A wild goose chase is a hopeless pursuit or foolish search after something that is in fact, pointless or unattainable. A wild goose chase is a frustrating enterprise that usually involves wasting a large amount of time. The idiom wild goose chase was first written down by William Shakespeare, in the play *Romeo and Juliet* in 1595: 'Nay, if thy wits run the wild-goose chase, I have done, for thou hast more of the wild-goose in one of thy wits than, I am sure, I have in my whole five.' Interestingly, the term wild goose chase was

first used to mean a type of horse race. In a wild goose chase horse race, the lead rider galloped across the open countryside in an erratic pattern. Subsequent riders were to follow at different intervals and had to follow the exact pattern of the lead rider. The idea is of geese flying in formation, following one leader..."[1]

So a wild goose chase is a hopeless quest for some ill-defined or poorly conceived undertaking. Galloping around in an erratic pattern was the perfect metaphor for how I felt after returning from Europe. In retrospect, I hadn't accomplished much during the past two months other than tick a few more boxes on a typical tourist must-see list. I had violated my own mandate to spend at least ten days in a place before passing judgment, and a month or more to begin to understand a place in more meaningful ways. Was the universe sending me a message via the office of Wild Goose Control? Am I doomed to fail??

CHAPTER TWENTY-SIX

WASHINGTON, D.C.

Sunday, July 3rd

Being in D.C. for another house- and petsit, with car privileges, was an opportunity to revisit the richness of our nation's capital. Decades earlier I'd explored many of D.C.'s public institutions, admired its landmarks, monuments, and architecture; and this mixed-income, inner-city-neighborhood housesit would allow me to experience D.C. more like a local. The anticipation was exhilarating, but first things first. I felt Hollywood-movie-deprived and went to a cineplex for the first time in four months, located in downtown D.C. I've driven in some of the world's most challenging places, São Paulo, Boston, Miami, and all over Poland and Costa Rica to name a few, and yet the D.C. driving culture was shocking. Was anybody paying attention to what they were doing, and would the car and I make it home in one piece? To build up my courage for the return drive, after sitting in the dark for two hours, I walked around the block to equilibrate. Ford's Theatre was in the distance, and I saw a long line of tourists waiting to get in. The idea of visiting the place where Lincoln was assassinated struck me as a little macabre, so I wanted to ask people standing in line why the Ford's was important to their D.C. experience and what it meant to them. I understand wanting to see interpretive exhibits, like at the excellent Sixth Floor Museum at Dealey Plaza in Dallas, but I don't think a lot of folks visit the actual spot where Lee Harvey Oswald's (and others'?) bullets connected with JFK's cranium. For Lincoln, the Ford's was this place. Were visitors hoping to snap a selfie from his balcony chair to put on their social media? I passed the Ford's by and kept my mouth shut, thinking I might incite a small riot or get shot at by someone who didn't appreciate the intrusion.

The Ford's website encourages visitors to attend a one-act play about Lincoln's assassination told from the point of view of two men who were there ("They grapple with the question, Could John Wilkes Booth have been stopped?") I called their information line for details, and when I asked if the play included an assassination reenactment, their representative disconnected the call. He must have thought I was pranking him, but I really wanted to know!

Tuesday, July 5th

While expectorating a mouthful of water after brushing my teeth, what looked like a tiny spider was among what dental hygienists refer to as "debris" that's left in your mouth following a meal. When I think of that word, I think of construction debris, so when I see chunks of leftover cereal and toast, I think of little pieces of brick and splinters of wood. But a spider? That was a new one.

So many history museums, including the Museum of Natural History (visited yesterday), have succumbed to the Disney model, the emphasis shifted from information to entertainment and aimed at a twelve-year-old's level of understanding. The visitor is forced to wade through confusing visuals and overlapping audio to get to the content of the exhibit. In the National Archive, one of the only rooms that is an exception is the Rotunda, where the Bill of Rights and the Declaration of Independence are exhibited. The Rotunda is kept at the temperature of a meat locker, and the lighting is so dim you think you're in the nocturnal animal exhibit at the zoo down the street. Those priceless documents used to be exhibited in a non-climate-controlled, sunlit place and, alarmingly, the ink faded and flaked off, hence the implementation of serious climate and light control. The exhibit explained that ink in those days was made of tannic acid from oak galls, bits of iron from nail scraps, and a gum arabic binder. Too bad the founding fathers didn't avail themselves of India ink, which they could have made by the gallons by collecting spent carbon from their lamps and mixing it with xanthan gum, derived from that wonder vegetable, corn. In the process of defining the future of our country, it seems like they forgot to consider the fugitive properties of the media used to immortalize their words.

Two large murals, called the *Charters of Freedom* (painted between 1933 and 1936) are also exhibited in the Rotunda and described inelegantly as each the size of a bus. The murals are allegorical portraits of the venerable (male) politicians who created the Declaration of Independence and the Constitution, and twenty-eight and twenty-five men, respectively, appear in the murals. Reminiscent of a high school play-reenactment of these events, most of the men stand downstage self-consciously in a straight line, facing the audience, in front of what looks like a painted backdrop that will be rolled up and stored in the ceiling of the theater when the production is over. The *Declaration*[1] mural features a large cloud suggesting the profile of Abraham Lincoln, as if he were lying on his bier and gazing up to heaven: a metaphor for the ephemeral nature of our laws, morals, and lives, in constant change, drifting with the wind. The artist was Barry Faulkner, a Raphael wannabe, and *The School of Athens*, clearly the murals' inspiration, these aren't.

Under the *Constitution*[2] mural, a few pieces of correspondence relating to the creation of the murals are on display. One letter is from Charles Moore—an architect, art historian, and a founding member of the United States Commission of Fine Arts—to Eric Gugler—a fellow architect and re-designer of the

White House's West Wing—about the defects in the Rotunda murals.

> . . . In the second figure from the right, how about those coattails! And must he display the same sort of a back that a matron of sixty exposes at the White House? Must Benjamin Franklin wear a belt under his protuberant stomach, and can he get more anatomy into his Jefferson? The gentleman in the light-colored toga standing against the column seems to wear such a garment as a doctor incases his patient in to save his clothes. . .

Charles Moore's evaluation of the murals was so spot-on that I was inspired to add to his response, in epistolary form. It was like indulging the feeling that moves you to write a love letter to a crush that you know you'll never deliver. Moore died in 1942.

> Dear Mr. Moore (may I call you Charles?),
>
> Thank you for your critique of the Barry Faulkner *Charters of Freedom* murals. I could not agree more with your assessments. I have a few observations of my own to add to yours, and I think you'll find our aesthetic convictions in perfect alignment.
>
> First, I'd like to comment on Washington, the central figure of the *Constitution* mural. His head is tiny, and his mantle is slipping off his right shoulder as if he's about to toss it off and *grand jeté* across the stage to Carl Maria von Weber's *Invitation to the Dance*. He looks like he's slept in his vest, and he's a little paunchy from too much cherry pie. Why is he so monochromatic and stiff while everyone else has at least a hint of color and gesture? One could imagine him playing the role of the Commendatore's statue in Mozart's *Don Giovanni*. And why the sourpuss? Is that a hint of a penis beneath his breeches that the fingers of his right hand touch? He's the only figure wearing boots (with

spurs); everyone else wears those black buckled shoes that say *Puritan;* it's clear who's boss. Alexander Hamilton's drawn sword rests on the thigh of Gouverneur Morris's left leg, drawing our eye to Morris's below-the-knee amputation, as if we'd miss it otherwise.

And the *Declaration* mural, the one with the clouds formed into Lincoln's profile (I think I see a couple of Tyrannosaurus rexes, too). Let me guess. This mural was painted second. It seems that Mr. Faulkner has run out of what little steam he had left after finishing the *Constitution.* The signers of the *Declaration* look like today's action figures—poseable, plastic microtoys based on fictional or historical characters—a phenomenon you missed by only a few years. (You may have appreciated G.I. Joe, an action figure inspired by the heroes of World War II.) Many of the men look as if they're not securely established on terra firma, as if they'll float up into the sky and join Lincoln among the clouds. The artist forces us to look and wonder at these odd meanings and provides no answers.

You and I would have been the perfect companions at the Prado. I can imagine what lively conversations we would have enjoyed, Charles.

With appreciation,
E.R.

Wednesday, July 6th

Before visiting the Hirshhorn Museum to see Yayoi Kusama's infinity mirror rooms,[3] I read about her work and familiarized myself with her bio. I'd heard of her but didn't know any of her history and discovered that she was part of the New York art scene in the late 1960s. The author mentioned her suicide attempts, motivated by upsets over others who were stealing her ideas. I guess no one told her that infinity mirror rooms in India waaaaay predated hers, like in the Amer Fort in Jaipur, built in the sixteenth century, and a mirror room in Delhi that was part of a Hindu temple I'd visited but can't remember the name of. It's not worth killing yourself over an idea you mistakenly think is original. As the author of Ecclesiastes wrote, incontestably, "There is no new thing under the sun."[4]

Thursday, July 7th

Strolling the National Gallery of Art for four hours was not nearly enough time to see it all, but when I'm pet-sitting, I never leave my charge(s) alone for more than five hours from the time I walk out the door to when I return. The National houses an excellent collection including many Goyas and El Grecos, complementing what's in the Prado, a small Bosch, several Botticellis. Vermeer's *Girl With the Red Hat*, Gilbert Stuart's *The Skater*. Some well-known Renoirs. One of Arcimboldo's vegetable and fruit portraits. The excellent John Singleton Copley's *Watson and the Shark*. The National owns the only Leonardo in the U.S., the *Ginevra Benci*.[5] Inside, there's a small version of the Pantheon—with an oculus—and a colonnade of huge black granite columns that describe a circle beneath the dome. The layout of one of the upper floors mimics Rome's Domus Aurea, with a central rectangular space surrounded by a colonnade and smaller, connecting rooms. Certain buildings in the D.C. Mall, especially the Museum of Natural History and the National Gallery, suggest what Imperial Rome may have looked like in its glory: Corinthian capitals, a triangular pediment with a sculpture-filled frieze, the shoebox shape. Immersed in this classical aesthetic felt like time travel back to the beginning of the first millennium. But seeing plus-size women in skintight leggings and crop tops, and grown men dressed like toddlers, broke the spell; too bad there's no dress code for entering, or merely walking in the vicinity of, these distinguished buildings. I remembered Rick Steves's whimsical suggestion and tried to imagine everyone in togas, covering all that excess, exposed flesh, but it didn't work.

Friday, July 8th

On the way to the local CVS, I walked past a large, white plastic trash container lying on its side, marked with dirty footprints and a large gash in the shape of a frown. Papers and junk mail, a woman's socks and underwear, and knick-knacks blanketed the grassy area between the sidewalk and the street. An unopened, handwritten letter, addressed to a local male resident, sat on the overturned container. What was the narrative here? It felt like an act of raw anger, as if someone in a fit of rage threw all these things into the trash, carried it out to the street, and gave the container a good, hard kick. Then someone else came along, found the unopened letter and, with empathy, laid it on top so that maybe the owner would see it and claim her stuff, or at least the letter. Curious about its contents, I was tempted to take it, but that would constitute mail theft and I could get five years in prison for that offense. Hey, I never considered JAIL as a possible domicile!

I visited the Phillips Collection, located in a pretty, leafy neighborhood near Dupont Circle. Renoir's *Luncheon of the Boating Party* is the standout of their collection; it was worth the trip just to see that in person. On my way there I'd noticed a Macy's, accessible directly from the Metro, so after visiting the Phillips in pursuit of great art, I visited Macy's in pursuit of a fashionable shirt. After some twenty minutes of frustrating meandering, I saw a possible candidate on a mannequin, the only one in my size. Since I've gotten in trouble before for removing clothes from mannequins, I politely asked a saleswoman if she would please remove it for me. She refused, saying cashiers weren't allowed to. I asked if she could check inventory to see if there was another one somewhere in the store. With a deep, audible sigh, she yanked the sales tag off the shirt and stomped over to her computer station. Pummeled the keyboard. NO. So I asked again, puleeze could I try on the shirt, while thinking, *Don't you want to make a sale for your employer?* Again, she refused, and another saleswoman joined in, escalating the dispute. I realized this wasn't about the shirt at all, it was class warfare. Fisticuffs were the next logical step, so I gave up and walked away. Around the corner another employee was dressing a mannequin. I asked him, Are you also allowed to *undress* a mannequin? Which must have sounded like the strangest question ever, but he said yes, and I explained that a shirt I wanted to try on, the only one available in my size, was on a mannequin. He agreed to help, and as we walked over to the mannequin, I asked another strange question. "Is your position unionized? What I mean is, is there a mannequin undressing union that mandates only certain store employees perform that task and no one else?" He said, "No, any employee may undress a mannequin." Both hostile saleswomen were elsewhere in the store, so they weren't witness to someone else overriding their authority. When they returned, though, they would notice the topless mannequin and see the crumpled shirt lying next to the cash register. This simple desire to buy a shirt had turned into an ugly Marxist contest of the bourgeoisie v. the proletariat, not at all my intention.

On my way home, three hours after I'd left, I emerged from the Metro and passed the plastic trash can that had vomited out its contents. The unopened letter was still there.

Washington, D.C., reminded me of an old joke: "You're from Tucson? I spent a week there one night!" I didn't have to experience the full ten days to know, definitively, that it didn't make the Location X short list. Twenty-four hours would have been plenty of time.

CHAPTER TWENTY-SEVEN

CAN ONE WORD BE ENOUGH TO KNOW WHERE?

Because no single place can fulfill all your requirements (see Appendix One, The List: Relocation Criteria) you're doing well if you get a 50 percent match. But would you base living or not living in a city on a single descriptor? I'll bet many people have and still do. Here are a few of these one-word descriptors, in alphabetical order.

Bars.
Bangkok, not Dublin, has the most bars of any city in the world. And if you're an older gentleman looking for a young Thai woman to take care of your many manly needs, this is also the place.

Beach.
Rio de Janeiro's Ipanema beach is not only world famous for both its beauty and a song that memorialized it, but also it's got a sidewalk made to look like waves of alternating black and white curves (modeled after Rossio Square in Lisbon), which actually look three-dimensional if you squint. Don't move here if you

have issues with dizziness, seasickness, balance, or the occasional petty theft.

Bookstores.
With 21 bookstores per 100,000 people, Hong Kong is the world's most enthusiastic consumer of the printed word. In the U.S., Portland, Oregon, is famous for its mega bookstore Powell's, but you have to navigate several city blocks' worth of homeless tent encampments to get inside.

Chill.
Stuttgart claims to be the city that's the most chill. I would have guessed Bangkok, city of bars and Buddhists, but neither drunks nor Buddhists are intrinsically chill, I guess.

Cinema.
Nope, it's not Hollywood. London is the city with the best cinemas and the most cinephiles.

Cold.
Don't like cold? Then avoid Yellowknife, Northwest Territories, Canada, one of the coldest inhabited places on Earth. But visit for a few days to see the aurora borealis, because it's one of the best places to have that experience. If you thrive in extreme cold, that's a great reason to move there.

Danger.
Tijuana, México, may be a haven for those seeking alternative medical treatments, but it's also a city with a spectacularly high murder rate at 138 people per 100,000, as of this writing. Danger may be your thing, but get your alternative medicine via the internet.

Diverse.
If what you love about a city is its diversity, Toronto is your place, with over 200 ethnic groups and 140 languages spoken. If you have your CELTA or TEFL certification, you should have no trouble at all getting a job.

Drivers.
If lowering your odds of dying in a car crash tops your list of places to live, Calgary ranks as the number one city in the world for great drivers. Who's the worst? Hint: during the colonial era this city was called Bombay.

Entertainment.
Las Vegas is synonymous with entertainment. It holds the world title for this dubious distinction.

Friendly.
In 2022, San Miguel de Allende, México, wrested the title from Rio de Janeiro, Brazil; San Sebastián, Spain; and Reykjavík, Iceland. San Sebastián and Reykjavík I can understand, but Rio? Friendly? Not the first word that comes to mind.

Golf.
Prague seems an unlikely place as the city with the best golfing; when Tiger Woods or the PGA come up in conversation, it's not the venue one thinks of, but there you are. If it were me, I'd move to Prague for the architecture; golf wouldn't even be on my radar.

Happy.
Helsinki, Finland, is considered the happiest city in the world, and it's no secret that all the Scandinavian countries rank among the happiest. What accounts for this? These countries take care of their people in all the important ways. For readers from the U.S., you may be interested to know that people in the Czech Republic are happier than you are. What could the U.S. possibly be doing wrong (wink)?

Healthcare.
Tokyo tops the list for best healthcare. Thanks to frequent earthquakes, tsunamis, volcanic eruptions, and Japan's experience with nuclear disasters (World War II and the Fukushima nuclear

power plant come to mind), their healthcare providers have had a lot of varied and challenging training and experience.

Hot.

For whatever spiritual credos or new-agey beliefs you may embrace, you may want to live near what California's Imperial County officially declared the center of the world. But Felicity, Arizona, near Yuma, is also one of the hottest places on Earth, with temperatures typically in the triple digits, and you may lose that chill vibe if you spend more than a few minutes outdoors.

Mountains.

The Himalayas, it's said, is the place you train for climbing the mountains outside Fort William, Scotland. Nelson, British Columbia, is Canada's first-place winner for the best mountains. If you're crazy about mountains, those are three crazy places to consider.

Noise.

Some people are unnerved by too much quiet, some by too much noise. Several contributors to expat forums have called Valencia, Spain, "noisy," specifically, the firecracker kind of noisy. A deal-breaker for me? No, unless I couldn't distinguish the difference between a firecracker and a firearm. However, any place with a rooster within earshot is definitely a NO.

Restaurants.

New York wins in the restaurant category, with over 10,000 restaurants serving any kind of food you can imagine.

Sad.

If wallowing in depression is your life's MO, by all means move to Lima, Peru. Herman Melville, the author of *Moby-Dick*, in chapter 42 entitled "The Whiteness of the Whale," called Lima "the saddest city thou can'st see":

> Nor is it, altogether, the remembrance of her cathedral-toppling earthquakes; nor the stampedoes of her frantic

seas; nor the tearlessness of arid skies that never rain; nor the sight of her wide field of leaning spires, wrenched copestones, and crosses all adroop (like canted yards of anchored fleets); and her suburban avenues of house-walls lying over upon each other, as a tossed pack of cards; it is not these things alone which make tearless Lima, the strangest, saddest city thou can'st see. For Lima has taken the white veil; and there is a higher horror in this whiteness of her woe...[1]

(The white veil is a perpetual white haze that hangs over the city.) Remind me never to visit Lima.

Unfriendly.
Some people just want to keep to themselves. Moscow is considered the world's most unfriendly city; Marseille, Atlantic City, and Los Angeles are close runners-up. Las Vegas makes this list, too. If you're looking to widen your circle of friends or start again from scratch, best to look elsewhere.

Wind.
For sailors and windsurfers, your place is Wellington, New Zealand. The windiest place on Earth, Wellington boasts a day and night average of 16.6 mph and gusts up to 154 mph. Couldn't you just lean into this place and give it a chance? Runners-up: Dodge City, Kansas; tornado alley in Oklahoma and North Texas; Santa Fe, New Mexico, in the winter and spring; Provence and the Mistral. Interestingly, Wellington ranks third in the overall well-being category, so maybe in the grand scheme of things, wind isn't that big of a deal?

One-word descriptors, alphabetized by city:

Bangkok = Bars
Calgary = Drivers
Felicity = Hot
Fort William = Mountains
Helsinki = Happy

Hong Kong = Bookstores
Las Vegas = Entertainment
Lima = Sad
London = Cinema
Moscow = Unfriendly
New York = Restaurants
Prague = Golf
Rio de Janeiro = Beach
San Miguel de Allende = Friendly
Stuttgart = Chill
Tijuana = Danger
Tokyo = Healthcare
Toronto = Diverse
Valencia = Noise
Wellington = Wind
Yellowknife = Cold

An overall winner in the Food category is not included in the list because it's too broad of a topic. Almost any civilized place is going to have *some* kind of good or at least edible food and both outstanding and good-enough places in which to get it. Art, music, architecture, and nature experiences are things of personal preference, and not easily quantifiable, so you're on your own with those, too.

CHAPTER TWENTY-EIGHT

SAN MIGUEL DE ALLENDE, MÉXICO

Sunday, July 31st

As of two days ago, I am officially a septuagenarian.

Before travelers are allowed to enter México from the airport, pushing a big red button sitting on a pedestal near the exit doors is mandatory. Successful pushing of the button is monitored by the last person in the long chain of immigration control. The device looks exactly like the novelty panic buttons available from your local Archie McPhee or Spencer's, but unlike those buttons that activate a scream or a guy who yells, "three, two, one, PANIC," this button doesn't seem to do anything. It doesn't sound or flash and cause yet another search of your bags, it doesn't trigger the exit doors to open, cause the airport to self-destruct, or launch a missile. So what's this about?

I'm not sure why it took nearly eighteen months of traveling for it to occur to me to visit the city of Archangel Michael, my designated guardian angel and occasional commentator on my process. But ominously, things were not getting off to a good start. During the flight's descent into Querétaro, making my way back to my seat from the lav, I tripped over someone's foot in the aisle, landed on my knees, and slid a few feet, catching both shoulders on armrests on either side of the aisle. My fellow passengers were aghast; I thought both shoulders were dislocated. Later, in a restaurant, while eating some corn, a crown fell off a back tooth. It's really hard to tell a kernel of corn from a crown, but I was able to retrieve it before it got swallowed. The hotel internet was *no funciona*, the phone number for the hotel didn't work so there was no one to report this to, and some guy down on the street cranked the engine of his car for more than four hours, trying to get it to start. It sounded like he was standing directly under my window with a metal trashcan full of nuts and bolts and other engine parts, shaking it with all his might.

Were these first-world inconveniences setting the tone for my six-week-long stay?

Friday, August 5th

Sunday, July 31st was an anomaly. Five days have elapsed, and I've had nothing but great experiences. Most people are open and friendly, greeting each other with buenos dias-es and generously sharing San Miguel's narrow sidewalks. A man who gives free orientations at the same restaurant every Thursday treated me to a one-on-one late yesterday afternoon, while I reciprocated with as many martinis as he could consume. He confirmed my hunch that Mexicans and gringos get along just fine here.

I'm in San Miguel not only to check it out as a possible place for relocation, but also to bump my Spanish up to the next level. I'm hoping four weeks of classes, two hours every day during the week, will do the job.

Something about San Miguel confers the ability to open up to others without a lot of self-consciousness getting in the way. I feel consistently happy here. A novel experience for me.

Sunday, August 7th

My big outing today was to the Mexican/American hybrid grocery store, La Comer. Happy doesn't exclude anxious, and why *was* I so anxious, what was the big deal? Like any place you've never been to, it seemed to take forever to get there, but Google Maps traced a dotted, blue-lined route only five and a half kilometers (less than three and a half miles) from the hotel. La Comer outshines any grocery store in a U.S. city of the same size (c. 175,000, about the same size as Rancho Cucamonga, California, home of the Smart & Final supermarket). Blueberries are available, and so are the same Italian truffles I bought in San Gimignano. The taxi driver took some interesting shortcuts on the way back, through the parking lot of an OXXO convenience store to avoid a roundabout and a long red light, and at a gas station where he pretended to be queueing up to fill his tank. Of the three or four taxis I've taken since I've been here, they all knew Calle Cuesta de Loreto and the location of the hotel without having to refer to their phones. I know it's not London or New York, but still, that's impressive.

Friday, August 12th

Lunch today was in the courtyard of the luxurious Rosewood Hotel, built in the early 2000s but made to look like a seventeenth-century colonial compound. A woman at the table next to me had brought a miniature felt teepee and assembled it next to her chair, and her two lion-cut Pomeranians were running in and out to get treats from their human.

Tonight, a multicolored light show was projected onto the Parroquia de San Miguel Arcángel (the parish church), adding a Disneyfying effect to a building that's already painted a fanciful pink.

Al pueblo pan y circo.
(To the people, bread and circus.)

The Parroquia looks like something that came out of a crystal-growing kit; it's as if two tectonic plates shifted suddenly and the building rose from inside the earth, piercing the sod with its many spikey, crystalline spires, growing and expanding into San Miguel's largest structure. The ringing of its bells denotes the time, I think? They're rung by hand by someone on the ground via thick ropes attached to the bells, and for days I've tried to decipher their meaning. For example, the bells will ring nine times—I'll check the time on my phone and it will match—but usually around 6:30 a.m. the bells will ring loudly and rapidly for thirty times or more. It sounds kind of panicked, as if making sure everyone wakes up and starts their day before too much of it slips away. Sometimes the bells will ring four times, pause, and ring once more. I think this extra ring may signal a fifteen-minute interval, so it could be 4:15 p.m. But in México, military time is observed, so shouldn't it ring sixteen times, pause, then add one more ring?

The bells of another church somewhere close by lack the full, sonorous sound of the Parroquia's and sound like someone's hitting a frying pan with a large metal spoon.

Monday, August 15th

San Miguel's cobblestone streets and narrow sidewalks are difficult to negotiate. There's no way to walk gracefully and with good posture on cobblestone, you must always have your head down anticipating your every step. If you lived in San Miguel long-term, you might develop a permanent slouch or a premature dowager's hump. While on the sidewalks, you must make yourself and your things as compact as possible so that every person you pass going in the opposite direction has the same amount of sidewalk real estate as you do. If you're carrying an open umbrella and a telephone pole appears in the middle of the sidewalk, there's barely enough room to turn the umbrella sideways and slip it through the space between the pole and the buildings. During an afternoon rain, you may get drenched in the process, and the next morning you may also get drenched by water draining off people's roofs through long pipes that empty out onto the sidewalks.

For the sake of research, I looked at a beautiful house for sale in a not-yet-gentrified neighborhood, and although I fell in love with the house, when I lay on the bed (out of sight of the realtor) and sat at the small kitchen table, I couldn't envision living there. From the rooftop terrace I made eye contact with a sad-looking, chunky pit bull that lived across the street, chained to a pipe on his rooftop terrace, and his expression said, Not your kind of neighborhood. I didn't hear any roosters, but it was three o'clock in the afternoon, not 3 a.m. Construction work was in progress close by, so I decided to circle the block on foot to see if there were fabrication businesses commingled with residences. Next to a car repair shop, someone had leveled a lot and was scraping the landscape bare with a mini-front loader, likely to build a brand-new home. The streets were slick from an afternoon rain, the steepest part of the street paved with tile that looked like leftover material from the construction of an industrial kitchen. The tile has no texture, and as I climbed the hill trying not to slip and fall, another woman passed me going in the opposite direction also trying not to slip and fall. To anyone without the agility of a twelve-year-old boy, staying upright in the streets and sidewalks of this neighborhood would be challenging. How could I consider living in a place where every time you venture out to do anything, your mind is completely preoccupied with staying vertical, your muscles so tense you move like a wooden doll? And would I be resented as a gringa interloper, one of the first to infiltrate one of San Miguel's last traditional neighborhoods?

Tuesday, August 16th

Spanish class is going well, and even though I signed up to be in a group, I'm getting one-on-one lessons with a teacher named Ramón. After class, I was walking toward the Parroquia and a guy started walking alongside me, keeping up for about a block. Finally he said, *Cómo estás?* And I answered, *Bien, gracias,* and repeated the greeting. He said, *Nosotros somos vecinos* (we are neighbors). We weren't really neighbors, or were we? I didn't remember having seen him on my street, but maybe he'd seen me? Did he mean it in a philosophical or a religious way? As in, we are all brothers and sisters in the great universal fraternity of humans? I giggled and said *tal vez* (maybe) and walked on. What did he want, I wonder?

August is rainy season in San Miguel, and currently there's a river flowing down the very steep Cuesta de Loreto. The two huskies that hang out on the roof of the house diagonally across are drenched, and one of them just took a dump in the two inches of water that has nowhere to drain.

Every day I try to think of Americanisms to tell Ramón, and he seems eager to have this insider knowledge. So far, the list has included: wicked cool, dope, dude, woke, and emo (drama queen). Tomorrow I'm going to introduce him to hot mess.

Wednesday, August 17th

Like in Rome, I must be losing my sense of time, because when I looked down at my hands this morning, my fingernails were shockingly long. Cutting fingernails is an activity I try to do on a dark-colored surface and while wearing the highest-magnification glasses in my possession. After every few snips, I round up the clippings into a small circle so that I don't lose track of the inventory. Because after I've finished, and I've been so very careful to collect and dispose of them properly, days after I'm still finding them under a sheet of paper or stuck in a banana when I lift it to my mouth to take a bite, or sometimes even in my bed. When I dispose of them in the trash, sometimes a few stick to the palm of my hand. One left behind can be really painful, like when I clench a fist in a moment of anxiousness or step on a stray toenail on my way to the bathroom, barefoot. Even with those procedures in place, a few still escape.

A midafternoon deluge drove patio diners indoors, filling the restaurant where I was having lunch. Everyone was drenched, and as they came inside, a few inches of water were dragged along with them. A couple who sat down at the table next to me had a companion German shepherd, huge and ferocious looking, and I hoped it wouldn't start shaking the water off its body and into my soup. San Miguel is lovely during these afternoon showers, and the locals know to stand under the dense, kelly green laurel trees, sculpted in shapes resembling upside-down flowerpots, that populate the Jardín (the town square).[1] No mussed hair, no big fuss about the rain; not a drop of water on themselves. They know when it will start and when it will end.

Thursday, August 18th

Today's phrases for Ramón the Spanish teacher: arm candy; what am I, chopped liver? Tomorrow I'm going to give him the Colbert Questionert, Spanish version.

This afternoon a little boy was trying to fly a giant, Day-Glo kite in the street next to some serious tangles of wires branching out from underneath an ancient transformer and leading to the surrounding houses. An afternoon thunderstorm was brewing. I hope the kid hasn't attached his house key to the kite string; surely he knows this is a bad idea?

Friday, August 19th

Yesterday I realized I lost the bracelet I bought at Pompeii. Small spheres made of black volcanic rock, four malachite spheres, and a single (fake) silver one, strung on a piece of elastic. I liked the idea of wearing it; for me, something about it signaled courage, like when a warrior killed a dangerous animal and wore its teeth around his neck. When laying my arm down on a hard surface, though, the little volcanic spheres dug into the flesh of my wrist and left red pockmarks behind, and after a few minutes it was painful. So sometimes I'd remove the bracelet, usually when typing or doing my Spanish homework. Never before washing my hands in a restaurant bathroom for fear of leaving it behind. But somehow, it disappeared. It had to be somewhere in the suite of rooms at the hotel, and before class I tore the place apart looking for it. It occurred to me that it could be one of my deceased husband's disappearing tricks that, mysteriously, he plays on me periodically. He died in 2015 and has been pestering me ever since.

Some people believe that you lose things when they no longer serve you, and maybe that's true. I considered the symbolic meaning of its loss, and maybe it means the end of the turista I've been suffering with for the past week. Both volcanic activity and diarrhea are associated with the word "explosive," so there's the metaphor. Or maybe those little volcanic spheres represented the number of years since my husband's death, and when those years were up, the bracelet would reach its expiration date and he would vanish for good, along with the jewelry.

Saturday, August 20th

I don't care what time it is, what day it is, and I have a few friends here already; these are good signs! Will I yearn for San Miguel when I'm back in the U.S.?

Several times now I've walked down Hidalgo Street, between the Jardín and Calzada de la Luz, and noticed an ancient man who does Aztec calendar readings in the back of his punched tin lighting store. He sits in a rusty folding chair and a single lantern illuminates his work space, sending patterns of colored light around the room and onto the ceiling. It felt impulsive when I stopped abruptly and hired him for a session.

He carefully opened his crumbling text to the page that corresponded to my birthday and showed me my personal glyphs, all birds. The vulture, the Eagle King, and the quetzal. He said, "You're a writer, a person who likes to investigate, a *perfectionista*. Recently indecisive." My color is blue. My guardian spirit, a bird-like figure, an Aztec version of St. Michael. And like a vulture, I've been circling my target in a recursive spiral when I need to locate my prey, fold my wings, and dive, feet extended, talons out, like an eagle.

Birds as my animals made so much sense. Especially the vulture. I do circle things, sometimes ruminating endlessly, I notice trash and it goads me, I notice the Wild Goose Control vehicle, a feather falls at my feet while I'm sitting under a concrete overhang. I had a powerful, visceral reaction to the wings of Angel Gabriel in *The Annunciation*, and the themes represented in *Leda and the Swan* intrigue me. I visit places expressly to birdwatch. I remembered the vultures I'd observed in Rome, how I counted twelve of them, an auspicious sign, and asked the question, Would I be settled somewhere in six months?

I'm clairaudient.

At the end of the reading, the man added, "In a few days, you'll receive a sign from your guardian spirit." Would Michael be paying me a visit?

Saturday, August 27th

Spanish classes have appropriated my life. I'm back in that seventh-grade place of wanting to please the teacher so badly that it short-circuits my ability to perform. So much for being unselfconscious. Why couldn't Ramón have been dull, unattractive, not-so-well-read, and unimaginative? He was the opposite of these things, and I wanted to connect with him on a more personal level despite our significant age difference. Still, I was tempted, and it showed in the thinly veiled stories and sentences I wrote for homework. (Note: Antonio means "priceless one.")

Antonio rompió todas las fotografías de su ex-novia.
(Antonio tore up all the photos of his ex-girlfriend.)

Hasta que conoció a una persona especial de los Estados Unidos, Antonio estaba triste porque nadie lo entendía.
(Until he met a special person from the United States, Antonio was sad because no one understood him.)

Antonio prefería las mujeres mayores y cuando encontró a la persona adecuada, una americana, se enamoró de por vida.
(Antonio preferred older women and when he found the right woman, an American, he mated for life.)

I wanted to hint at a shared mischievous streak:

Antonio y yo salimos temprano de la fiesta y corrimos por el parque Benito Juárez bajo la lluvia.
(Antonio and I left the party early and ran through Benito Juárez Park in the rain.)

Ramón taught me some choice *dichos* (sayings) and other words/phrases I might find useful:

Ser candil de la calle; oscuridad de la casa.
(You are a chandelier on the street, but in your house, darkness.)

Dar una bofetada con guante de seda. (To give a slap with a silk glove.)

No es tu asunto. (None of your business.)

No soporto... (I can't stand..., stronger than "I don't like...")

¡Qué payaso! (What a clown!)

El tráfico me choca. (I clash with–hate–traffic.)

Estoy frito. (I'm fried, I'm in big trouble.)

Irse a la goma. (Erase yourself, bugger off.)

Empalagoso. (Twee)

Es un aprovechado. (A person who takes advantage of someone for personal gain.)

Me dejó plantada. (Stand someone up, not show up, like for a date.)

Yo no soy florero. (I am not a flower vase; i.e., "What am I, chopped liver?")

I wondered if Ramón wrote our Spanish text. It's sometimes dark, brooding, deeply pessimistic, accusatory, judgmental.

Él comió muchísimo ayer, por eso está enfermo.
(He ate so much yesterday that today he's sick.)

Nosotros bebimos mucho anoche, por eso nos levantamos muy tarde.
(We drank a lot last night so we got up really late.)

¿Por qué no me llamaste antes de venir?
(Why didn't you call me before you came?)

Yo no toqué el timbre lo tocaron los niños y corrieron.
(I didn't ring the doorbell; the kids rang it and ran.)

¿Alguna vez chocaste manejando tu automóvil?
(You crashed while driving your car?)

¿Alguna vez rechazaste algo de lo que más tarde te arrepentiste?
(Have you ever rejected something that you later regretted?)

An entire exercise read like an Edgar Allan Poe poem:

Lo hice sin querer.	I did it without wanting to.
Lo dije sin pensar.	I said it without thinking.
Lo supe sin querer.	I knew it without wanting to.
Lo escogí sin observar.	I chose it without observing.
Lo dije sin saber.	I said it without knowing.
Lo tuve sin merecer.	I got it without deserving it.

The student supplies the verbs in a story about a park inhabited by a giant monster who scares children off who want to play. Is Ramón a Cynic, a Mexican Diogenes??

My heart pounded as I anticipated his answers to the Colbert Questionert, the "15 questions to cover the full spectrum of human experience." Question number three: "What is the animal you're most afraid of?"

He answered, "Birds." Surprising and inauspicious.

Number six: "What happens when you die?" His answer: *Se acabó todo.* It's over. Number thirteen, "If you had to listen to a single song for the rest of your life, what would it be? Pink Floyd's "Another Brick in the Wall." And number fifteen, "Describe the rest of your life in five words: "Shameless, indifference, sickness, decrepitude, and books." Gosh, I think I'm right.

Every night I was required to write a brief story, my choice, and knowing he likes the book *The Great Gatsby*, I wrote about when I was a twenty-two-year-old ballet dancer living in Rhode Island (I didn't disclose the date) and working in movies off and on, both things true. A talent scout, a caricature of the bald-pated, rotund, cigar-smoking padrino straight out of a *Godfather* movie, had come to town looking for people to cast in a dance scene, so I auditioned. I got one of the (many) parts, but he told me I had to cut my luxurious, long hair into a 1920s flapper bob, short with bangs. The end of the hippie era was approaching, but even so, it was a decidedly uncool hairstyle, so I declined. The purpose of the story was not the narrative, but the imagery. I wanted Ramón to picture me in my glamorous youth. After writing that story, I noticed I was sitting up straighter in class and trying not to slouch so much in the streets of San Miguel, difficult when you're trying to look over your Covid mask at the sidewalk to evaluate potential trip hazards.

On another occasion, he asked me to write a story about him, an opportunity at which I leapt. During class he had shared that he's obsessed with the American South, specifically the Mississippi River, and Mark Twain's *Huckleberry Finn*. Taking my inspiration from Twain, I wrote a four-hundred-word work packed with pathos, action, brotherly love, and finding home, following the three-act structure of the Hero's Journey. I hoped it would move him to tears, but it barely elicited a reaction. Not even a shrug.

Today's story started with, This morning when I woke up (so he would picture me in bed), I was thinking about the movie *The Loneliest Planet*. The Mexican actor Gael García Bernal betrays his girlfriend with an inappropriate reaction to a danger they suddenly faced, and the relationship implodes in that instant. At the end of the story, I pose the question, Has this sudden destruction of respect ever happened to you? It was intended as an information-gathering story. After three weeks now, I still can't tell what his orientation is. If he throws the question back at me, I'm willing to reciprocate.

The intensity of our eye contact reminds me of tango. When he rises to walk to the whiteboard, he holds my gaze; the few times I've risen from my desk to hand him something, gliding dramatically toward him, I hold his. Maybe my next story will be about the suggestive meanings of tango's ultrastylized body positions and sexual overtones.

At the end of class, he handed me his special black book and asked for my contact info. I forgot to breathe.

An impromptu party erupted on the Cuesta de Loreto tonight: a brass band complete with a horn section, trombones, a tuba, and a one-man percussionist, the musicians in white sparkly costumes, neighbors drinking beer and dancing. Nobody cared that it was pouring rain. How do you say *joie de vivre* in Spanish?

Wednesday, August 31st

The lost bracelet has not rematerialized. Not yet. But it's somewhere in the suite of rooms, I'm sure of it. The very thorough housekeeper who cleans the room daily hasn't found it either, but I tell myself, it's likely I'll see it again.

For the past two days I've been noticing an orange aura in the palms of Ramón's hands. I've never seen an aura in anybody's hands before and figured Google could weigh in.

> . . . Orange is the colour of the belly chakra, associated with things like childhood, the inner child, the parent/child relationship, reproduction/birth, and so on. . . an orange aura can mean things like a good sense of humour, spontaneity, flow, adaptability, social connection, hope, playfulness. . .[2]

None of this really fit Ramón's cynical personality, so maybe he's on a strict carrots, cantaloupe, sweet potatoes, and pumpkins-only diet, which could account for the orange color on his hands. As I stood across the street from the school today, a flatbed truck chock-full of freshly harvested carrots passed by so closely I could have reached in and grabbed a handful. Maybe they were on their way to his place to make a delivery.

Thursday, September 1st

Today I packed to move to a different hotel, loading up a suitcase opened on the bed. I turned around and looked at the sofa, and the bracelet was sitting dead center on one of the cushions. This makes half a dozen times that objects have disappeared and reappeared under mysterious circumstances. I know it's my departed husband attempting contact. But what's he trying to say? I wish I knew what to make of these events. Maybe another consultation with one of my sources can clear things up.

San Miguel's two most understated street musicians sit on the curb of a street near the Parroquia. The guy, an old man who mostly smokes cigarettes and mutters, looks back and forth as if watching a slow-motion tennis game and periodically blows a single note on a trumpet. Accompanying him is a woman with a single maraca, shaking it to Mexican music playing from the world's tiniest loudspeaker. I wonder if they're a couple. And are they feuding? They're always sitting several meters apart.

A friend fluent in Spanish encouraged me to say *¿Cómo amaneciste?* (How did you greet the dawn?) to Ramón today. He said Mexicans lovvvvve this, and that it would impress him. Ramón just gave me a funny look. Was I really saying, "I wish you'd been in bed with me this morning when I greeted the dawn?" I told Ramón that it was a friend's suggestion. Ramón said, "Why?" (Well, isn't it more interesting than the conventional *buenos dias?*) Not much of a response. He is so inscrutable!

While composing tonight's epic for Spanish class (I needed to use Google translate a lot), a troubling mistranslation occurred: "While I was walking down a sidewalk yesterday, I was thinking about Dostoyevsky's work *Notes From Underground* and the character called Kevin." Kevin, the name substituted in the translation for Dostoyevsky's character the Underground Man, was the name Michael assigned the Devil. Was its appearance an inauspicious sign?

Friday, September 4th

Today was the last day of Spanish class. I was determined to make meaningful, unhalting conversation with Ramón. All the way to class I practiced the sentences I would say to him when he asked, *¿Qué hiciste ayer después de clase?* (What did you do yesterday after class?) But today, the question didn't come. Instead, he asked me to read my composition right off the bat. And by the end of it, those practiced sentences had completely vaporized. The remaining hour and a half of class went smoothly enough, going through exercises in the book, but then came the dreaded enforced conversation where, historically, I become mute. But not today. In a previous class I'd told Ramón about a miscreant who had carjacked my son-in-law Fabiano in São Paulo, and I decided to add something new to that thread. So I made it up. I'm not sure I've ever deliberately lied on the spot like that. The words I could use in a possible scenario were colliding in my brain: *estaba caminando, la playa, el ladrón, mi bolsa, me escape*:

> I was walking on the beach in Rio when a thief tried to steal my purse, and I ran away.

I pulled it off, and he bought it. *Las palabras fluyeron de mi boca cuando no pienso demasiado*. (The words flow out of my mouth when I don't think too much.)

Saturday, September 3rd

Today was the first time in four weeks that I've woken up without my stomach tied in knots. Could it be because Spanish class is over? Being the introvert that I am, it was really hard to be "on" for two hours every day with Ramón, and I must say, I don't think I did a very good job. However, because I was required to provide short, written works for every class, that's where I shone.

In these pieces of writing, I:

—compared the (chill) San Miguel strolling-the-narrow-sidewalks experience with Dostoyevsky's "Apropos of the Wet Snow" from *Notes from Underground*, where the Underground Man engages in a contest with a soldier for sidewalk supremacy.

—wrote a commentary about Anish Kapoor's twisty, bright red London sculpture that Boris Johnson turned into a tourist attraction by adding a spiraling slide to its center support.

—cited a story about a doctor who, after being struck by lightning, woke up with a newfound ability to read music and play performance-level piano, comparing it to my desire to be struck by lightning and wake up speaking fluent Spanish.

—wrote about Cato and his belief that cabbage was a superfood and how, in his work *De Agricultura* (a two-thousand-word document all about the salutary effects of cabbage), he claimed that cabbage cured headache, bad vision, bruises, and broken bones; that inhaling the fumes of cooking cabbage improved fertility; and that bathing in the urine of a person who eats a lot of cabbage can cure just about anything.

—as mentioned previously, wrote about my brush with movie stardom when I tried out for a part in the ballroom scene in *The Great Gatsby*. Ramón was obsessed with Fitzgerald, whose name he endearingly pronounced Fiz-HAIR-al, so I knew he'd be interested in this bit of movie trivia.

—also as mentioned previously, examined the sudden betrayal of loyalty and loss of respect, the theme of the film *The Loneliest Planet*. The story's final sentence was an open-ended question, wherein I hoped to trigger an intimate exchange of personal betrayal experiences (a nonstarter). Followed by the story about his obsession with the Mississippi River and wanting to run away with a big Black man, hoping to trigger a discussion of sexual orientation. Another nonstarter.

—and, finally, the anecdote about how, on the very day I was publishing my first book *Travel for STOICs*, my friend Len in Seattle texted with the heads-up that my (previous) pseudonym was already taken by an author of soft-core porn, with such titles as *Pregnant and Horny: My Husband's Hot Paralegal* and *Submissive Office: Kinky Office Series, Book 1*.

I owe Ramón a huge debt of gratitude, and not just for the Spanish lessons. For years I'd felt like protective spikes were growing out of my heart, more and more the longer I was married, fortifying me against the emotional and physical attacks of my abusive husband and, by association, men in general. Selling my house, the one we had lived in together, and roaming around searching for Location X, was not only a quest for place, but also it was my way to heal. And after four weeks with Ramón, two hours a day, not only did he teach me some Spanish, but he knocked those spikes off one by one until there were none left.

Monday, September 5th

On my walk around town this afternoon, a guy on a motorcycle sped around a corner, barely making the turn, and a machete flew out of his backpack. It spun in the street and came to a stop, pointing in the direction of the Parroquia. Another guy bolted from his *tienda*, picked up the machete, and went running after him.

This was the sign from Archangel Michael, the machete a stand-in for his sword. I hope he's not suggesting that I convert. Regardless, I headed in the direction of the Parroquia.

I turned the corner from Aldama onto Nemesio Diez, and yellow barricade tape blocked my route. A policeman waved me away. I took another route, and when passing a woman walking in the opposite direction with her companions, I heard her say, "I just missed getting into the crossfire." I arrived at the intersection of Hernandez Macias and Codo, the location of a wall fountain where water pours out of an earthen jug into a pair of cupped bronze hands, collecting in a semicircular pool below.

Half a dozen cops stood sentinel in their riot gear, and more barricade tape blocked that end of the street. They were going after the cartel. I felt neutral about it all, not caring if I happened to take a stray bullet or not, I'd be happy to die in San Miguel. I walked around the corner to Café Zenteno on Hernandez Macias, sat down, and Michael slipped into the seat opposite me.

"And where have *you* been for the past month?"

"Do you realize you've met one of your relocation criteria?" he replied excitedly.

"Huh? What do you mean?"

"You just said it. 'I'd be happy to die in San Miguel.' That's criterion number three: 'Can I envision taking my final breath here without reservation?' By the way, in case you need reminding, I'm the city's patron saint, so I have a lot of obligations. Multiply that by the 258 other places in the world named San Miguel, and maybe next time you'll be a little more enthused when I show up."

"Thanks for making time for me in your busy schedule."

"What about the other two?"

"The other two what?"

"Criteria! 'Can I envision my life in this place?'"

"Well, I'm about to sign a yearlong lease on a rental here. I can envision my life in San Miguel for at least the next twelve months."

"And 'Will I be able to connect to my adopted community in meaningful ways?' Criteria number two."

"The clock starts tomorrow with a reading of *Travel for STOICs* at the library, and I'm donating 100 percent of the box office. If only twenty people show up, that's 2,000 pesos, $100 U.S."

Is this the end of my quest for Location X and, thus, the book? Yes, I think it is!

THE END

With gratitude

Anatha Attar for her cheerful company while walking the Camino Francigena
Alaine Ball for putting up with me for three months in São Paulo
Andy Bridge for his outstanding cover design
Dale Conner for 55 years of mentoring and friendship
Guadalupe Hernández Hernández for polishing the Spanish
Courtney Kerr and Caitlin McHugh for sharing their Santa Fe home for three weeks
Susan Matthews for reading and commenting on an early draft
Laurie Mercier for urging Anatha and me to keep putting one foot in front of the other on the camino
Geoffry Oshman for helping underwrite *Location X*
Sheri Quirt for her outstanding proofreading skills
Suzie Russell, base camp Fort Worth
Evelyne and Tim Taylor, base camp Santa Fe

APPENDIX ONE

THE LIST:
RELOCATION CRITERIA
not in order of importance

- Natural beauty
- Interesting architecture and good urban planning
- Affordable housing and food
- A place with good stories
- A place with good sounds
- Museums I may like to visit again and again
- A town large enough to provide multiple and diverse events and activities, esp. musical events and films
- A good bus/train/metro system
- Reliable Uber/taxis and food delivery
- Mild winters/not-too-hot summers/minimal wind
- Low possibility of dying in a tsunami
- Low possibility of dying in an earthquake
- Proximity to volcanoes okay
- A friendly, nonracist, multicultural population where I am not considered a gringa interloper
- No legal private gun ownership

- Great medical, dental, geriatric care (I'm heading in that direction)
- Bougainvillea must be able to grow in this place
- Close to some kind of water, but not in a hot, sticky environment
- Readily available drinking water
- An international airport nearby
- Within a three-to-five-hour flight to family and friends
- Clean public places and spaces (this is relative)
- Reliable internet
- Opportunities to contribute to the welfare of the community
- A personal purpose

APPENDIX TWO

NOTES

All photographs copyright 2023, Laurie McDonald, unless otherwise indicated. Where public domain "U.S. tag" is indicated, it refers to: https://commons.wikimedia.org/wiki/Commons:Copyright_tags/Country-specific_tags#United_States_of_America

Introduction
1. https://tarotx.net/tarot-card-meanings/marseilles/9-de-deniers.html

During the Tarot reading, the three cards I chose from the deck were: the Two of Wands; the Chevalier des Batons, right side up; and the Nine of Pentacles.

Two of Wands
The Two of Wands is inspired by a great idea and makes it ripe towards the true path to follow. You have been able to give an idea a new dimension that will allow you to succeed. Now you are going to put a plan in place to make sure that idea comes true as you wish. This Ace card also bodes well for discovery, especially when you step out of your comfort zone, explore new worlds, and try new experiences. Taking the first step may require a little courage, but it gives you confidence. You have identified your goal, and you know where you are guiding your creative process, so you have faith in the final result.

You have already made good progress, but now you feel ready for change, this time with your long-term future in mind. You may be considering overseas travel, to increase your knowledge and development, and broaden your horizons beyond your current environment. Careful organization and a realistic approach will put the odds on your side to succeed in the future.

You know that the world can offer you something larger or more constructive, but you are also aware that to maximize this opportunity, you must leave your familiar environment. Even if you have already invested heavily in the current situation in order to develop and maximize your potential, it is imperative that you embark on this new world and explore your options. This card focuses on patience.

Chevalier des Batons, right side up
Riding on a white horse, symbolizing the desire to control, the Knight of Wands has tamed his horse and could force it to turn. Chevalier des Batons reveals the implementation of a new idea. Many actions are taken by this rider who invests all of his energy without hesitation to ensure that his ideas will be applied. His courage is incredibly tenacious, and he is afraid of nothing. He is willing to exploit his intentions and visions to make things happen.

This Knight is impatient and impulsive with unshakable faith. He embarks on a headlong journey and often crashes for lack of a clear plan of attack, which can have a negative impact on his chances of long-term success. He almost forgets to prepare in advance and keep an eye on reality.

This card can also indicate an event that happens in your life quickly and unexpectedly. An important problem is likely to occur in your life and to demand your attention until its resolution. Rather than resist him, take the time to give him all of your vigilance. Often, this Knight card may indicate a hasty change in residence, work, or any other lifestyle. You must be ready to react quickly and follow the current flow because any resistance will be useless.

Nine of Pentacles
A material stage has been completed, from which new birth is born. It is also a material detachment; one has left everything to start a new life or a profound financial transformation leads to a new project.

The Nine of Pentacles indicates that you have reached a point in your life where you feel confident, autonomous, independent, and free. By acting on your own, you have achieved a well-deserved success, and you can now enjoy the property, recreation, pleasure, material comfort, and rest. You appreciate what is available to you at the moment and that the difficulties are behind you. You also know that you can accomplish everything with a little confidence, self-discipline, and patience. This card means it's time to enjoy the good life and fruits of labor. You have worked hard to get there, so now let's sit back, relax and enjoy the luxuries of life. You deserve it!

You are about to reach your goal, so get ready for what will come next. Sometimes, however, this card may indicate that you are close to achieving your goal, but you have not done yet. You show great self-discipline and conviction to make sure you get where you want to go.

2. Refer to Wikipedia's article on Anamorphosis: https://en.wikipedia.org/wiki/Anamorphosis. Note Hans Holbein the Younger's *The Ambassadors* to see a 16th-century example of this distortion phenomenon.

Chapter 1: Diogenes
1. https://en.wikipedia.org/wiki/Diogenes; reference 30. Laërtius, Diogenes (1972) [1925]."Διογένης (Diogenes)". Βίοι καὶ γνῶμαι τῶν ἐν φιλοσοφίᾳ εὐδοκιμησάντων [Lives of eminent philosophers]. Vol. 2. Translated by Robert Drew Hicks (Loeb Classical Library ed.). Cambridge, Massachusetts: Harvard University Press. ISBN 978-0-674-99204-7.

Chapter 2: São Paulo
1. The Witch House.

2. Beco do Batman (Batman Alley).

3. Pixação. Author: LiaC.
https://commons.wikimedia.org/wiki/File:Sao_vito1.JPG
link to license:
https://en.wikipedia.org/wiki/GNU_Free_Documentation_License

4. The orquidarium in the Parque Villa-Lobos.

5. Museo de Arte de São Paulo. Author: Lucas Oriolo Rodrigues.

https://commons.wikimedia.org/wiki/File:Masp_-_S%C3%A3o_Paulo.jpg
link to license: https://creativecommons.org/licenses/by-sa/4.0/deed.en;
photo edited by Laurie McDonald

6. Calçada outside the Pinacoteca de São Paulo.

7. A mesa radiônica and a 1956 TV test pattern/camera registration chart (unattributed graphics).

8. Reni, Guido. *Archangel Michael defeats Satan*. Between ca. 1630 and ca. 1635, oil on canvas. Santa Maria della Concezione dei Cappuccini, Rome.
https://commons.wikimedia.org/wiki/File:GuidoReni_MichaelDefeatsSatan.jpg; Public domain.

9. Oscar Niemeyer Cathedral and Bell Tower, Brasília.

10. President Juscelino Kubitschek posing with Marlon Brando dressed as Mr. Christian from *Mutiny on the Bounty*.

11. Pirenópolis's friendly Minotaur.

12. Removing scuff marks with a tennis ball on a pole, Shopping Cidade São Paulo.

Chapter 4: México City

1. Immobilized in traffic, on the hop-on-hop-off bus, in a México City tunnel.

2. Palacio de Bellas Artes. Author: Timothy Neesam.
https://commons.wikimedia.org/wiki/File:Palacio_de_Bellas_Artes,_México_City,_MX.jpg
link to license: https://creativecommons.org/licenses/by-sa/4.0/deed.en;
photo edited by Laurie McDonald

3. Rivera, Diego. *Man at the Crossroads* or *Man, Controller of the Universe*, 1934, fresco, Palacio de Bellas Artes, México City.

4. http://www.calledtocommunion.com/2010/12/our-lady-of-guadalupe/?_ga=2.201905297.1095802920.1671557606-1420464496.1671557606

5. A fascinating article on the miraculous image in the Basilica of Our Lady of Guadalupe: https://www.wordonfire.org/articles/st-juan-diegos-miraculous-proof/

6. Our Lady of Guadalupe. Photograph by Mike Peel, www.mikepeel.net, edited by Laurie McDonald https://commons.wikimedia.org/wiki/File:Basilica_of_Our_Lady_of_Guadalupe_-_Wiki_Loves_Pyramids_tour_101.jpg
https://creativecommons.org/licenses/by-sa/4.0/deed.en

The moving walkway.

Chapter 7: El Paso, Texas

1. *El Equis* (The X). Unattributed photograph. https://www.borderreport.com/hot-topics/la-feria-poised-for-comeback-juarez-plans-mass-outdoor-entertainment-event-in-august/

2. Memorial to the U.S. Troops killed in Kabul, Afghanistan, 8/26/2021, Starbucks.

Chapter 9: Guadalajara

1. The "Riad," Calle San Felipe 39, Guadalajara.

2. Orozco, José Clemente. *El pueblo y sus falsos líderes* (The townspeople and their false idols). 1935, true fresco. Museo de las Artes (MUSA) de la Universidad de Guadalajara.

Orozco, José Clemente. *El hombre creador y rebelde* (The creative and rebellious man). 1935, true fresco. Museo de las Artes (MUSA) de la Universidad de Guadalajara.

3. Houses designed by Luis Barragán. Avenida de la Paz 1877 is now a small hotel called Petit María José.

4. Conservation team working on a Jesus figure, the Basilica of Our Lady of Zapopan.

5. Venus glyphs, Chichén Itzá, Yucatán.

6. Rossolatos, George. "The moribund syntax of Hula Hoop dancing (2014)."
https://www.researchgate.net/publication/257946025_The_moribund_syntax_of_Hula_Hoop_dancing_2014

7. Querétaro aqueduct Los Arcos, author unknown. Ca. 1905/1910, photograph from a glass plate negative. California Historical Society Collection, 1860–1960. https://commons.wikimedia.org/wiki/File:Aqueduct_at_Queretaro,_Mexico,_ca.1905-1910_(CHS-643).jpg; Public domain.

8. Urban dictionary, Sean. https://www.urbandictionary.com/define.php?term=Sean

9. https://myfirstname.rocks/baby-names/sean

Chapter 12: Uncertain, Texas: A Housesit
1. https://en.wikipedia.org/wiki/Cynicism_(philosophy)

Chapter 13: Costa Rica
1. The Bongolow, Sarchí.
2. Coffee cart wheel, Sarchí.
3. Resplendent quetzal, Rescate Wildlife Rescue Center, Alajuela Province.
4. https://en.wikipedia.org/wiki/Jehovah%27s_Witnesses
5. Sloth, Jaguar Rescue Center near Puerto Viejo de Talamanca, Limón Province.
6. http://www.thehistoryblog.com/archives/47593
7. Zorbing, near Arenal.
8. Swimming pool at the Los Lagos Hotel, Spa, & Resort; Alajuela Province.
9. Manuel Antonio beach, Quepos.

Chapter 14: Arenal
1. The Arenal volcano.

Chapter 15: Panamá
1. A mola, handmade textile designed and fabricated by the Guna women of Panamá.

2. Wagua, Orgun. *Guna women drinking chicha and dancing, Ustupa, Guna Yala Region*. 2016. Museo de la Mola, Panamá City.

3. The F&F Tower, Panamá City.

4. One of the 350 islands of the San Blas archipelago.

5. Molas and the Guna flag, San Blas Islands.

6. Guna mother and son, Albrook Mall, Panamá City.

7. Young Embera man showing painted tattoos and wearing traditional dress re-created in plastic beads, Embera Village, Gamboa.

Chapter 17: Granada
1. Plastic film toilet seat cover, O'Hare Airport, Chicago. Author: Nskrill.
https://commons.wikimedia.org/wiki/File:High_tech_toilet.JPG
Public domain photo, February 13, 2011.

2. https://www.npr.org/sections/thetwo-way/2013/01/29/170570621/those-hygienic-toilet-seats-at-ohare-may-not-be-so-clean

3. Catedral de Granada, interior painted white, and its two organs.

4. The Alhambra and the Generalife.

5. Street sign, Granada.

6. Muqarnas or "stalactite" vaults, the Alhambra.

7. Rūmī, Jalāl al-Dīn Muḥammad, translated by Coleman Barks. *Rumi: The Book of Love, Poems of Ecstasy and Longing* (HarperOne; Illustrated edition; January 1, 2002).
https://sufispirit.com.au/feature/what-was-said-to-the-rose/

Chapter 18: Madrid
1. Angelico, Fra. *The Annunciation*. Ca. 1426, tempera on panel. Museo Nacional del Prado, Madrid; detail of birds and Gabriel's wings.
https://commons.wikimedia.org/wiki/File:La_Anunciaci%C3%B3n_(Fra_Angelico-Prado).jpg; Public domain; U.S. tag.

2. Tintoretto, Domenico. *Portrait of a woman revealing her breasts.* Ca. 1570, oil on canvas. Museo del Prado, Madrid. https://commons.wikimedia.org/wiki/File:Jacopo_Tintoretto_-_Portrait_of_a_Woman_Revealing_Her_Breasts_-_WGA22692.jpg Public domain.

3. Quellinus, Erasmus. *The Rape of Europa.* 1635, oil on canvas. Museo del Prado, Madrid. https://commons.wikimedia.org/wiki/File:Erasmus_Quellinus_(II)_-_The_Rape_of_Europe.jpg Public domain; https://en.wikipedia.org/wiki/Creative_Commons

4. Tintoretto, Jacopo. *Susana y los viejos.* Ca. 1552–1555, oil on canvas. Museo del Prado, Madrid. https://commons.wikimedia.org/wiki/File:Susana_y_los_viejos,_por_Tintoretto.jpg; Public domain; U.S. tag.

5. Vecellio, Tiziano (Titian). *Venus and Organist and Little Dog.* Ca. 1550, oil on canvas. Museo del Prado, Madrid. https://commons.wikimedia.org/wiki/File:Venus_and_organist_and_little_dog.jpg; Public domain; U.S. tag.

6. Machuca, Pedro. *La Virgen y las ánimas del Purgatorio* close-up, edited by Laurie McDonald. 1517, oil on wood. Museo del Prado, Madrid. https://commons.wikimedia.org/wiki/File:Pedro_Machuca_-_The_Virgin_and_Souls_in_Purgatory_-_WGA13802.jpg Public domain; U.S. tag.

7. Goya y Lucientes, Francisco de. *La maja desnuda.* Between 1775 and 1800, oil on canvas. Museo del Prado, Madrid. https://commons.wikimedia.org/wiki/File:Maja_desnuda_(museo_del_Prado).jpg; Public domain.

8. Rubens, Peter Paul. *Diana and Callisto* and detail. Ca. 1635, oil on canvas. Museo del Prado, Madrid. https://commons.wikimedia.org/wiki/File:Peter_Paul_Rubens_-_Diana_and_Callisto_-_WGA20326.jpg; Public domain.

9. Rubens, Peter Paul, and workshop. *Achilles discovered by Ulysses among the daughters of Lycomedes* and detail. 1617–1618, oil on canvas. https://commons.wikimedia.org/wiki/File:Achilles_discovered_by_Ulyss

es_among_the_daughters_of_Lycomedes_-_modello.jpg
Public domain; U.S. tag.

10. Giordano, Luca. *Capture of a Stronghold*, detail. Ca. 1697, oil on canvas. Museo del Prado, Madrid.

11. Rubens, Peter Paul. *The Judgment of Paris*, detail. Ca. 1638, oil on canvas. Museo del Prado, Madrid.
https://commons.wikimedia.org/wiki/File:Peter_Paul_Rubens_115.jpg
Public domain, U.S. tag.

12. Goya y Lucientes, Francisco de. *Las floreras o La Primavera*. Between 1786 and 1787, oil on canvas. Museo del Prado, Madrid.
https://commons.wikimedia.org/wiki/File:Las_floreras.jpg
Public domain.

13. Goya y Lucientes, Francisco de. *Saturno devorando a su hijo*. 1820–1823, mixed method on mural transferred to canvas. Museo del Prado, Madrid.
https://commons.wikimedia.org/wiki/File:Francisco_de_Goya,_Saturno_devorando_a_su_hijo_(1819-1823).jpg
Public domain, U.S. tag.

14. Sanzio, Raffaello. *Le Grand Saint Michel*. 1518, oil transferred from wood to canvas, Musée du Louvre, Paris.
https://commons.wikimedia.org/wiki/File:Le_Grand_Saint_Michel,_by_Raffaello_Sanzio,_from_C2RMF_retouched.jpg
Public domain.

15. Young adult mandible and reconstructed model of *Homo georgicus*. National Archaeological Museum, Madrid.

Chapter 19: Rome
1. Urbino, Raffaello Sanzio da (Raphael). *The School of Athens* and detail. 1509, oil on canvas. Vatican Museums, Rome.
https://commons.wikimedia.org/wiki/File:Escola_de_Atenas.jpg
Public domain; U.S. tag.
https://commons.wikimedia.org/wiki/File:%22The_School_of_Athens%22_by_Raffaello_Sanzio_da_Urbino_(cropped).jpg; Public domain.

2. Buonarroti, Michelangelo. *The Last Judgment* detail. Between 1537 and 1541, fresco. The Vatican Museums, Rome.
https://commons.wikimedia.org/wiki/File:Michelangelo,_Giudizio_Universale_31.jpg; Public domain; U.S. tag.

3. Buonarroti, Michelangelo. *The Creation of Adam*. Ca. 1511, fresco. The Vatican Museums, Rome.
https://commons.wikimedia.org/wiki/File:Michelangelo_-_Creation_of_Adam_(cropped).jpg
Public domain; U.S. tag.

4. Realized by Giuseppe Sacconi. Monument to Victor Emmanuel II. Built between 1885 and 1935.

5. Works in the Capitoline Museums.
Equestrian Statue of Marcus Aurelius. Artist unknown. Erected 175 CE, bronze. With Capitoline Wolf. Artist unknown. Etruscan, 11th or 12th century–wolf, late 15th century–twins, bronze.
The colossal foot of Constantine.
Bernini, Gian Lorenzo. *Bust of Medusa*. Ca. 1638–1648, marble.
The Dying Gaul. Copy of a lost sculpture from the Hellenistic period (323-31 BC), marble.
Caravaggio, Michelangelo Meresi da. *The Fortune Teller*. Ca. 1594, oil on canvas.
https://commons.wikimedia.org/wiki/File:The_Fortune_Teller_(1594)_Caravaggio.jpg; Public domain; U.S. tag.

6. Fanelli, Giovanni. *Roma: Portrait of a City*. "Girl Scouts decorate a young officer on leave in a street in Rome with a small tricolor cockade in the colors of the flag, June 1915." Anonymous. TASCHEN; Multilingual edition (January 18, 2018), page 133.

7. Commissioned by Marcus Agrippa. The Pantheon. A former Roman temple and since 609 CE a Catholic church.

8. Plaster casts of figures found at Pompeii.

9. Grounds of the Museo Nazionale Romano.

10. Works in the Borghese Gallery and Museum.
Bernini, Gian Lorenzo. *David*. 1623–1624, marble.

Bernini, Gian Lorenzo. *Abduction of Proserpina*. 1621–1622, marble.

Bernini, Gian Lorenzo. *Apollo and Daphne*. Between 1622–1625, marble.

From the circle of Leonardo da Vinci, probably Cesare da Sesto. *Leda and the Swan*. Ca. 1510–1520, tempera grassa on panel.

11. Water features and water organ, Villa D'Este, Tivoli.

An explanation of how the water organ works: https://gardenofeaden.blogspot.com/2011/05/rome-water-organ-at-villa-deste.html

A good paper about the water organ: https://www.academia.edu/35151274/The_Organ_of_the_Villa_d_Este_in_Tivoli_and_the_Standards_of_Pneumatic_Engineering_in_the_Renaissance

12. SPQR monogramming, Rome.

Chapter 21: Walking the Camino Trail: the Via Francigena

1. View from the Hotel Miravalle, San Miniato, Italy.

2. Logo representing the Via Francigena.

3. https://www.onefootabroad.com/blog/explanation-via-francigena/

4. Map of the Via Francigena through Tuscany. Author: Paulusburg. https://commons.wikimedia.org/wiki/File:VF_(region)_4IT-5_Toscana.svg
https://creativecommons.org/licenses/by-sa/4.0/deed.en

5. San Gimignano.

6. Jesus with skinned knees.

7. Vaca, Álvar Núñez Cabeza de. *Cabeza de Vaca's Adventures in the Unknown Interior of America*. Translated by Cyclone Covey. Collier Books: January 1, 1961.

8. Interior of the Siena Cathedral.

9. Caravaggio, Michelangelo Merisi da. *Judith Beheading Holofernes*. Ca. 1599, oil on canvas. Galleria Nazionale d'Arte Antica, Rome. https://commons.wikimedia.org/wiki/File:Caravaggio_Judith_Beheadin

g_Holofernes.jpg
https://commons.wikimedia.org/wiki/Commons:Copyright_tags/Country-specific_tags#United_States_of_America

Biondo, Giovanni del. *Triptych of Saint Sebastian* detail. Ca. 1370, tempera on wood panel. Museo dell'Opera del Duomo, Florence.

Botticelli, Sandro. *Salome with the Head of St. John the Baptist* detail. Ca. 1488, tempera on panel. Uffizi Gallery, Florence.
https://commons.wikimedia.org/wiki/File:Sandro_Botticelli_-_Salome_with_the_Head_of_St_John_the_Baptist_-_WGA02736.jpg
Public domain; U.S. tag.

Chapter 22: Florence

1. Botticelli, Sandro. *The Birth of Venus*. Ca. 1485, tempera on canvas. Uffizi Gallery, Florence.
https://commons.wikimedia.org/wiki/File:La_nascita_di_Venere_(Botticelli).jpg; Public domain.
https://commons.wikimedia.org/wiki/File:La_nascita_di_Venere_(Botticelli).jpg

2. Caravaggio, Michelangelo Merisi da. *Medusa*. 1597, oil on canvas mounted on wood. Uffizi Gallery, Florence.

3. Francesca, Piero della. *Diptych of Federico da Montefeltro and Battista Sforza*. Between ca. 1473 and 1475, tempera and oil on panel. Uffizi Gallery, Florence.
https://commons.wikimedia.org/wiki/File:Piero,_Double_portrait_of_the_Dukes_of_Urbino_03.jpg; Public domain.

4. Caravaggio, Michelangelo Merisi da. *Bacchus*. Ca. 1596, oil on canvas. Uffizi Gallery, Florence.

5. Cimabue (Cenni di Pepi). *Crucifix*. Ca. 1265, distemper on wood panel. Basilica di Santa Croce, Florence.

Chapter 23: Porto

1. Pasteis de nata.

2. The Sé do Porto.

3. Azulejos, the Sé do Porto.

4. Unknown Italian artist. Archangel Michael and close-up showing spear aimed for his foot. Sé do Porto chapter house.

5. Diorama illustrating a scene from Jesus's life; angel, old town square, Guimarães.

6. The Capela das Almas (Chapel of Souls) with azulejos, Porto.

7. Café Majestic. Author: António Amen. https://commons.wikimedia.org/wiki/File:Santo_Ildefonso-Caf%C3%A9_Majestic.jpg

Chapter 24: Lisbon
1. The prison cell Airbnb accommodation.

2. Sardine hats and green wigs.

3. https://passportsandspice.com/a-special-time-to-visit-lisbon-the-sardine-festival/

4. "A unique art form first seen in Lisbon at the end of the 15th century. In the transition from the Gothic era to the Renaissance, an architectural style influenced by Moorish elements began to come into use in the palaces in Lisbon and Sintra, as well as in the construction of the monastery of Jerónimos and Torre de Belém. During the reign of King Manuel I, countless monuments, windows and doorways were built that were more or less influenced by a Naturalist style responsible for more architectural structures than decorative motifs. The size and depth of the arches and twisted framing cornices, façades and vaults distinguish the pure Manueline style, which began to wane with the Renaissance from 1517 onwards. The style is part of the history, richness and glory of this unique period in Portuguese history."
https://www.visitlisboa.com/en/places/manueline-architecture

5. Photos from the Saint Anthony parade: pincushion float, cell phone marchers, Saint and Baby Jesus in a boat.

6. Quake: Lisbon Earthquake Center. Unattributed photograph. Tripadvisor. https://en.tripadvisor.com.hk/Attraction_Review-g189158-d23957745-Reviews-Quake_Lisbon_Earthquake_Centre-Lisbon_Lisbon_District_Central_Portugal.html

Chapter 25: A Wild Goose Chase
1. https://grammarist.com/idiom/wild-goose-chase/

Chapter 26: Washington, D.C.
1. Faulkner, Barry. *The Charters of Freedom: Declaration of Independence*, and close-up showing the Lincoln cloud. 1936, oil on canvas. Rotunda of the National Archives, Washington, D.C.
https://commons.wikimedia.org/wiki/File:Barry_Faulkner%27s_1936_Declaration_of_Independence_mural_in_the_rotunda_of_the_National_Archives,_Washington,_D.C_LCCN2011633882.tif
No copyright restrictions.

2. Faulkner, Barry. *The Charters of Freedom: Constitution*. 1936, oil on canvas. Rotunda of the National Archives, Washington, D.C.
https://commons.wikimedia.org/wiki/File:Barry_Faulkner%27s_1936_%22Constitution%22_mural_in_the_rotunda_of_the_National_Archives,_Washington,_D.C_LCCN2011633883.tif
No copyright restrictions.

3. Kusama, Yayoi. *Infinity Mirrored Room—One With Eternity*.
2013, wood, metal, mirrors, plastic, acrylic, rubber, and LED lighting system. Hirshhorn Museum and Sculpture Garden.

4. The thing that hath been, it is that which shall be; and that which is done is that which shall be done: and there is no new thing under the sun. Ecclesiastes 1:9

5. Works cited from the National Gallery.
Vermeer, Johannes. *Girl With the Red Hat*. Ca. 1665-1666, oil on panel.
https://commons.wikimedia.org/wiki/File:Johannes_Vermeer,_Girl_with_the_Red_Hat,_c._1665-1666,_NGA_60FXD.jpg
Universal Public Domain Dedication.
Stuart, Gilbert. *The Skater (Portrait of William Grant)*. 1782, oil on canvas.
https://commons.wikimedia.org/wiki/File:GSskater.jpg; Public domain.
Copley, John Singleton. *Watson and the Shark*. 1778, oil on canvas.
https://commons.wikimedia.org/wiki/File:Watsonandtheshark-original.jpg; Public domain.

Vinci, Leonardo da. *Ginevra Benci*. Between 1474 and 1478, oil on canvas.
https://commons.wikimedia.org/wiki/File:Ginevra_de%27_Benci_-_National_Gallery_of_Art.jpg; Public domain.

Chapter 27: Can One Word Be Enough to Know Where?
1. http://www.literaturepage.com/read/mobydick-201.html

Chapter 28: San Miguel de Allende
1. The Jardín, Centro. Unattributed photo from Tripadvisor. https://www.tripadvisor.com/Tourism-g151932-San_Miguel_de_Allende_Central_México_and_Gulf_Coast-Vacations.html

2. https://omanisa.com/2011/11/28/reading-aura-colours-around-the-hands/

ABOUT THE AUTHOR

Eva Rome (Laurie McDonald) is a writer and a media artist. She has published three books, written feature-length screenplays and short stories. Her narrative nonfiction book *Travel for STOICs* empowers the solo traveler who is obsessive, introverted, and compulsive, informed by ancient Stoicism; and her collection of semiserious semiotic essays *What It Means: Myth, Symbol, and Archetype in the Third Millennium, Vol. 1* examines how myth, symbol, and archetype manifest in everyday American life in the early third millennium.

She has designed books, graphics for print and video, built websites, and manages a blog called Our Childhood Homes: Stories About Place (www.childhoodhomestories.com). In the early 1970s, she was a founding member of the video art collective

Electron Movers, and her video art can be viewed here: www.lauriemcdonald.net. She has received a Fellowship from the National Endowment for the Arts and four American Film Institute/NEA Fellowships, and her video art has been exhibited internationally. Visit www.bluemorphopress.net for more information about her publications.

www.ingramcontent.com/pod-product-compliance
Lightning Source LLC
Chambersburg PA
CBHW042049290426
44110CB00001B/1